Linda Seiler address ion and gender identity confu esearch. Having experienced personal transformation herself, she serves as an able guide to help others find wholeness.

**Michael Brown, PhD,**
host of the Line of Fire radio broadcast and
author of *Can You Be Gay and Christian?*

I give thanks for Linda Seiler and this book, both for the candor of her testimony and for her faithfulness in staying true to God's will for her life and not compromising the gospel. She offers sensitive and sensible advice from her own experience and from Scripture on how to navigate LGBTQ matters.

**Robert A. J. Gagnon, PhD,**
professor of Bible and theology at Houston Christian University,
author of *The Bible and Homosexual Practice: Texts and Hermeneutics*
and co-author of *Homosexuality and the Bible: Two Views*

God has raised Linda Seiler up for such a time as this! She is to the LGBTQ movement what Paul was to the keepers of the Old Jewish Law—someone from that background who encountered God and is now equipping the church to respond with clarity and recover those who have been deceived. Linda is bold, insightful, and led by the Lord. I highly recommend her book *Trans-Formation*!

**Rick Dubose,**
Assistant General Superintendent of the Assemblies of God, USA

Trail-blazing, hope-filled, insightful, and a thorough resource—all are true of Linda's book, *Trans-Formation*. All who seek to be overcomers out of LGBT, as well as parents, pastors, and counselors will find this an invaluable resource!

**Anne Edward,**
Executive Director of Restored Hope Network and
author of *Restoring Sexual Identity: Hope for Women Who Struggle with Same-Sex Attraction* and coauthor of *Love Won Out*

Dr. Linda Seiler has given the church a courageously honest and needed gift. *Trans-Formation* incorporates a sound biblical theology of sexuality along with solid academic research, making it a ground-breaking resource for ministers, counselors, parents, and friends of those who struggle with gender identity and LGBTQ issues.

**Beth Grant, PhD,**
Founder of Project Rescue, a ministry
to sexually exploited women and children

Theologically and scientifically, Linda adeptly addresses critical issues today's culture is pressing on the church, including "gay Christian" ideology and origins, while offering practical application regarding spiritual warfare, loving LGBTQ-identified friends and family, and how to navigate gay weddings and transgender pronouns. Every leader who desires to be kingdom relevant must read this book.

**E. Scott Martin, Dmin,**
Senior National Director of Chi Alpha Campus Ministries, USA

I love this book! It sounds like Jesus to me. Not only is it well-written, it is practical, comprehensive, and reflects the heart of someone who has struggled with these very issues and found freedom in Christ. Moreover, I love how it integrates the entire counsel of Scripture with counseling, discipleship, and sound principles of inner healing (or the healing of the soul). This is a great equipping tool for the body of Christ!

**David Kyle Foster, Dmin,**
author of *Love Hunger* and producer of
*Such Were Some of You, How Do You Like Me Now?* and *TranZformed*

Our nation is filled with LGBTQ voices, each one louder and angrier than the one before. Dr. Linda Seiler is the trusted voice that our culture needs today. Uncompromising truth delivered with experience and expertise is the hallmark of *Trans-Formation*.

**Phil Schneider,**
Superintendent of the Illinois District Assemblies of God

Dr. Linda Seiler has masterfully taken the lessons from her testimony and combined them with biblical principles to provide us with *Trans-Formation*. It is obvious we are witnessing a serious moral revolution . . . culture pivoting away from a biblical view on human sexuality. This book is timely and a much-needed resource for the church, equipping believers to respond to the LGBTQ issues that we face.

**Doug Clay,**
General Superintendent of the Assemblies of God, USA

At a time when secular culture has pivoted so dramatically around issues of sexuality and human identity, *Trans-Formation* stands out in its courageous clarity, unwavering conviction, and heart-felt compassion. I shall be recommending it widely.

**James T. Bradford, PhD,**
Lead Pastor of Central Assembly of God in Springfield, MO

What an excellent book filled with hope, radical honesty, spiritual wisdom, and practical resources! Linda's scholarly yet readable explanation of the "why" behind same-sex attraction and gender dysphoria are made even more potent since she has experienced freedom from both. Transformation is possible, and this book lights the way to uncompromisingly agree with the gospel and how God intended for our genders to reflect His glory.

**Kimberley D. Knochel,**
Christian Counselor and Consultant, newdayinitiative.com

I have personally observed Linda's life and the transformation Jesus worked in her. Her testimony and the biblical principles in *Trans-Formation* reinforce the good news that applies to all believers: our divine nature empowers us to live a changed life and walk in victory over sin.

**Donald Gifford,**
Former Superintendent of the Indiana District Assemblies of God

In answer to an increasingly popular idea—that love is authored only by the divorce of kindness and uncompromising truth—Linda has written a book that draws us toward the author of both kindness and truth. She proclaims a paradox—that the marriage of kindness and truth is the true wellspring of love . . . and of sexual wholeness. Linda herself is a refreshing paradox. Her steadfastly loving heart has endeared her even to persons whose actions she steadfastly opposes. This unfailing love and her credible testimony imbue her clear, straightforward message with the same palpable authority that marks the author of us all.

**Mark Sandford,**
Executive Director of Elijah Rain Ministries and
author of *Deliverance and Inner Healing*

A FORMER TRANSGENDER **RESPONDS TO LGBTQ**

**Linda A. Seiler, PhD**

*Trans-Formation*


Published in the United States of America by Credo House Publishers, a division of Credo Communications, LLC, Grand Rapids, Michigan
credohousepublishers.com

ISBN: 978-1-62586-260-0



Cover and interior design by Frank Gutbrod
Editing by Andrew Sloan and Emily Irish

*Printed in the United States of America*
First edition

*To my parents, Jan and Jerry Seiler,*
*whose love and support have made all the difference.*

*Do not conform to the pattern of this world,*
*but be transformed by the renewing of your mind.*
*Then you will be able to test and approve what God's will is—*
*his good, pleasing and perfect will.*
—Romans 12:2

# CONTENTS

**Foreword** by Rev. James T. Bradford, PhD *1*

**Introduction** *5*

**1.** Trans-Formed: My Story *9*

**2.** How Our Sexuality Images the Gospel *27*

**3.** What About Sexual Orientation and Gender Identity? *43*

**4.** The Bible and Homosexuality: "Did God Really Say . . . ?" *57*

**5.** What Science Says: Are People Born Gay/Trans? *83*

**6.** How Same-Sex Attractions Develop *95*

**7.** How Transgender Desires Develop *111*

**8.** How Transformation Happens: Theologically Speaking *125*

**9.** How Transformation Happens: Practical Application *139*

**10.** Redemptive Relationships: Addressing the Fruit *159*

**11.** Inner Healing: Resolving the Root *167*

**12.** The Five Streams: Differing Responses to LGBTQ *191*

**13.** Spiritual Warfare: What's Fueling the Cultural Shift? *225*

**14.** How to Engage LGBTQ-Identified Friends and Loved Ones *237*

**15.** Cultural Conundrums: Church Involvement, Weddings, and Pronouns *251*

**Conclusion:** Reclaiming the Rainbow *269*

**Appendix A:** Quick Guides for Ministry Leaders *271*

**Appendix B:** When Someone Says, "I Experience Same-Sex Attractions" *273*

**Appendix C:** When Someone Says, "I Struggle with My Gender Identity" *277*

**Appendix D:** Rapid-Onset Gender Dysphoria (ROGD): Why Teen Girls Transition *281*

**Glossary** *285*

**Acknowledgments** *291*

**About the Author** *295*

**Endnotes** *297*

# FOREWORD

It is difficult, as a pastor, to know where to begin processing the seismic moral, social, and cultural shifts taking place today, especially regarding sexuality. The secularization of Western culture has placed the traditional biblical view of sexuality in stark contrast to a broadly based acceptance of LGBTQ ideology—creating a dividing line by which we are judged.

The fallout is everywhere. Christians are increasingly stereotyped as hateful, bigoted, and intolerant. Respectful disagreement is now considered hate speech. As a Christ follower, it is easy to feel out-muscled by the culture and out-voiced by the media. For a growing number of churches, addressing issues of sexual immorality and brokenness has become taboo due to fear or social accommodation. Meanwhile, society is decaying all around us. The people we serve pastorally are struggling with addictions, depression, sexual confusion, and hopelessness like never before.

Yet I believe there is a hopeful way forward. Our response to LGBTQ requires a posture of both pastoral compassion and biblical conviction. Compassion without compromise means that we stand on the grounds of love: hating no one and victimizing no one. We follow the way of Jesus, who taught us to care for and serve everyone, even those with whom we disagree or who oppose us. At the same time, Jesus warned that there are pathways of darkness and deception that lead to the death of the human soul. It is there that our conviction of what is true and biblical must never waver. Alignment with God's creative design cannot be subservient to whatever might be celebrated as "normative" in the media, the academy, or the culture at large.

That is why we need this book. With both compassion and conviction, Dr. Linda Seiler provides an incisive and thoughtful biblical response to LGBTQ. Dr. Seiler's response is also disarmingly transparent. The credibility of her work is tied not only to her significant scholarship but also to her personal story. From a place of both gender dysphoria and same-sex attractions to that of healing and freedom, Dr. Seiler's own journey is inspiring and hope-filled. This is not a quick-fix book, but it does provide an in-depth look at the deceptions that can take root in the human heart while, at the same time, elevating the transforming love and power of Jesus.

*Trans-Formation* is built on a carefully crafted biblical theology of sexuality, which I find to be very accessible and insightful. We must think theologically and not emotionally about these issues if we are to stay anchored and redemptive. Additionally, Dr. Seiler's chapter on the five streams of differing responses to LGBTQ in the church today is invaluable.

I have personally known Dr. Seiler for years, first in her role as a university campus pastor and now as the executive director of ReStory Ministries, which is dedicated to resourcing pastors and churches to address LGBTQ. Dr. Seiler is respected not only as a compelling public speaker but as a gifted leader, ministry consultant, and writer. I am personally grateful for her life, her courage, and her influence.

I will always keep Trans-Formation nearby as a valued pastoral resource. May it be for you as well.

Rev. James T. Bradford, PhD
Lead Pastor, Central Assembly of God
Springfield, Missouri

# INTRODUCTION

I was in Chicago in June of 2002. The inner healing conference I had been attending was nearly over, and I stood in the back corner of the auditorium, disheartened. I had been seeking freedom from unwanted transgender desires and same-sex attractions for eight long years—but nothing seemed to change. As I turned toward God in my discouragement, I sensed His still, small voice speaking a hope-filled promise to my heart: *Your healing is not just for you, and it's not just for a few . . .*

That didn't make sense to my natural mind. I still longed to be a man and was attracted exclusively to women. And yet my spirit bore witness: *Someday God will redeem my struggle in such a way that it will help others.*

As I persevered in pursuing the Lord, He eventually fulfilled His promise to me, and I experienced profound transformation beyond anything I could have ever asked or imagined. After an eleven-year journey of transformation, I couldn't wait to tell others what I had experienced, but the Lord instructed me to stay silent and wait on His timing to share publicly. One year passed . . . then three years . . . then five years. It ended up being eight years after my transformation before He gave me the green light.

During that season of waiting, God called me to study for a master's degree at the Assemblies of God Theological Seminary (AGTS). While researching the topic of homosexuality for an ethics class, I thought to myself, *This is so much fun! I'd read this stuff in my spare time, even if it wasn't required for class!* At that moment, I sensed the presence of the Holy Spirit come upon me, and the Lord spoke to my heart: *This is why I called you to AGTS. I want you to continue studying for a PhD; and I'm going to use your testimony, combined with the latest academic research, as a one-two gut punch to the enemy.*

It was a holy moment, pregnant with destiny.

This book is a compilation of my journey of transformation, which began nearly three decades ago, along with highlights from my master's and PhD research. I wrote this book for pastors, missionaries, and lay leaders—though I hope it is a blessing to others as well. Many of us have congregation members, friends, or loved ones who are looking to us for answers on LGBTQ matters. And that's when the panic sets in: *There wasn't a credentialing class on this!*

We have to figure this out as we go. What does the Bible say about sexual orientation, gender identity, and "sex-reassignment surgery"?[1] How should we respond when someone says they feel like they were born gay or trans? What about those who tried to change and can't? Why are teenagers adopting LGBTQ identities at alarming rates? Does transformation mean all temptation disappears? What about "celibate gay Christians"? How do we respond to LGBTQ-identified loved ones who accuse us of bigotry because we affirm God's design for sexuality? Should a Christian attend a gay wedding? What about transgender pronouns?

This book addresses these questions and more, starting first and foremost with a biblical theology of sexuality that serves as the foundation for the rest of the book. After examining Scripture, I discuss the latest research regarding the origin of same-sex attractions and transgender desires. The latter half of the book moves into practical application, integrating truths from Scripture, science, and my personal experience. Chapter twelve on the five streams is one of the most important chapters of the book, synthesizing truths from the previous chapters to inform our pastoral care and mission to the lost. If you're the parent of a child who identifies as LGBTQ, I include a specific word to you at the end of chapter seven.

Each chapter ends with discussion questions useful for personal reflection, staff team development, or small group interaction. I also include valuable resources in the endnotes and appendixes, plus a glossary of LGBTQ terms. If you're interested in reading a more robust thesis, you can access my PhD dissertation online.[2]

May the Holy Spirit guide you as you read, filling you with the knowledge of His will through all spiritual wisdom and understanding so that you can respond to LGBTQ matters—and, most importantly, to the people whom God loves—by demonstrating Christ's compassion without compromising the good news of His transforming power.

# 1

# TRANS-FORMED: MY STORY

It was nearly time to get up for kindergarten, but I decided to stay in bed a bit longer to do some business with God. If He really did exist, and He could do anything, then certainly He could change me into a boy before I got out of bed. So, I put my request in with God, dropped my pajama bottoms, and waited.

And waited some more.

I gave Him a good ten to fifteen minutes.

Eventually, I got out of bed, a disappointed little girl who doubted God's love for her.

I have zero childhood memories of being content in a female body. I had never heard the terms *transgender* or *gender dysphoria*[3]—those weren't common in the 1970s. Somehow, I just knew I was born in the wrong body and that I wouldn't be complete unless I had male anatomy. I was a tomboy in every sense of the word and was often mistaken for a boy, which always made my day. My parents and older sister knew nothing of my secret ambition and probably thought I would grow out of my tomboy phase, as many girls do. But to me, this was no phase: *masculinity was my destiny.*

Or so I thought.

When I was about nine years old, I heard about "sex-change operations,"[4] and I decided that was the answer to my dilemma. I charted out my plan: As soon as I was old enough and had enough money, I would change my name to David (which is what my parents would have named me if I had been a boy), get a sex change, and live happily ever after.

During that school year, a classmate pushed me into the boys' bathroom, and I saw a wall of urinals. I had no idea how the other half lived, if you know what I mean. I became mesmerized by urinals, which became a symbol of the forbidden world that I so desperately longed to join. From that point forward, I snuck into men's restrooms and pretended to use a urinal. No one batted an eye because I looked so much like a boy. That eventually developed into a fetish for urinals that dominated my life for decades. In addition to visiting men's restrooms for the sexual high, I spent hours alone in my room, drawing urinals and male body parts. At one point, I considered becoming an architect so that I could design men's restrooms.

When I was about ten years old, some childhood friends introduced me to the Playboy Channel, which prematurely awakened my sexual desires. I became fascinated with the men in those movies and longed to have a male body so that I could act out sexually as a man. That developed into rampant sexual addictions that would span the next twenty-plus years.

In junior high, when all the other girls were interested in makeup and boys, I wanted nothing to do with that world. I despised my own body that began showing signs of femininity. I was intensely jealous of the boys around me whose voices were changing, and I mourned the fact that my voice wouldn't change like that. Instead, I was stuck in a female body, subjected to stupid training bras and inconvenienced by monthly periods. Being female was a curse. I became depressed and even began to entertain suicidal thoughts.

It was around this time that I discovered, to my horror, that I was sexually attracted to women.

I didn't choose that.

I didn't want that.

But I felt helpless to change it.

My attractions didn't start with sexual feelings. Initially, I just wanted the attention of older, nurturing women who had a certain quality of maternal strength about them. I wanted them to notice me, to connect with me, and to hold me in a motherly embrace. I spent hours alone in my room fantasizing scenarios where I was in distress, drowning in a river, and one of the women I admired would come to my rescue and hold me. When my adolescent hormones kicked in, that desire for emotional and physical connection became confused with my normal sex drive. It felt like I had been born attracted to women instead of men.

I still remember my first sexual attraction. I was taken by surprise when I felt butterflies in my stomach and extreme excitement upon seeing a certain female junior high teacher who paid special attention to me. After a while, I realized what those feelings were. Little did I know that teacher was grooming me and drawing me into an inappropriate relationship that compounded my sexual confusion.

I was ashamed of my attractions, and I dared not tell anyone. Adopting an LGBTQ identity wasn't trendy in the 1980s like it is today. In fact, those who "came out" were ridiculed and ostracized. I didn't feel like I could talk to my parents. I had to figure it out on my own. I reasoned to myself, *If I truly am a man trapped inside a female body, then I should be attracted to women; that just makes me a straight man. I just need to hold out for the sex change, and my whole world will make sense.*

Near the end of junior high, I started to consider the ramifications of getting a sex change in a way I hadn't thought through as a nine-year-old. How would I tell my family? I couldn't just leave the house one day as Linda and come back the next day as David. Of course, I knew nothing about the then-required counseling, hormone replacement therapy, and living as the opposite sex for two years before surgery. In my juvenile mind, I literally thought I could go to the hospital as a woman and leave the next day as a man. I started to think from my family's perspective: What would my parents think? What would my sister think? What would the neighbors think? What would my *grandparents* think?

Fearing rejection, I concluded that I had only two options: run away from home, have the surgery, and live happily ever after; or don't have the surgery, never tell my family, and do my best to conform to societal norms so that no one would ever know my deep, dark secret. I remember the day I was walking down a hall in junior high and consciously chose option B—because my family was all I had. I didn't have friends. I wasn't "one of the girls," and I wasn't officially a boy. I felt like a third sex that didn't fit in anywhere. I loved my family, and I knew they loved me and would be heartbroken if I ran away and never spoke to them again. The thought of leaving my family and living alone—even if I got to live as a man—was daunting.

From that point forward, I decided that I had to do whatever it took to pass as a girl without being too "frilly." But deep inside, I still longed to be a man. The attractions to women became increasingly difficult to resist, and I was still enslaved to sexual addictions and the urinal fetish.

When I started high school, I let my hair grow long and began making more of an effort to appear female, taking cues from my older sister. But for me it was more of a means of survival than of embracing my true identity as a woman. By my junior year, I decided that maybe I wasn't attracted to guys because I had never tried dating. Perhaps experimenting sexually would awaken dormant attractions to men. In a grand scheme to "cure" myself, I asked a guy from my physics class to go to the turnabout[5] dance with me. I borrowed a dress from my sister and played the role of a girl dating a boy. I have a picture of me standing in that dress like a football player next to my date. No sparks were flying that night; it was awkward on every level. Dressing up always felt like wearing a costume, like I was a man dressing in drag.[6]

Over the course of high school and college, I tried dating guys and experimenting sexually with them in hopes that it would awaken something in me, but my plan backfired. The more I fooled around with guys, the more jealous I became; I wanted to be the *man* with the woman, not the *woman* with the man. I concluded I must have been born this way, and nothing could change that.

During my junior year in high school, a friend invited me to an evangelistic outreach, where I heard the gospel for the first time. Though I had been raised going to church, I thought I had to earn my salvation through good works. It was news to me that I could simply trust in Jesus's completed work on the cross and receive His righteousness as a gift. I surrendered my life to Jesus that night and sincerely believed that when I woke up the next morning all of my illicit desires would go away. Much to my disappointment, I woke up the next morning still attracted to women and desiring to be a man—only now I was in a dilemma because no one in the church seemed to be talking about LGBTQ. I would have to work even harder to fool everyone and fit in.

Despite my sexual desires not changing, I did have a genuine salvation experience. I started attending my church youth group and, for the first time in my life, felt like I had friends who loved me. But the closer I got to females, the more I struggled with my attractions and sexual addictions. I was miserable, yet I didn't feel like I could tell anyone.

In college, I joined a campus ministry and developed a deeper relationship with Jesus. I started reading my Bible regularly and sharing Christ with the lost. I eventually became a student ministry leader. No one knew that behind closed doors I still longed to be a man, was sexually attracted to my female mentor, and was enslaved to sexual addictions. I remember kneeling on my college dorm floor and begging God to please take away my same-sex attractions and the desire to be a man.

But nothing changed.

In fact, things grew worse.

During my senior year in college, I heard a sermon about overcoming habitual sin. The speaker quoted James 5:16—"Confess your sins one to another and pray for each other so that you may be healed"—stressing how important it is to bring sin into the light to be free. I was deeply convicted and knew I would never be free unless I took what was in the dark and exposed it in the light with a trusted leader.

It took all the courage I could muster to finally tell my campus pastor, John. I was twenty-one at the time, and no one on planet earth—not even my parents—knew my lifelong secret. I so feared rejection that I momentarily considered suicide as a way out of my appointment with John. By God's grace, I didn't follow through.

When I finally met with John and told him my deep, dark secret, I expected him to react with shock, disgust, or condemnation when he heard one of his student leaders was living a double life. Instead, John looked me straight in the eyes and said, "Thank you for sharing your struggle with me. I know that took a lot of courage, and I want you to know that doesn't change our opinion of you. We love you. We see the hand of God on your life. And we want to get you the help that you need."

That was a phenomenal response for 1994. I can never thank God enough for John's pastoral compassion. Had he responded any differently, I might not be alive today.

I walked away from that conversation stunned. I expected rejection yet was met with love. As I reflected on what just happened, I sensed the still, small voice of the Lord saying, *What you just saw is a picture of My heart. That's how I feel about you, Linda. I love you. I'm sad that you're hurting, and I want to get you the help that you need.*

God's response astounded me. I had always felt He hated me because of my sin. John's reaction revealed a side of the Father I had never experienced before.[7] For the first time in my life, I discovered that being completely transparent with another person was tremendously healing.

That day was the first step in what would be an eleven-year journey of transformation. I didn't know it would be eleven years, or I probably wouldn't have signed up for the trip! Suffice it to say, transformation takes time and isn't so much about the "finished product" as it is about growing in intimacy with Jesus as we face our struggles with Him.

After I confided in John, he met with me a few times and eventually connected me with a professional counselor. When I told my counselor I wanted to be a man, she responded by saying, "Well, we all probably wonder at times if the grass is greener on the other side."

I never brought that up again with her.

I met with that counselor for about a year and felt like I hit a plateau. My desires weren't changing, and I felt hopeless. I had recently gotten involved in an Assemblies of God campus church with students on fire for the Lord, and I wanted to know God like they did. They introduced me to the baptism in the Holy Spirit. It took me a while to get filled because I had been told that speaking in tongues was demonic. But I couldn't deny the presence of the Lord in this little campus church. After studying the Scriptures, I became convinced that the baptism in the Spirit is a gift for today, and I wanted everything God had to offer. I was alone in a room when the Spirit filled me; and second to salvation, that encounter changed my life forever.[8]

The following spring, our church hosted a guest speaker from Texas whom I had never met. We called her "Mama Carol" because she was old enough to be our grandma and because she loved college students. My friends urged me to come hear Mama Carol because she "moved in the prophetic" and could "read your mail." I had no idea what that meant, but I was so hungry for more of God that I went to the meeting.

During her presentation that night, Mama Carol stepped off the platform, walked up to my seat, and asked my name. I freaked out. But Mama Carol calmly said, "Linda, the Lord wants you to know that when you were born, He wanted another little girl and not a boy . . . " And for the next nine minutes she "read my mail"! God spoke things through Mama Carol that I had never told another person, including how I thought women in the Bible were second-class citizens and how I was resisting God's call on my life.

Mama Carol shared my private thoughts in such detail that I knew the Lord was interrupting my existence and speaking through this woman I had never met. The prophetic message ended with, "There is going to come a day when you look in the mirror and say, 'I like me' instead of 'I hate me.'"

My mind couldn't comprehend that, yet my spirit knew it was true. The Lord used that prophetic message to plant a supernatural seed of faith in my spirit that someday, somehow, my sexual brokenness would be a thing of the past.[9]

The next decade was full of ups and downs as I met with multiple counselors, read books on sexual brokenness, attended conferences, and listened to cassette tapes, one of which helped me realize I was experiencing transgender desires. It was a slow process, as I wasn't aware of many resources to help people like me. One well-meaning Christian counselor told me he had worked with people who had same-sex attractions but never anyone with transgender desires. He said, "I'll do my best to help you cope this side of heaven. Just know that when you die, you'll be free." Because of the supernatural seed of faith deposited in me through Mama Carol's prophetic message, I disregarded the counselor's comment and thought to myself, *I don't know how, and I don't know when—and God's probably not going to use you—but there will come a day when I'm totally free.*

Nevertheless, I thirsted so deeply for female nurture that I seemed to get worse (i.e., acting out sexually with another woman) before I got better. I was disillusioned when I realized my fantasy of being a man who slept with women would never fill the deep ache in my soul. I broke off that relationship, repented before my pastor, and received his help to focus on the Lord and get connected to accountability.

Seven years into my healing journey, I met a counselor who specialized in helping those with transgender desires, with which he himself used to struggle. I still remember our first phone conversation. He described what it's like to feel intense envy of the opposite sex and the anguish of feeling trapped in the wrong body. For the first time in my life, I felt a connection with someone who understood my unique struggle. I wasn't alone anymore. And if God could help this man, surely He could help me.

Through that counselor I came to realize that my sexual addictions were merely fruit from a deeper root. The evil one had taken advantage of wounds of rejection to lure me into believing lies about my sexuality. The path to resolving the pain in my heart was to renounce the lies, receive God's truth, and find comfort in my heavenly Father instead of in the arms of another woman. I had met with multiple Christian counselors prior to that point, but we did more talking than praying about the roots of my disordered desires. I started to meet with several prayer ministers and began to see incremental changes along the way, but it was a slow process that seemed to take forever. I can remember at times curling up in the fetal position on the floor and screaming because I couldn't stand the inner anguish. It was a grueling process, but I resolved not to give up. God had spoken, and I believed Him. *There is going to come a day when you look in the mirror and say, "I like me" instead of "I hate me."*

As I continued to pursue the Lord, He put a spiritual mom in my life to walk alongside me. Pastor Nan was only a few years older than I but much more spiritually mature. She and her husband, Russ, pastored the campus church where I was newly on staff. As I got to know Nan and grew spiritually under her pastoral care, I found myself sexually attracted to her. It became increasingly difficult to be around her due to the strong temptation.

Eventually, I decided to get everything in the light and met with Pastor Russ and Pastor Nan to confess my struggles. I told them they should fire me so I could get away from Pastor Nan. Pastor Russ disagreed. He said temptation would arise no matter where I went, and if I left, I would be disconnected from community, making my struggles more difficult to overcome. Then he dropped a zinger that changed my life forever: "Linda, you got hurt in relationship, and you'll get healed in relationship."

I found his statement both reassuring (that he and Nan were committed to helping me) yet also terrifying because it was so difficult to be around Nan. Prior to that point in my life, if I found myself attracted to a woman, I would cut off relationship with her to eliminate the temptation. But clearly my cut-and-run strategy wasn't working.

Russ and Nan assured me that they weren't fazed by my attractions; Nan's heart was for Russ with no sexual inclinations toward me. From that point forward, they began to invest in me relationally in a wholesome way, like spiritual parents. I started to realize that my sexual attractions were rooted in my own insecurity as a female, and my attempt to bond sexually with Pastor Nan was a subconscious effort to become one with her femininity in order to complete what I deemed lacking in myself.[10]

I found myself wanting to be just like Nan, much like a daughter might want to emulate her mother. I missed that crucial stage in childhood development because I rejected my mom early on, perceiving her as weak and emotional. I wanted to be more like Dad, who seemed strong and stable. Instead of imitating Mom, like most girls do, wearing her heels or trying on her makeup, I imitated Dad, pretending to shave and mow the lawn. I had no idea that rejecting my mother created a vacuum for feminine love that I sought to fill with other women.

As I experienced wholesome love from Pastor Nan, I saw more clearly how my attractions were simply fruit from a deeper root: a thirst for feminine love that had become confused with my God-given sexual desires. God used my relationship with Pastor Nan to draw me into the world of women and help me complete the developmental milestone I had missed earlier in life. Soon I *wanted* to start dressing more like a woman—this time not to fool anyone, but to genuinely embrace who God created me to be. My outward appearance changed as I ventured into the world of women and discovered my God-given identity. Nan played a vital role in that process, helping me find my own sense of style and giving me advice about makeup, mannerisms, and approaching life from a feminine perspective. It also helped to have the affirmation of a small group of women and men from my church who affirmed me both as a woman among women and as a woman distinct from, yet cherished by, men.

All the while, I continued to pursue Jesus in the secret place, met with Christian counselors, and experienced inner-healing prayer sessions. My desires diminished somewhat, but they weren't fully resolved. I still wanted to be a man, was still attracted to women, and still battled sexual addictions and the urinal fetish. After nearly eleven years of seeking God and contending for transformation, I had hit my limit and was ready to give up.

Through a series of events, the Lord led me to an exceptionally gifted prayer minister who offered week-long prayer intensives. I was desperate to try anything, so I flew thousands of miles to attend a one-on-one intensive. Before I left, I gathered a team of forty intercessors to pray for me during the sessions that week. I'm so grateful I was part of a church that knew how to pray and battle in the spiritual realm. Their intercession was crucial to the transformation I experienced.

During the prayer intensive, the Holy Spirit revealed wounds of rejection that I didn't even know existed, which fueled the lie that it's better to be a man than a woman. (I'll give specific examples in a later chapter.) As the Lord exposed each wound, I forgave those who hurt me, let go of bitterness, renounced inner vows, and repented of my sinful responses to rejection. In doing so, we took back the legal ground I had given to the evil one. As I came out of agreement with the enemy's lies, I was able to receive God's life-giving truth that transformed me from the inside out.

After one of the prayer sessions, I went back to my room to seek the Lord and began to cry, which was uncharacteristic for me. I thought to myself, *My crying sounds weak and womanly, just like my mother.* I sensed the Lord saying, *I'm not turned off by your emotions. You can be as weak and as womanly as you want, falling apart into a million pieces, and I will be right here to pick up each piece.* My heavenly Father's compassionate response made me cry all the more. And the more I cried, the more He drew near—so close that it was as if I could feel His hands holding my heart. My lifelong yearning to be held and comforted by a woman was met in that intimate moment, in the tender arms of my heavenly Father.

As I experienced inner healing prayer and intimate encounters with the Lord, I discovered a newfound contentment in being a woman. I no longer felt the pull to be held by a woman, as that thirst had been met in the presence of my heavenly Father. I experienced freedom from the urinal fetish and sexual addictions, which were essentially a counterfeit of the comfort I could only find in my heavenly Father's love.

As I continued to walk out my healing over the next several years, sexual attractions to men began to emerge. It was as if I were going through a delayed emotional puberty in my late thirties—which was both awkward and thrilling at the same time! God had transformed me from the inside out and accomplished the impossible. I still feel like I'm living a dream!

Each day that I walk with Jesus I walk further away from my past and step into greater wholeness as the unique woman God created me to be. I like to dress up and look pretty, but I also like to wear a ballcap and play sports. I enjoy fellowship with women, but I'd still rather watch football than go to a baby shower. Instead of a purse, I carry a backpack. (I'm a missionary to college students, after all!) I may not fit all the cultural stereotypes, but I'm secure in who God created me to be; and I no longer desire to be a man, nor am I compelled to bond sexually with women. That thirst has been met in legitimate ways, "for he satisfies the thirsty and fills the hungry with good things" (Psalm 107:9).

The transformation I've experienced doesn't erase my history or my vulnerabilities. There are times I still hunger for maternal love, and God has graciously provided spiritual moms who meet that need in legitimate ways. I'm still discovering how some of my relational conflicts in the present are connected to unresolved wounds from my past, and I'm still learning to seek refuge in my heavenly Father's love instead of finding comfort in food. But that's all part of the process of progressive sanctification. The good news is that God never gives up on us; and no matter how much we struggle, there is always more growth and transformation available in Jesus. Always.

Healing from sexual brokenness is rarely instantaneous—it's more like peeling back the layers of an onion, one at a time. But if we will determine to hold fast to the truth of God's Word, lean on God's family, and allow His healing touch into the deepest wounds of our heart, we can experience the transformation that Jesus died to give us. I am a living example of what the Bible says: "Such *were* some of you."

> Or do you not know that the unrighteous will not inherit the kingdom of God? Do not be deceived; neither fornicators, nor idolaters, nor adulterers, nor effeminate, nor homosexuals, nor thieves, nor the covetous, nor drunkards, nor revilers, nor swindlers, will inherit the kingdom of God. *Such were some of you;* but you were washed, but you were sanctified, but you were justified in the name of the Lord Jesus Christ and in the Spirit of our God. (1 Corinthians 6:9–11, NASB, italics mine)

## DISCUSSION QUESTIONS

1. What are your thoughts about Linda's story?
2. What questions do you still have?
3. How might Linda's story be an encouragement to someone who struggles with their sexuality?
4. What concepts do you see in Linda's story that might encourage someone who struggles in an area other than sexual brokenness?

2

# HOW OUR SEXUALITY IMAGES THE GOSPEL

Today's younger generation doesn't want to hear *that* homosexuality is wrong; they want to know *why*. If sex is merely a physical act, and "love is love," then who are gay people hurting when they "marry" each other? Why in the world is homosexuality a hill Christians must die on?

The answer lies in our understanding of and submission to God's ultimate design for our sexuality. God created us in His image with sexed bodies for a purpose: to reflect His character and nature and point toward the good news of the gospel. The following three questions will serve as a guide in this chapter to help us understand God's design for sexuality and why it matters:

1. Who is God?
2. Who are we in light of who God is?
3. What do the answers to the above have to do with sex?

## Who Is God?

For the sake of simplicity, let's look at just three aspects of God's nature that appear in the first chapter of Genesis:

First, God is a Creator who brings all of life into existence: "In the beginning God created the heavens and the earth" (Genesis 1:1).

Second, God is a relational God: "Let us make mankind in *our* image" (Genesis 1:26, emphasis added). The *us* and *our* are taken by multiple scholars and early church writers as veiled references to the Trinity.[11] In that sense, God exists in a divine community of holy love between Father, Son, and Holy Spirit.[12] As a relational Creator, God invites us to participate in His divine community of holy love, which is the ultimate goal of the gospel: restoring our broken relationship with Him. The gospel isn't merely about praying the "sinner's prayer" so that we can go to heaven when we die; it's an invitation to turn away from self-rule and be restored to relationship with our Creator. It's about joining His divine community of holy love and living wholly yielded to our benevolent King in such a way that we persuade others to join us in worship around His worthy throne. God is all about relationship.

Third, God's Trinitarian nature is a paradoxical mystery. A paradox occurs when two seemingly contradictory statements are both true. God is a paradox because He exists as three distinct persons (Father, Son, and Holy Spirit), and yet He is one God.

Another way of describing this mystery is to say that God exists as "unity in diversity." The Hebrew words used in Deuteronomy 6:4 reveal the mystery of unity in diversity: "Hear, O Israel: The Lord our God [*elohim*—plural word, translatable as 'gods,' as in Father, Son, Holy Spirit all are God], the Lord is one [*echad*—understood in this verse as one in essence, not one in number]." We generally think of unity as indicating sameness. But the mystery of the Trinity is that God exists as three distinct persons who remain wholly unified: unity in diversity.

So, who is God? He is a relational Creator who welcomes us to participate in His divine community of holy love that exists as unity in diversity. Again, I'm oversimplifying here for the sake of argument. The mystery of God, especially as it relates to the Trinity, is not something we can fully understand this side of heaven.

## Who Are We in Light of Who God Is?

According to Scripture, we are made in the image of God: "Then God said, 'Let us make mankind *in our image*, in *our* likeness'" (Genesis 1:26, italics mine). An image reflects the original. For example, when you look in the mirror, you see a reflection of yourself. The image in the mirror reflects you, but it is not you. In the same way, we are made in the image of God. We are not God, but we reflect what God is like. As His creation, we reflect the three aspects of God mentioned above: creativity (as in the ability to create), relationality, and unity-in-diversity.

We reflect God's creativity as procreative beings. Just as God creates life and rules over the universe, God designed human beings to image their Creator by procreating and ruling over the earth:

> God blessed them and said to them, "Be fruitful and increase in number; fill the earth and subdue it. Rule over the fish in the sea and the birds in the sky and over every living creature that moves on the ground." (Genesis 1:28)

We reflect God's relational nature in that we were designed to exist in community: "It's not good for man to be *alone.* I will make a helper suitable for him" (Genesis 2:18, italics mine). God created us for relationship, out of which comes the possibility of procreation. The exclusive relationship of husband and wife has the potential to extend beyond them as they produce children and invite them into their family, just as God created us and invites us to participate in His divine community of holy love.[13]

Finally, we reflect God's unity in diversity as indicated by Genesis 1:27: "So God created mankind in his own image, in the image of God he created them; *male* and *female* he created them" (italics mine). As human beings made in the image of God, we are united in our humanity yet diverse in our sexuality as male and female. While this is true of all humanity, there is a deeper dimension to that reality in human marriage, describing the union of husband and wife.

The word *echad*, used in Deuteronomy 6:4 to describe God's unity in diversity, is the same word used in Genesis 2:24 to describe the mystery of unity in diversity imaged in human marriage: "That is why a man leaves his father and mother and is united to his wife, and they become one flesh [*echad*—meaning one in essence here, not one in number]." All humanity, and especially the marital union, images the mystery of God's unity in diversity.

## Christ and His Bride

According to Scripture, the earthly marriage between male and female is not an end in and of itself but rather a reflection of the greatest marriage of all: that of Christ and His Bride, the church. The same three characteristics—procreativity, relationality, and unity in diversity—characterize the relationship between us and Christ.

First, procreation happens in the spiritual realm when we place our faith in Christ and are born of God: "Yet to all who did receive him, to those who believed in his name, he gave the right to become children of God—children born not of natural descent, nor of human decision or a husband's will, but born of God" (John 1:12–13). No one comes into the kingdom unless they are "born again" (John 3:3). Scripture refers to newborn believers as spiritual babes and new creatures in Christ (1 Corinthians 3:1–2; 2 Corinthians 5:17) who mature through discipleship.

Second, God's relational nature is reflected in the Great Commission and the process of discipleship. Just as

Jesus became flesh and dwelled among us (known as the Incarnation), we are to live "incarnationally" among the lost. Through relationship, we influence others to become born again; and we welcome them into the body of Christ, just as God welcomes us into His divine community of holy love. We then disciple (or "spiritually parent") new babes in Christ by teaching them to obey everything Christ has taught us (Matthew 28:19–20; 1 Corinthians 4:15; 1 Thessalonians 2:11). In that sense, we pass on our "spiritual DNA" to the next generation. The whole process is intensely relational; and as we continue to invest in relational discipleship, God's kingdom grows exponentially.

Last, our relationship with Jesus reflects God's unity in diversity. Jesus is fully human, just like us; and yet He is also fully God, unlike us. Thus, the marriage between Christ and His Bride images the paradox of unity in diversity. Paul compares the spiritual union of Christ and the church to the mystery of physical oneness between male and female:

> Do you not know that he who unites himself with a prostitute is one with her in body? For it is said, "The two will become one flesh." But whoever is united with the Lord is one with him in spirit. (1 Corinthians 6:16–17)

I believe this is one of the reasons Jesus never married. He wasn't looking for an earthly partner; His sights were set higher. Everything points toward the ultimate marriage between Christ and His Bride, the church:

> "For this reason a man will leave his father and mother and be united to his wife, and the two will become one flesh." This is a profound mystery—but I am talking about Christ and the church. (Ephesians 5:31–32)

Throughout Scripture God uses marriage to describe the kind of relationship He wants with His people. In the Old Testament, He compares wayward Israel to an adulteress and expresses His desire to betroth Israel to Himself: "I will betroth you to me forever; I will betroth you in righteousness and justice, in love and compassion. I will betroth you in faithfulness, and you will acknowledge the Lord" (Hosea 2:19–20). In the New Testament, He describes the ultimate fulfillment of His relationship with us as "the wedding of the Lamb" (Revelation 19:7).

## How Sexuality Images God's Love

Comparing our relationship with Christ to earthly marriage doesn't mean God wants to have sex with us. God is spirit (John 4:24), so the category of biological sex doesn't apply to Him.[14] However, as our Creator, God is the source of all things male and female, and He uses our understanding of biological sex to reveal Himself to us in ways we can understand. For instance, we can relate to God as Father because we understand what a father-child relationship looks like.

God also uses feminine imagery to describe His attributes. For example, He compares Himself to a mother who comforts her children (Isaiah 49:15; 66:13), a bear robbed of her cubs (Hosea 13:8), and a hen who gathers her chicks (Matthew 23:37). Scripture even speaks of God giving birth (Deuteronomy 32:18; Isaiah 42:14; James 1:18), which aligns with the concept of being "born again" (John 3:3).

This is not to say that God is female. Again, God is spirit and is not confined to our concept of biological sex and is therefore neither anatomically male nor female.[15] No human analogy can fully contain God, for God is "*sui generis*, wholly other than anything else in the created order."[16] And yet we understand what God is like through the lens of what we know: a shepherd who cares for his sheep, a father who welcomes his prodigal son, a mother who comforts her child, and a groom who pursues his bride.[17]

We refer to God as "Him" not because God is a biological male but because God reveals Himself relationally to us as our Father.[18] In a spiritual sense, we are born again from above as God places His spiritual seed (in Greek, *sperma*) in us: "No one who is born of God will continue to sin, because God's seed [*sperma*] remains in them; they cannot go on sinning, because they have been born of God" (1 John 3:9). To further the analogy, God is the initiator and giver of all life, and we are the recipient of His seed. In that regard, God is forever masculine toward us, and we are forever feminine toward Him. We are collectively called the Bride of Christ, an analogy that includes both anatomical males and anatomical females.

While God reveals Himself with both male and female attributes, that doesn't mean God is transgender or a hermaphrodite (having both male and female reproductive organs);[19] God is spirit and is therefore not constrained by biological anatomy as we are. As humans, our physical bodies, including our biological sex, are sacred symbols that reflect God's nature and demonstrate the kind of relationship He wants to have with us. Just as the bodies of a husband and wife come together in a covenantal sexual union to form a deep and intimate bond, so too God wants to know us in the most intimate way possible: spirit touching Spirit. One author explains how our sexuality reflects God's desire for intimate communion in this way:

> Sexuality as part of God's image . . . is the human drive toward intimate communion. More than a mere physical itch that needs scratching, it urges us "to experience the other, to trust the other, and to be trusted by [that other person], to enter the other's life by entering the vital embrace of his or her body." Of course, the search toward mutual trust and self-disclosure is also present in friendships and family relationships at their best. But with the urge for sexual intercourse there comes the added

> dimension of passion, ecstasy and throwing-off of restraint. Thus, sexual intimacy involves, at one time, the maximum degree of risk (if it goes badly) and the maximum promise of communion (if it goes well).[20]

The fact that God desires such intimate communion with His creation is not nearly as astounding as the idea that God would figuratively throw off restraint, become vulnerable with us, and risk total rejection. And yet, that's who God is—One who invites us into relationship with Him to experience mutual trust and self-disclosure, with the added dimension of throwing off all restraints to know and be fully known. God uses our sexuality to reveal the depths of His intimate, risk-taking, all-consuming love. In this way, human marriage images the kind of exclusive, monogamous relationship God wants to have with His people: "You shall have no other gods before me" (Exodus 20:3).

The way our sexuality images God is not limited to marriage. In contrast to the exclusivity of the marital covenant, singles image God's all-inclusive love to welcome "whoever believes" (John 3:16) to participate in His divine community. Rather than forming exclusive bonds with the opposite sex, single people can form platonic friendships with multiple members of the opposite sex, the same way God opens His heart to those still outside of His kingdom. In this way, singles image God's desire to inclusively welcome everyone to be in relationship with Him, while marriage images God's desire for an exclusive, intimate relationship. In this way, both marriage and singleness image the beauty of God's holy love.

## What Does This Have to Do with Sex?

Many Christians skip the nature of God as a starting point on the topic of sexuality and instead look at sex through the lens of rules—i.e., a list of what we *should* and *shouldn't* do. We tell our Christian teenagers, "Don't have sex until you get married," without giving them the larger context as to how our sexuality is a sacred symbol of the gospel. When it comes to homosexuality, we quote Leviticus 18:22: "You shall not sleep with a male as one sleeps with a female; it is an *abomination*" (NASB, italics mine). And yet some don't even know what an *abomination* is, much less why the homosexual act is referred to as such. (I will address the meaning of *abomination* in chapter 4.)

If our starting point for sexuality focuses on following all the rules, we'll lack motivation to obey them because rules apart from relationship lead to rebellion. God didn't create us as robots to follow rules; He created us to be in relationship with Him, out of which flows our motivation and resulting actions. In short, God didn't create sex to serve a set of rules; instead, sexuality reveals things about God to us and the kind of relationship He wants to have with us. Our sexuality images the good news of the gospel so that as we live out our sexuality according to His design, our lives persuade others to accept His invitation to participate in His divine community of holy love.

Thus, instead of looking at sexuality through the lens of *dos* and *don'ts*, let's look at how our sexuality images the characteristics of God that I mentioned earlier in this chapter: creativity, relationality, and unity in diversity. For the sake of clarity, I'm going to start with unity in diversity and go in reverse order.

### How Our Sexuality Images God

First, Scripture reveals that God's design for sexual intimacy involves unity in diversity and forbids any sexual act that falls short. For example, divorce is not part of God's design for marriage because it images dis-unity, not unity in diversity. Dennis Hollinger writes, "Just as the oneness of the divine Trinity cannot be broken or pulled apart, so the oneness from the covenant relationship, sealed by the sexual union, is not to be pulled apart."[21] God designed marriage as a lifelong, monogamous covenant to image the kind of exclusive relationship He wants with us for all eternity.

Similarly, Scripture forbids the homosexual act because two humans of the same sex image unity in sameness, not unity in diversity. This is the fundamental reason *why* the Bible forbids homosexuality. It's not a matter of whether two people of the same sex have romantic feelings for each other. Rather, what we do with our bodies is meant to be a sacred symbol of unity in diversity, pointing to the ultimate marriage between Christ and His Bride, the church. This is also why bestiality (sex with animals) is forbidden: a human and an animal image only diversity, not unity. When Adam named the animals, no suitable helper was found for him (Genesis 2:20), which resulted in God forming Eve out of Adam's side, foreshadowing the birth of the church out of Christ's side on the cross.

Second, Scripture reveals that God's design for sexual intimacy involves a lifelong covenant relationship and forbids any sexual act that does not. This includes adultery, fornication (sex before marriage), and any other kind of sexual activity outside of a lifelong, one-man-with-one-woman covenant. Rape violates God's design because it does not image the kind of mutual love relationship God desires; God would never violate you for His selfish purposes and then discard you. Pornography violates God's design in that it is devoid of relationship and commitment; it is impossible to have an intimate relationship with an image on a screen. Similarly, masturbation falls short of God's design for sex, as it is an act done in isolation, separate from relationship and lifelong covenant with another person.

Finally, Scripture reveals that God's design for sexual intimacy involves procreative capacity and forbids any sexual act that does not. God blessed Adam and Eve and commanded them to "be fruitful and increase in number; fill the earth and subdue it" (Genesis 1:28). Only a heterosexual union can fulfill that mandate. Again, this is why the homosexual act, along with bestiality, is prohibited. Under no circumstances can two humans of the same biological sex create life, nor can the union of a human and an animal create life. Likewise, pedophilia is not God's design for sexual behavior, since a child cannot reproduce, nor does an adult imposing his or her desires upon a vulnerable child reflect God's heart for a mutual covenant relationship.

Incidentally, this does not refer to infertile couples, couples who choose not to have children, or older couples who have aged beyond their childbearing years. We know that under normal circumstances the sexual act between a man and woman of childbearing age carries with it the capacity for procreation. Because we live in a fallen world, there are biological males and females who lack the ability to procreate. Infertile couples often seek medical advice to find out why they are infertile, because we know procreation is normative for a male-female sexual union. In contrast, couples in a same-sex sexual union never seek medical advice as to why they are unable to procreate, since they know that childbearing is anatomically impossible.

## The Why Behind It All

In sum, our physical bodies are temples of the Holy Spirit (1 Corinthians 6:19–20), designed by God to reflect His character and nature and to point to the good news of the gospel. That's why the Bible forbids any sexual act that does not image God's creativity, relationality, and unity in diversity, as reflected in a covenantal marriage between a man and a woman and ultimately realized in the marriage between

Christ and His Bride, the church. Consequently, we steward our sexuality based on relationship, not rules. For example, my motivation to abstain from having sex before marriage is not because of a random rule but because my sexuality is a sacred symbol of the gospel. If Jesus can wait more than two thousand years for His Bride, I can wait a few months or years to make a lifelong covenant with my earthly mate.

Clearly, Western culture has strayed far from God's design for sexuality, insisting that "love is love" and introducing concepts, such as "sexual orientation" and "gender identity," which do not appear in Scripture. The next chapter helps us understand how to approach those concepts from a scriptural perspective.

## DISCUSSION QUESTIONS

1. How does our sexuality image God and ultimately point to the gospel?
2. What are your thoughts on approaching sexuality from the starting point of relationship (i.e., how we image God) versus starting with rules (i.e., what we should/shouldn't do)?
3. Based on what you've learned in this chapter, if a young person were to ask you why homosexuality is wrong, how would you answer?
4. Offer an example of how you steward your own sexuality in a way that reflects the message of the gospel.

3

# WHAT ABOUT SEXUAL ORIENTATION AND GENDER IDENTITY?

In an attempt to explain sexual brokenness, contemporary secular psychologists created categories to differentiate one's biological sex (anatomy), gender identity (subjective feeling of being male or female), gender expression (external appearance, mannerisms, etc.), and sexual orientation (sexual attractions). See "The Genderbread Person"[22] diagram on the next page. According to those four categories, a female (biological sex) could think of herself as a male (gender identity), dress like a male (gender expression), and be attracted to females (sexual orientation). Or a male (biological sex) could think of himself as a male (gender identity), dress like a male (gender expression), yet be attracted to males (sexual orientation).

## The Genderbread Person

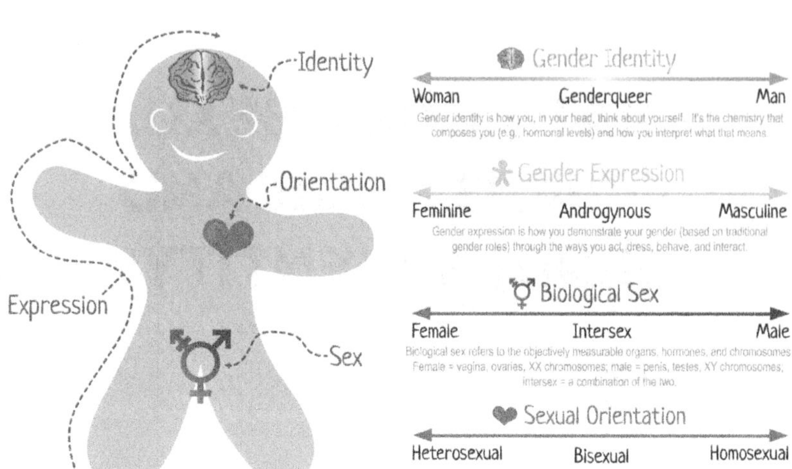


http://bit.ly/genderbread. Used with permission.

While the four categories may help secular psychologists explain sexual brokenness, they are human constructs that have only come about in recent history to justify same-sex unions and transgender ideology. For instance, the term *homosexual* originated in the 1860s to decriminalize sodomy,[23] marking a dramatic shift in culture. Whereas *sodomy* describes an action of the body, *homosexual* became a means of describing an internal identity of the soul that exists independent of one's biological sex. Theologically speaking, this is a subtle form of the dualism embraced by Gnosticism,[24] divorcing the soul from the physical body. This divide between soul and body set a precedent for contemporary distinctions between one's biological sex (body), gender identity (mind), and sexual orientation (mind/heart). There is really no such thing as a "sexual orientation." This is simply a human construct created to describe disordered desires and to justify sinful behavior.

The concept of *gender* developed even more recently. Prior to the 1950s, the term *gender* was only used in linguistic contexts, such as in the Spanish language where nouns and adjectives can be masculine or feminine. In the 1950s, sexologist John Money introduced the term *gender* to describe whether someone with an intersex condition (formerly called hermaphroditism) identifies as male or female despite having ambiguous genitalia.[25] This normalized the term for use with those who identify as transgender because their mental concept of their gender remains at odds with their biological sex.

You may not have noticed, but prior to this chapter I have avoided using the word *gender*. Instead, I have used *male/female* and the category of *biological sex*, which more closely align with Scripture. God describes humans simply as *male* and *female* and makes no concession for changing one's sex based on one's mental perception of his or her gender. Despite our culture's attempt to differentiate between biological sex and gender, linguistically, the two concepts are directly related, as Christopher West notes:

> Gender shares the same root as the words generation, generous, genre, and—how 'bout it—*genitals*. The origin of the word can be taken to mean: "the

> manner in which we generate" or "with what genitals we generate." Even more literally, we determine our "gender" by asking with what genre of genitals we generate. It's so simple and obvious. Why hadn't I seen that before? Contrary to those who want to make gender a malleable social construct, *gender* is, and always has been, determined by our *genitals*.[26]

In contrast to the Genderbread Person, God's original design for sexuality is that our biological sex, gender identity/expression, and sexual attractions would all align. For example, God created females to understand themselves as female in their minds, present as female in their bodies, and experience attractions to males. Likewise, God created males to understand themselves as male in their minds, present as male in their bodies, and experience attractions to females. If a person's biological sex does not align with their gender identity/expression or sexual attractions, it is not an indicator that they were born that way or that God made a mistake. Rather, it is an indicator that something is out of alignment in their soul (mind, emotions, and will) since their mental perception (gender identity) doesn't align with their God-given body (biological sex).

Because God created us as triune beings (spirit, soul, and body), our mental/emotional development can influence our physical drives and desires. In other words, painful experiences in childhood can contribute to the development of same-sex attractions and transgender desires. Psychologists refer to the link between our minds and our sexual desires as "psychosexual development." Interestingly, the New Testament Greek word for "soul" is *psuche*, the same root from which we get the words *psyche* and *psychology*.

In my case, I reacted to painful experiences in my past by becoming jealous of men and viewing women as second-class citizens. In my mind, males were superior to females. As a result, I longed to identify as male and despised my female body. Additionally, because I rejected my own mother (despite her best attempts to nurture me), the emotional deficit in my heart for motherly nurture became sexualized and aimed at females when I hit puberty. My desire to bond sexually with other women was a subconscious attempt to complete the formative step of connecting meaningfully with my own gender. I skipped that step during my formative years, so my sexuality became confused. My story is only one example of how misalignment occurs. Since we are complicated beings who live in a fallen world, there are countless ways that Satan can distort our sexuality.

## The Body Is Part of the Gospel Story

God created us as spirit beings who have a soul and live in a physical body. Therefore, the fall affects us in every regard—spirit, soul, and body. Some mistakenly think that the body itself is evil and of no value to God and that only the soul and the spirit matter to God. The result of such thinking leads to the heresy of gnostic dualism, which limits salvation to the spiritual realm and discounts the material world. If you follow that gnostic mindset, you could conclude that acting out homosexually or undergoing sex-reassignment surgery has no bearing on what it means to be made in God's image. However, the image of God in us includes our physical bodies and our sexuality, which was distorted by the fall. Because of the fall we rebel against God's design for our sexed body. Consequently, God's plan of redemption deliberately includes our physical bodies.

Consider how our physical bodies are part of the gospel story of creation, fall, redemption, and restoration:

1. *Creation:* God creates us with sexed bodies that image God's unity in diversity and have the capacity to procreate additional image-bearers and invite them into community.
2. *Fall:* The fall not only impacted our spiritual relationship with God; it distorted our sexuality as well. After the fall, we see the introduction of sexual deviations such as polygamy (Genesis 4), homosexuality (Genesis 19), incest (Genesis 19), and rape (Genesis 34). And that's only the first book of the Bible! The fall corrupted all human relationships and defiled all human beings with a distorted view of sexuality.
3. *Redemption:* Human sexuality plays a vital role in our salvation in that a female gave birth to a Savior who inhabited a gendered physical body. As Albert Mohler states,

> We must note that one of the most important aspects of our redemption is that it came by way of a Savior with a body. "The Word became flesh and dwelt among us" (John 1:14; cf. Phil. 2:5–11). Human redemption is accomplished by the Son of God incarnate—who remains incarnate eternally.[27]

Thus, the body is indispensable to God's plan of salvation.

4. *Restoration:* Those in Christ will experience bodily resurrection and have glorified bodies for the rest of eternity, just as Jesus lives eternally in a glorified body. Some think that Jesus's reference to there being no more marriage in heaven (Matthew 22:30) means that the redeemed will have genderless bodies for eternity. However, Jesus's glorified body retained his male gender, and when we see him, we will be like him (1 John 3:2).[28] Mohler explains that while we will retain our gender, the purpose for sexual activity will be fulfilled:

> In terms of our sexuality, while gender will remain in the new creation, sexual activity will not. It is not that sex is nullified in the resurrection; rather, it is fulfilled. The eschatological marriage supper of the Lamb, to which marriage and sexuality point, will finally arrive. No longer will there be any need to fill the earth with image-bearers as was the case in Genesis 1. Instead, the earth will be filled with

> knowledge of the glory of God as the waters cover the sea.[29]

When I was struggling with transgender desires, I would have been devastated to learn that I would remain in a female body for eternity. I despised my female anatomy, and were it not for the grace of God, I would have gone through with my plans to become "David" and live happily ever after—or so I thought. It may not have ended well when I realized that rearranging the skin on my body did nothing to resolve the anguish in my soul.

The gospel response to transgender desires is not to change one's body to match one's fallen mind, equating to rebellion against our Creator. As Isaiah writes, "Shall what is formed say to the one who formed it, 'You did not make me'? Can the pot say to the potter, 'You know nothing'?" (Isaiah 29:16). Nor is the universal solution simply to "white-knuckle it" until we experience freedom in heaven. The good news of the gospel is that Jesus—who redeems our spirit, soul, and body—is able to provide peace with our God-given gender *in this life*. Rather than changing our body to match our fallen mind, we renew our fallen mind to match the body God gave us. The answer is not transitioning, but *transformation* by renewing the mind (Romans 12:1–2).

The reason why some people experience transgender desires is not because God gave them the wrong body. Rather, it is because they have wounds in their soul, resulting in lies that influence their mental concept of their sex, persuading them that living as the opposite sex would be superior to living as their God-given sex. The root issues are idolatry and intense jealousy, which have more to do with the soul (mind, emotions, and will) than the physical body.

Similarly, for those who experience same-sex attractions, the attractions themselves are merely a red-flag indicator that something is off in the soul. At their root, same-sex attractions are not a sexual issue but most often an emotional-relational deficit or root of rejection that becomes sexualized. Therefore, the answer lies not in adjusting one's theology to affirm gay "marriage"[30] but in addressing lies in the soul that may contribute to the development of disordered desires. Because the fall affects every part of our being—spirit, soul, and body—God wants to redeem us on every level. As the Apostle Paul said to the believers in Thessalonica,

> May God himself, the God of peace, *sanctify you through and through*. May your *whole spirit, soul and body* be kept blameless at the coming of our Lord Jesus Christ. The one who calls you is faithful, and *he will do it*. (1 Thessalonians 5:23–24, emphasis mine)

## What About Gender Stereotypes and Intersex?

While we affirm the biblical categories of male and female, we must be aware that gender stereotypes can unwittingly perpetuate gender insecurities that may contribute to the development of same-sex attractions and transgender feelings. I will address that more fully in later chapters but suffice it to say here that some males do not fit the world's "macho" stereotype because God created them with a sensitive temperament, artistic abilities, or a preference to cook instead of play football. Likewise, some females do not seem as "girly" as others because God gave them a bold temperament, athletic ability, or a preference for climbing trees instead of playing with dolls.

When boys and girls don't fit into cultural gender stereotypes, they may feel as if something is deficient about their sexuality. Sensitive boys are often teased as "sissies" and struggle to feel masculine. Strong girls are sometimes considered "butch" and struggle to feel feminine. It's important to affirm the God-given personality types and gift sets in children without forcing them into cultural gender stereotypes that are incongruent with how God made them. To be clear, a boy is masculine because he is a male human being—not because his personality type or gift set conforms to a societal ideal. Likewise, a girl is feminine because she is a female human being—not because her personality type or gift set conforms to what our culture considers feminine. Interestingly, the Bible refers to God creating males and females but never offers a definition of masculinity or femininity.

While we shouldn't pigeonhole males and females into cultural gender stereotypes, we are not contending for androgyny or a blurring of the distinctions between the sexes. Both the Old Testament and New Testament affirm gender differences. Pagan rituals often involved blurring the distinctions between male and female, which pertains to the context of Deuteronomy 22:5: "A woman must not wear men's clothing, nor a man wear women's clothing, for the LORD your God detests anyone who does this."

Therefore, regardless of personality temperament or gifting, we still recognize the inherent differences between males and females, including their approach to life[31] and their anatomical and genetic differences. Even if a biological male undergoes so-called "sex reassignment surgery," that does not turn him into a female. It merely rearranges the skin on his body, literally mutilating his genitals to make them appear more like those of a female—yet he will always have XY chromosomes. Similarly, if a female undergoes surgery to appear male, her chromosomes remain XX.[32]

Granted, there are intersex conditions in which a baby who appears externally female has XY chromosomes (known as AIS, androgen insensitivity syndrome) or a baby who appears externally male has XX chromosomes (known as CAH, congenital adrenal hyperplasia). Such conditions in which the sex chromosomes (genotype) conflict with the external appearance (phenotype) are extremely rare—less than 0.02 percent of the population.[33] Still, LGBTQ[34] activists seek to include the "I" in their alphabet (LGBTQI, for example), insisting that intersex conditions form a bridge to explain the transgender phenomenon. However, intersex conditions differ from transgender feelings in that intersex conditions often involve a misalignment between one's chromosomes and external appearance, whereas someone with transgender feelings has chromosomes that match their God-given external anatomy, yet in their minds they feel as if they are the opposite sex. In that sense, transgender feelings are psychological, whereas intersex conditions are physiological. Intersex conditions happen because we live in a fallen world and are not an indicator that God intended to create more than two sexes.

## Closing Thoughts

The concepts of "sexual orientation" and "gender identity" are human constructs created to justify homoerotic behavior and transgender ideology. While the Bible describes homosexuality as an action of the body—"men who have sex with men" (1 Corinthians 6:9) and "women who exchanged natural sexual relations for unnatural ones" (Romans 1:26)—the creation of a "homosexual orientation" turns the action into a state of being, an inherent identity at odds with God's design for sexuality. In addition to creating false constructs to justify sinful behavior, pro-gay advocates take Scriptures out of context to support their position, as detailed in the next chapter.

## DISCUSSION QUESTIONS

1. Summarize how the term *homosexual* came about and why it leads to a subtle form of gnostic dualism (dividing the soul/mind from the physical body).
2. Summarize how the term *gender* came about and how that plays into the concept of gender identity.
3. When individuals experience transgender desires, that doesn't mean God made a mistake and put them in the wrong body. Explain what's happening from a biblical perspective.
4. What's the difference between intersex and transgender?

4

# THE BIBLE AND HOMOSEXUALITY: "DID GOD REALLY SAY . . . ?"

The previous chapters explain the overarching reason *why* God forbids homoerotic behavior: Two same-sex persons cannot image unity in diversity in a covenant relationship with procreative capacity which reflects the gospel message. If the gospel and the mission of God are not our starting point, then anyone can take a few Bible verses out of context to make them say what they want them to say. That is exactly what is happening today. "Progressive" Christians who claim to follow Jesus yet want to justify gay partnerships argue that Christians have, for two thousand years, wrongly interpreted Bible verses about homosexuality, echoing the serpent's age-old question: "Did God really say . . . ?" (Genesis 3:1). This chapter addresses the most common revisionist arguments (i.e., attempts to revise Scripture to condone homoerotic behavior) and reveals the faulty reasoning behind such claims.

## The Bible Mentions Homosexuality Only a Few Times

Revisionists highlight the fact that there are only six biblical passages that explicitly mention homoerotic behavior: three in the Old Testament and three in the New. Since so few references exist, they reason, homosexuality must not be that important to God. However, the Bible wasn't written as a treatise on sexuality but rather as a revelation of who God is, His design for creation, and His missional plan to redeem fallen humanity and restore our relationship with Him. That's why we must look first at whether the homosexual act aligns with the gospel message itself, as explained in the previous chapters. Because it is incongruous with the gospel, homosexuality need not be mentioned repeatedly throughout the Bible, except to note its deviation from God's original design for our sexuality to image the gospel.

Michael Brown uses the analogy of a cookbook for diabetics that features recipes without sugar. The cookbook only needs to mention the word *sugar* a few times in the beginning, since the rest of the book explains how to avoid the use of sugar. It would be inaccurate to say that because the word *sugar* is only used sparingly, avoiding sugar isn't important to the author. In fact, the exact opposite is true: Avoiding sugar is so important to the author that none of the recipes in the cookbook include that ingredient.[35]

So it is with the Bible. Our Creator's design for sexuality images the unity in diversity present in the Trinity. This theme permeates the Bible from beginning to end in reference to both human marriage and the ultimate marriage between Christ and His bride, the church. Deviations from God's design need only be mentioned a few times as an aberration from His original plan. This is true of homoerotic behavior, incest, and bestiality—all of which deviate from God's design but are mentioned sparingly.

To conclude that the Bible condones homoerotic behavior, revisionists must first ignore how our sexuality images the gospel and then construct arguments to discredit straightforward Scripture verses that condemn the homosexual act. There isn't a single positive reference to homosexuality in all of Scripture. Every time it's mentioned, it's explicitly condemned. The same cannot be said of sex between a man and a woman. While there are passages that condemn adultery and sex before marriage, there are also passages that explain how men and women can engage sexually in a way that images the gospel (i.e., one man with one woman in a lifelong covenant marriage). You won't find any passages blessing homoerotic behavior because, at its root, the act itself is incongruent with the gospel. Still, revisionists contend that Christians who hold to a traditional sexual ethic have taken Scripture out of context or have disregarded the original Hebrew or Greek words that give a passage its meaning.

## The "Clobber Passages"

Revisionists refer to the six passages prohibiting homoerotic behavior as the "clobber passages" because, unfortunately, some Christians have used those verses in a haughty and legalistic manner to condemn LGBTQ-identified people. For example, a Christian might read Leviticus 18:22, which describes the homosexual act as an "abomination," and use that to infer that God hates gay people. Many Christians don't know what an abomination is—they just know it's bad—and they errantly conclude that *abomination* must mean that homoerotic behavior is worse than any other sin. Some even go so far as to label homoerotic behavior as an unpardonable sin. However, if you read the Bible carefully, you'll discover that all of us are guilty of committing an abomination, as revealed in Proverbs 6:16–19:

> There are six things the Lord hates,
> seven that are detestable [an abomination] to him:
> haughty eyes,
> a lying tongue,
> hands that shed innocent blood,
> a heart that devises wicked schemes,
> feet that are quick to rush into evil,
> a false witness who pours out lies
> and a person who stirs up conflict
> in the community.

No one can claim they've never been proud, or lied, or stirred up conflict. An abomination is not an unpardonable sin. Rather, it's described as something that God hates because it's incongruent with His character and nature.

For example, why does God hate pride? Because He's the humblest being in the universe, who took on flesh and humbled Himself to the very point of death (Philippians 2:5–11). Why does He hate lying? Because He is the truth (John 14:6), and He will never lie or deceive us. Why does He hate stirring up contention? Because He is the Lord of peace, not strife (2 Thessalonians 3:16). Why does God hate the homosexual act? Because it conflicts with His character and nature as a creative, relational being who exists as unity in diversity.

To be clear, Scripture says that God hates the homosexual *act*. It does *not* say that He hates the *person* who *experiences* same-sex attractions or engages in homosexual acts. This is where the body of Christ has often missed it. While we don't want to compromise the truth of Scripture, we need to learn how to communicate God's truth in a way that demonstrates His love for everyone—including those who embrace a gay or trans identity and who commit sexual sin. Jesus died for them just as much as He died for us.

Most revisionist interpretations can be traced back to John Boswell, former professor of history at Yale, who was gay himself. His book *Christianity, Social Tolerance, and Homosexuality*, published in 1980, once functioned as the "bible" of the "gay Christian" movement.

In recent years, Matthew Vines, author of *God and the Gay Christian: The Biblical Case in Support of Same-Sex Relationships*, has led the cause in reiterating Boswell's arguments. Vines adds his own perspective as a gay man, including an emotional appeal as to why it's unfair—even unloving—for Christians to insist that gay individuals, like him, remain celibate for the rest of their lives. Vines contends that the writers of Scripture knew nothing about the concept of sexual orientation and that we need to update the Scriptures accordingly. He likens the "discovery" of sexual orientation to the "Copernican Revolution,"[36] when astronomers discovered that the sun, not the earth, is the center of our solar system.[37]

Further, Vines misapplies Matthew 7:18—"a good tree cannot bear bad fruit"—suggesting that the traditional biblical ethic forbidding homoerotic behavior cannot be from God because it harms people and produces bad fruit.[38] In essence, he elevates the command to love your neighbor above the first and greatest commandment (to love God). Vines also gives his take on the "clobber passages." I'll include some of his and Boswell's arguments below as I quote the six Scripture passages, summarize the revisionist interpretations, and explain why their arguments don't hold up under scrutiny.

## Passage #1: Genesis 19:4–8

> Before they [the two angels visiting Lot] had gone to bed, all the men from every part of the city of Sodom—both young and old—surrounded the house. They called to Lot, "Where are the men who came to you tonight? Bring them out to us so that we can have sex with [*yada*] *them*."

> Lot went outside to meet them and shut the door behind him and said, "No, my friends. Don't do this wicked thing. Look, I have two daughters who have never slept with a man. Let me bring them out to you, and you can do what you like with them. But don't do anything to these men, for they have come under the protection of my roof."

### Revisionist Interpretation

Revisionists argue that Sodom's primary sin was inhospitality, in that Lot failed to get permission from the city's elders to entertain guests within the city walls. They further claim that scholars mistranslated the Hebrew verb *yada* as "to have sex with," when the proper translation should be "to know," apart from sexual connotations.[39] This is why Ezekiel 16:49–50 only mentions Sodom's sin as inhospitality:

> Now this was the sin of your sister Sodom: She and her daughters were arrogant, overfed and unconcerned; they did not help the poor and needy. They were haughty and did detestable things before me. Therefore I did away with them as you have seen.

Another revisionist interpretation contends that Genesis 19 condemns gang rape, not the homosexual act itself.[40]

### Response

While it is true that *yada* is translated "to know" in the majority of the 943 times it appears in the Old Testament, it appears fifteen times in an explicitly sexual sense, and six of those fifteen instances occur in the book of Genesis.[41] Additionally, *yada* used with a personal direct object, as in this case of "Bring them out to us so that we can [know] *them*," clearly carried a sexual connotation.[42]

Furthermore, the context of Genesis 19 contradicts revisionist interpretations. If *yada* were being used without a sexual connotation, it wouldn't make sense for Lot to offer his two daughters "who have never slept with a man." Clearly, the context is sexual.

The argument that Genesis 19 solely condemns gang rape, not the homosexual act, is likewise illogical. Lot's reply to offer his two daughters as a less wicked alternative would still constitute gang rape. The context implies that the homosexual act itself is wicked. Additionally, Jude 7 states that Sodom and Gomorrah "gave themselves up to *sexual immorality* and *perversion*. They serve as an example of those who suffer the punishment of eternal fire" (italics mine). In other words, God judged the cities for their aberrant sexual practices. The Greek word translated "perversion" literally means "going after strange flesh,"[43] implying a violation of God's design for sexuality.[44] Robert Gagnon, author of *The Bible and Homosexual Practice*, concurs:

> Since the story is used as a type scene to characterize the depths of human depravity in Sodom and Gomorrah and thus to legitimate God's decision to wipe these two cities off the face of the map, it is likely that the sin of Sodom is not merely inhospitality or even attempted rape of a guest but rather attempted homosexual rape of male guests.[45]

While inhospitality may have played a part, an honest reading of Genesis 19 reveals that homosexual acts were included among the sins that brought God's judgment on Sodom and Gomorrah.

## Passage #2: Judges 19:22–24

> While they were enjoying themselves, some of the wicked men of the city surrounded the house. Pounding on the door, they shouted to the old man who owned the house, "Bring out the man who came to your house so we can have sex with [*yada*] him."
>
> The owner of the house went outside and said to them, "No, my friends, don't be so vile. Since this man is my guest, don't do this outrageous thing. Look, here is my virgin daughter, and his concubine. I will bring them out to you now, and you can use them and do to them whatever you wish. But as for this man, don't do such an outrageous thing."

### Revisionist Interpretation

Revisionists use similar arguments regarding Judges 19:22–24, insisting that the primary sin is inhospitality, based on misinterpretation of the verb *yada*.

### Response

Just as in Genesis 19, the old man's reply to offer his virgin daughter and his guest's concubine implies that *yada* refers to sexual relations. Additionally, the man calls the homosexual act "vile" and "outrageous"—which is quite a statement coming from a man who would offer up his own virgin daughter to be raped.

The last line of Judges describes the cultural context of Judges: "In those days Israel had no king; everyone did as they saw fit" (Judges 21:25). Like the story of Sodom and Gomorrah in Genesis 19, Judges 19 reveals that homosexual behavior is one of the natural outcomes of a culture that insists on following its own desires instead of submitting to God's design. The same correlation between rebellion and homosexuality occurs in Romans 1, which I will address in the section on New Testament passages.

## Passage #3: Leviticus 18:22 and Leviticus 20:13

> Do not have sexual relations with a man as one does with a woman; that is detestable [an abomination]. . . .

> If a man has sexual relations with a man as one does with a woman, both of them have done what is detestable [an abomination]. They are to be put to death; their blood will be on their own heads.

### Revisionist Interpretation

Although Leviticus clearly condemns the homosexual act, labeling it an abomination, revisionists argue that the Hebrew word for abomination, *toevah,* does not refer to something intrinsically evil, but rather something that is ceremonially unclean, like eating pork.[46] They further contend that *toevah* can sometimes imply idolatry. In that sense, the homosexual act is only condemned when joined with idol worship or male temple prostitution. Therefore, revisionists reason, God would condone monogamous gay marriage because homoerotic behavior itself is not inherently evil—only homosexual acts associated with cult prostitutes are condemned.

### Response

The Hebrew word used to describe the homosexual act in Leviticus 18 and 20 is *shakab,* which refers to sexual copulation—the same term that is used in regard to husband and wife. If these verses were referring to male temple prostitution, the accurate term would be *qadesh,* which is the word used to refer to cultic temple prostitution in Deuteronomy 23:17; 1 Kings 14:24, 15:12, 22:46; and 2 Kings 23:7.

Second, pro-gay advocates ignore the context of the Levitical prohibition of homoerotic behavior. Chapters 18 and

20 fall within the framework of a larger block of laws in Leviticus 17–26 that some scholars refer to as the "Holiness Code."[47] The purpose of this code was to ensure that God's people would live set apart from the pagan nations surrounding them, reflecting the purity of their Creator. The Ten Commandments form the crux of the Holiness Code, as Gagnon notes:

> Most of Leviticus 18 through 20 can be thought of as an expanded commentary on the Ten Commandments, with prohibitions against idolatry and witchcraft, stealing and lying, adultery and incest; and commands to honor one's parents, keep the Sabbath, and "to love one's neighbor as oneself."[48] (Leviticus 19:18)

Accordingly, Leviticus 18 expands on the commandment not to commit adultery by listing specific actions which break that command, including incest (vv. 6–18), adultery (v. 20), homosexuality (v. 22), and bestiality (v. 23). Leviticus 20 describes the punishment for breaking the commands listed in chapter 18. Incest, adultery, homosexuality, and bestiality incur the penalty of death because they relate to God's moral law (e.g., the Ten Commandments), which transcends time and culture.

The ceremonial laws, which are bound by time and culture, do not incur the death penalty but involve lesser indictments, such as temporary prohibition from worship, barrenness, or, at the worst, excommunication. By equating eating pork with homoerotic behavior, revisionists ignore the context of the Holiness Code and the distinction between moral and ceremonial laws. Breaking God's moral law carries with it a stricter penalty (i.e., death), from which one cannot recover—as opposed to being unclean, for which a ceremonial remedy exists.

The commands based on the moral law, which transcends time and culture, are reaffirmed in the New Testament, which prohibits incest (1 Corinthians 5:1), adultery (Matthew 5:27–28; Romans 13:9; James 2:11), and homoerotic behavior (Romans 1:26–27, 1 Corinthians 6:9; 1 Timothy 1:10). However, the New Testament overturns Levitical commands that are part of the ceremonial law, which *is* bound by time and culture. For example, Jesus repealed ceremonial food laws by declaring all foods clean (Mark 7:19), and the Apostle Paul declared the Old Testament practice of physical circumcision null and void now that every new-covenant believer experiences a circumcision of the heart (Romans 2:29). The ceremonial laws in Leviticus do not apply to the believer today, but the moral laws—which are rooted in the timeless truths of the Ten Commandments—still apply, as evidenced in the New Testament prohibitions of homoerotic behavior.

## Passage #4: Romans 1:26–27

> Because of this, God gave them over to shameful lusts. Even their women exchanged natural sexual relations for unnatural ones. In the same way the

> men also abandoned natural relations with women and were inflamed with lust for one another. Men committed shameful acts with other men and received in themselves the due penalty for their error.

### Revisionist Interpretation

First, revisionists argue that the word *natural* refers to homosexual acts committed by heterosexual individuals—for whom the act would then be *unnatural.*[49] Second, some revisionists insist that Romans 1 only condemns gay sex rites associated with first-century idol worship and does not serve as an indictment against monogamous gay sex in modern times. In fact, some go so far as to suggest that God's command to love one another supersedes any prohibition against homosexuality because first-century writers were unaware of loving, monogamous gay relationships now common in today's culture.[50]

### Response

The idea that homosexual desires come "naturally" to some conflicts with the context of Romans 1, which is that God's design for creation can be "understood from what has been made, so that people are without excuse" (Romans 1:20). In other words, even if one disregards Scripture altogether, the very nature of creation itself reveals God's design for sexuality since only male-female copulation can produce offspring. To deny that reality is to "suppress the truth" (Romans 1:18).

Furthermore, the Greek words *theleiai* and *arsenes*, which Paul uses respectively for "females" and "males" in Romans 1:26–27, place the emphasis on the biological sex of those participating in homosexual acts.[51] Thus, Paul stresses the fact that homoerotic behavior was unnatural to them *as males* and *as females* because of their God-given anatomical design—not because of their "sexual orientation."

The authors of Scripture never mention the concept of "sexual orientation" because they presuppose opposite-sex marriage as the Creator's original design. Every male is designed to be attracted to females and vice-versa. As discussed in previous chapters, same-sex attractions are not an indicator of God's original design for the body but rather serve as a red-flag warning that something is out of alignment in the soul.

Imagine if we used the same concept of "orientation" for the other sins Paul condemns at the end of Romans 1, such as greed, envy, and arrogance:

"Greed comes naturally to me, so I identify as a greedy Christian."

"I can't help it that I envy others; I have an envious orientation."

"I was born arrogant. I do my best to abstain and walk in humility, but I still identify as an arrogant Christian."

When we put it in those terms, it sounds silly to apply the modern construct of sexual orientation and identify as a "gay Christian." As a new creation, a Christian is not oriented toward sin but toward righteousness in Christ.

Additionally, Romans 1 describes what happens when humans reject their Creator and worship created things instead. The context implies that the root of homoerotic behavior is self-willed determination that rejects the Creator and His authority in our lives. Similarly, the Apostle Peter links the sin of the citizens of Sodom and Gomorrah to self-will and insubordination:

> If he condemned the cities of Sodom and Gomorrah by burning them to ashes, and made them an example of what is going to happen to the ungodly; and if he rescued Lot, a righteous man, who was distressed by the depraved conduct of the lawless . . . then the Lord knows how to rescue the godly from trials and to hold the unrighteous for punishment on the day of judgment. This is especially true of those who *follow the corrupt desire of the flesh and despise authority.* (2 Peter 2:6–10; italics mine)

In response to the argument that first-century writers were unaware of loving, monogamous gay relationships, Gagnon observes,

> The notion that mutually caring same-sex relationships first originated in modern times sounds absurd. Are we to believe that nobody with homosexual or lesbian urges in all of antiquity was able to provide a healthy example of same-sex love?

> In fact, moving statements about the compassionate and beautiful character of same-sex love can be found in Greco-Roman literature. Among the examples are the speeches in Plato's *Symposium*.[52]

Plato's *Symposium* predates the letter to the Romans by several hundred years. Surely the Apostle Paul would have been aware of Plato's work since he was both a Roman citizen and an elite scholar who debated with the Athenians about contemporary Greek philosophy and culture (Acts 17).

Our culture is not the first that has sought to normalize homosexuality. To argue that God condones homoerotic behavior so long as it's in the context of a loving, monogamous relationship is akin to saying that God condones any of the other twenty-plus sins Paul lists at the end of Romans 1 that result from rejecting our Creator, so long as we practice them "in love." Be greedy and arrogant, murder others, and cause strife—as long as you do so in a loving way. That defies logic.

## Passage #5: 1 Corinthians 6:9–11

> Or do you not know that wrongdoers will not inherit the kingdom of God? Do not be deceived: Neither the sexually immoral nor idolaters nor adulterers nor men who have sex with men nor thieves nor the greedy nor drunkards nor slanderers nor swindlers will inherit the kingdom of God. And that is what

> some of you were. But you were washed, you were sanctified, you were justified in the name of the Lord Jesus Christ and by the Spirit of our God.

### Revisionist Interpretation

Revisionists argue that the word *homosexual* never appeared in an English Bible until 1946, and that it's a mistranslation of the Greek word *arsenokoites.*[53] They argue that Paul made up the Greek term, since it never appeared in Greek literature until after Paul used it in the Scriptures. Were Paul referring to homosexuality, he would have used a common Greek term for homoerotic behavior instead of coining a new word. Therefore, the passage in 1 Corinthians could be referring to pederasty, the common first-century practice of a master having sex with his boy slave, as opposed to loving, monogamous gay relationships like we see in today's culture.[54]

### Response

While Paul did coin the Greek word *arsenokoites*, neologisms (the creation of new words or phrases) were commonly practiced by the apostle. In fact, he coined 179 words in the New Testament.[55] Rather than discounting a neologism because of its origins, we should look more closely to see *how* Paul constructed the term to discern its intended meaning.

*Arsenokoites* is a compound word consisting of two Greek words: (1) *arsen*, meaning "male" or "man" and (2) *koite* (from which we get the English word *coitus*), which appears only twice in the New Testament, referring to a "bed" or "couch" in a sexual context (see Romans 13:13 and Hebrews 13:4). Revisionists insist that the words *male* and *bed* could refer to any sexual sin, including sex between a man and a woman. However, the Septuagint (the Greek translation of the Hebrew Old Testament, which Paul often quoted in his writings) provides a clue as to how Paul coined the term *arsenokoites*. The root words *arsen* and *koite* that Paul used to form *arsenokoites* appear in Leviticus 18:22 and Leviticus 20:13, the only two verses in the Holiness Code that prohibit homoerotic behavior. Clearly, Paul intended *arsenokoites* to refer to the sin of the homosexual act, not just any sexual act involving a man and a bed.

Moreover, the use of the word *malakos* in 1 Corinthians 6:9 supports the fact that *arsenokoites* refers to homoerotic behavior of any kind. *Malakos* refers to the passive partner in the homosexual act, and *arsenokoites* refers to the active partner.[56] Had Paul been referring to pederasty only, he could have used more specific Greek words, "such as *paiderastai* (lover of boys), *paidomanai* (men mad for boys), or *paidophthoroi* (corrupters of boys)."[57] First Corinthians 6:9–11 clearly references the homosexual act between two males and implies the possibility of complete deliverance from such immorality: "that is what some of you *were*."

Paul's word choice is significant. He doesn't say "that is what some of you *used to do*," but "that is what some of you *were*." The Corinthians' new identity in Christ meant their lives were no longer marked by enslavement to sinful desires that used to dominate them. This is another reason why calling oneself a "gay Christian" is incongruent with Scripture. Once we are in Christ, we are a new creation, no longer identified by the life we used to live, nor defined by our temptations and vulnerabilities.

There's a vast difference between identifying as a "gay Christian" versus a Christian who is tempted by disordered sexual desires. It's not a sin to be tempted, but to embrace our fallen nature as our identity implies that Christ has no power to transform our lives, such that our fallen desires dictate our identity and determine our destiny. Again, consider the example of a person who struggles to overcome a porn addiction and therefore identifies as a "lustful Christian." That's wholly incongruent with the good news of the gospel.

## Passage #6: 1 Timothy 1:9–11

> We also know that the law is made not for the righteous but for lawbreakers and rebels, the ungodly and sinful, the unholy and irreligious, for those who kill their fathers or mothers, for murderers, for the sexually immoral, for those practicing homosexuality, for slave traders and liars and perjurers—and for whatever else is contrary to the sound doctrine that conforms to the gospel concerning the glory of the blessed God, which he entrusted to me.

### Revisionist Interpretation

In 1 Timothy 1:10, Paul again uses *arsenokoites* to refer to "those practicing homosexuality." Pro-gay advocates echo the same arguments from 1 Corinthians 6:9–11, saying that Paul made up the word *arsenokoites* and that it has been mistranslated to refer to homoerotic behavior.

### Response

Because *arsenokoites* is a compound word consisting of the same two Greek words that occur in the Greek translation of Leviticus 18:22 and 20:13, the original readers would have understood Paul to have been reiterating the original Levitical prohibition against homoerotic behavior.

## Jesus and Homosexuality

Revisionists note that Jesus never mentioned homosexuality in any of his teachings. While technically that's true, an argument from silence doesn't support their case. Jesus was silent on other issues that clearly violate God's moral law, such as incest, rape, pedophilia, abortion, and human trafficking, to name a few. We must take into consideration what Jesus *did* say:

1. Jesus quoted Genesis 2:24 and affirmed marriage between one man and one woman as God's original design for sexuality:

   > "Haven't you read," he replied, "that at the beginning the Creator 'made them male and

> female,' and said, 'For this reason a man will leave his father and mother and be united to his wife, and the two will become one flesh'? So they are no longer two, but one flesh. Therefore what God has joined together, let no one separate." (Matthew 19:4–6)

By affirming male-female marriage, Jesus implicitly condemned homoerotic behavior as a violation of the Creator's original design.

2. Jesus, who said He came not to abolish the law but to fulfill it, referred to the Ten Commandments in the Sermon on the Mount: "You have heard that it was said, 'You shall not commit adultery.' But I tell you that anyone who looks at a woman lustfully has already committed adultery with her in his heart" (Matthew 5:27–28). As previously noted, Leviticus 18 and 20 are an expanded commentary on the Ten Commandments. Jesus would have been well aware of the prohibition against homoerotic behavior included in the Holiness Code.
3. Homoerotic behavior is not the only sexual sin forbidden in Scripture. Jesus condemned all forms of sexual activity outside the bounds of a male-female marriage: "What comes out of a person is what defiles them. For it is from within, out of a person's heart, that evil thoughts come—*sexual immorality* [italics mine], theft, murder, adultery, greed, malice, deceit, lewdness,

envy, slander, arrogance and folly. All these evils come from inside and defile a person" (Mark 7:20–23). The Greek word for "sexual immorality," *porneiai*, closely related to the English word porn, functions as a catchall term describing any kind of sexual activity outside of marriage. Thus, Jesus's hearers would have understood *porneiai* to include all forms of sexual immorality prohibited in the Old Testament—including incest, adultery, bestiality, and homosexuality.

## What About Eunuchs?

Some revisionists contend that Jesus's commentary about eunuchs in Matthew 19:12 refers to those born with a gay orientation or transgender feelings: "For there are eunuchs who were born that way, and there are eunuchs who have been made eunuchs by others—and there are those who choose to live like eunuchs for the sake of the kingdom of heaven."

However, revisionists ignore the context of Jesus's statement, which is in response to whether a man can divorce his wife "for any and every reason" (Matthew 19:3). Before talking about eunuchs, Jesus quotes from Genesis, reaffirming that God's design for marriage involves a biological male with a biological female, who together form a one-flesh union that should not be separated by divorce (Matthew 19:4–6). He goes on to say that "Moses permitted you to divorce your wives because your hearts were hard," yet goes on to say, "it was not this way from the beginning" (Matthew 19:8). In other words,

God's original design for marriage never included divorce as a concession.

Jesus answers their question: If a man does divorce his wife "for any and every reason" (i.e., anything less than sexual immorality on her part) and marries another woman, he commits adultery (Matthew 19:9). In response to Jesus's high standard for the marriage covenant, the disciples suggest that perhaps it's better not to marry at all. Jesus replies that not everyone can accept that word (meaning most people will marry), but there are a few who won't—and he offers eunuchs as an example.

Biblically speaking, a eunuch refers to a man who lacks the ability to procreate, whether because of castration, accident (Leviticus 21:20), or congenital birth defect. In other words, being a eunuch has to do with one's organs, not "orientation"—which is a modern construct foreign to the first-century context. Jesus uses the term *eunuch* in a literal sense to describe those who do not marry/procreate because of a physical condition. He also uses it in a figurative sense to describe those who choose not to marry/procreate because they want to devote themselves to kingdom work.

Paul reiterates the same idea of committing oneself to kingdom work in 1 Corinthians 7:32–34: "An unmarried man is concerned about the Lord's affairs—how he can please the Lord. . . . An unmarried woman or virgin is concerned about the Lord's affairs: Her aim is to be devoted to the Lord in both body and spirit." To suggest that Jesus's reference to eunuchs is a concession for a gay "orientation" or a transgender identity is to impose a twenty-first-century interpretation that is absent from the original context.[58]

## Closing Thoughts

While they may sound cunning at first glance, revisionist arguments fail to stand under scrutiny. Scripture consistently condemns the homosexual act as an aberration from God's original design for sexuality. Those who hold to revisionist arguments typically do so because they are looking for a way to justify their subjective experience (i.e., either they or someone they love embraces an LGBTQ identity) over the objective truth of Scripture.

## DISCUSSION QUESTIONS

1. How would you respond to the argument that the Bible only mentions homosexuality a few times, so it must not be important to God?
2. How would you respond to the argument that the primary sin of the cities of ancient Sodom and Gomorrah was inhospitality?
3. How would you respond to the argument that the Levitical prohibition of homosexuality is no longer valid because Christians can now eat shellfish and pork?
4. How would you respond to the argument that Jesus never mentioned homosexuality?

5. How would you respond to the argument that the Apostle Paul didn't know about the modern concept of "sexual orientation"?
6. How would you respond to the revisionist argument that 1 Corinthians 6:9 and 1 Timothy 1:10 are not referring to homosexuality?

5

# WHAT SCIENCE SAYS: ARE PEOPLE BORN GAY/TRANS?

Lady Gaga's song "Born This Way" echoes today's cultural narrative:

> No matter gay, straight, or bi', lesbian, transgender life
> I'm on the right track, baby. . . . I was born this way.[59]

This song so resonated with the masses that more than one million downloads were sold in its first five days, setting a Guinness World Record for the fastest-selling single on iTunes.[60]

Though many believe the born-this-way message, scientists have yet to find a biological origin of same-sex attractions or transgender feelings. In fact, research suggests that environmental factors play a significant role. What follows is a summary of the latest studies regarding the origins of disordered sexual desires, including three areas of research:

the search for a "gay gene," the brain structure theory, and the hormonal influence theory.[61]

## The Search for a Gay Gene

For decades scientists have searched for a gay gene. In 1993, Dean Hamer published a study claiming that he had discovered a link to a gay gene on the X chromosome. Since both males and females carry an X chromosome, Hamer's findings would explain how homosexual propensities are passed on to future generations.[62] However, other researchers weren't able to replicate Hamer's findings.[63]

Identical-twin studies offer the best opportunity to discover a gay gene, since identical twins share the same DNA. If homosexuality were entirely genetic, like eye color, hair color, or biological sex, then if one identical twin is gay, the other twin would also be gay. Yet identical-twin studies indicate a low correlation between genetics and same-sex attractions. One of the most comprehensive twin studies to date showed that when one male twin was gay, his identical-twin brother was gay only 9.8 percent of the time.[64] The researchers from that study concluded that sexual preferences must be influenced more by external environments than by genetics.[65]

Today we have more sophisticated technology, involving genome-wide association studies (GWAS) that enable us to study millions of gene variants at once to see if there's a link between a certain gene and a particular trait. A 2012 GWAS involving 23,000 participants found no link of statistical significance corresponding to homosexual orientation.[66] Similarly, a 2019 GWAS involving nearly half a million British, American, and Swedish residents found no genetic influence of statistical significance. The authors concluded,

> There is certainly no single genetic determinant (sometimes referred to as the "gay gene" in the media).[67] . . . Many uncertainties remain to be explored, including how sociocultural influences on sexual preference might interact with genetic influences.[68]

The 2019 GWAS study suggests that nongenetic influences like personality temperament, family upbringing, and adverse childhood experiences may play a greater role than genetics in shaping our sexuality.

Another theory involves epigenetics, which is the study of how environmental influences affect the expression of genes. Researchers hypothesize that epigenetics may explain why one identical twin is gay when the other is not.[69] However, without the discovery of a gene linked to homosexual desires, it remains impossible to study how the environment affects expression of the undiscovered gene, making epigenetic hypotheses speculative at best.

Despite decades of research and advancements in technology, researchers have yet to discover the elusive "gay gene." Lisa Diamond, psychology professor at the University of Utah and self-identified lesbian, urges people to abandon the argument that same-sex attractions are inborn and immutable, since "higher estimates of heritability [i.e., inherited through genes] . . . have been found for a range of characteristics that are not widely considered immutable, such as being divorced, smoking, having low back pain, and feeling body dissatisfaction."[70]

An honest look at the evidence reveals that Lady Gaga has it wrong: Science does not indicate that people are "born this way."

## The Brain Structure Theory

Another hypothesis is that the hypothalamus, a region of the brain that influences our sexual drives and desires, hardwires our sexual desires from birth. In 1991, Simon LeVay published a study claiming that a region of the hypothalamus in homosexual men was smaller in size than the same region in heterosexual men, similar to that of women versus men.[71] *Newsweek* trumpeted LeVay's study as evidence of a biological origin for same-sex attractions.[72] However, like Hamer's X-chromosome study, researchers haven't been able to replicate LeVay's findings. His study has since been discredited, and he eventually recanted:

> It is important to stress what I didn't find. I did not prove that homosexuality is genetic or find a genetic cause for being gay. I didn't show that gay men are

> born that way, the most common mistake people make in interpreting my work. Nor did I locate a gay center in the brain.[73]

It turns out that LeVay was a gay-identified man with an agenda: He admitted he wanted to find a gay gene so he could educate society about homosexuality and influence religious and legal attitudes that are opposed to it.[74]

Fast-forward thirty-plus years, and we now know that brain structures are not static from birth, but rather that they change over time in response to environmental influences—a concept known as neuroplasticity. For example, violinists, who rely on their left hand, develop larger brain areas that control the left hand, as opposed to pianists, whose brains develop more evenly for both hands.[75] The brains of those who learn to juggle change over time; but when they stop practicing, their brains change again.[76]

The concept of neuroplasticity is especially relevant to our sexuality. Research shows that the brain changes in response to pornography addiction, affecting both the gratification and reward systems, in addition to affecting one's ability to have real sex.[77] Sex and the brain are inextricably linked. This comes as no surprise, since 1 Thessalonians 5:23 reveals that God created us as triune beings: spirit, soul, and body. What goes on in our soul (mind, emotions, will) affects our physical body and even our spirit. That's why Scripture emphasizes taking our thoughts captive (2 Corinthians 10:5), renewing our minds (Romans 12:2; Ephesians 4:23), and meditating on God's Word so that we may not sin against Him (Psalm 119:11). What we dwell on with our minds will affect our sexual desires and behaviors.

A study of sexually abused girls revealed a link between changes in the brain and the age at which the abuse occurred, indicating brain regions may have unique windows of vulnerability to trauma.[78] If the abuse happened between ages three to five, the hippocampus changed. If the abuse happened between ages nine and ten, the corpus callosum changed. If the abuse happened between ages fourteen to sixteen, the frontal cortex changed. The study only measured changes in brain structure, but we know from observation that abuse victims suffer emotional trauma and that past abuse can often affect one's sexual responses. We must not overlook the interrelatedness of spirit, soul, and body. The good news is that neuroplasticity works both ways. Just as pornography use can forge new neural pathways that lead to addiction, so renewing one's mind and abstaining from pornography can forge new neural pathways; and the old, unused neural pathways will eventually disappear.[79]

Transgender activists embrace the outdated static brain structure theory, noting that brain scans show male-to-female transitioners[80] have more "feminized" brains, while female-to-male transitioners[81] have more "masculinized" brains. However, such studies do not take neuroplasticity into consideration. As Mayer and McHugh note in their 2016 meta-analysis on sexuality and gender (which is a must read), "In most cases transgender individuals have been acting and thinking for years in ways that, through learned behavior and associated neuroplasticity, may have produced brain changes that could differentiate them from other members of their biological or natal sex."[82] It's possible that a scan of my brain would appear more masculine than a typical female since I spent decades wanting to become a man. However, that would merely indicate that my brain changed in response to my attempts to emulate men, not that God created me to have a male brain and a female body.

## The Hormonal Influence Theory

The most popular theory today is the hormonal influence theory, which presupposes a link between prenatal hormonal exposure and sexual orientation. The theory is based upon research from the 1950s known as the Phoenix hypothesis,[83] which involved injecting animals with sex hormones and observing resulting changes in sexual behavior. Researchers then extended the findings in animals to human intersex conditions involving hormonal imbalances. They theorized that hormonal influences may affect sexual orientation by either "masculinizing" or "feminizing" the brain without affecting the body's physical development, as can happen with intersex conditions. The hormonal theory is debatable for several reasons:

1. The Phoenix hypothesis doesn't apply uniformly to rats, ferrets, and mice due to structural brain differences and varied hormonal reactions in each species. If the hypothesis doesn't apply across animal species, it's highly speculative that it would apply to the complexity of human sexuality.
2. The physical abnormalities associated with prenatal hormonal abnormalities don't occur at elevated rates among the general LGBTQ population. In other words, most people who develop same-sex attractions or gender dysphoria do not have intersex conditions (also known as disorders of sexual development), wherein the external genitalia do not match the internal gonads—an extremely rare condition.[84]
3. Studies measuring the impact of diethylstilbestrol, a synthetic female hormone used from 1940 to1970 to prevent miscarriages, indicate excess exposure to the female hormone did not result in boys developing higher rates of homosexual tendencies, contradicting the Phoenix hypothesis.[85]
4. The hormonal theory, which suggests the brain is permanently "masculinized" or "feminized" by the hormonal environment in the womb, offers no explanation for people like me who experience a change in their sexual attractions and resolution of gender dysphoria in adulthood. If the brain were permanently altered, such change would not be possible.

Although decades-old studies show that prenatal hormones affect sexual behavior in lower animals, it's a leap to apply the Phoenix hypothesis to the complexity of human sexuality. Similarly, there's insufficient evidence that hormonal abnormalities associated with rare intersex conditions apply to those with same-sex attractions and gender dysphoria.

Perhaps the strongest argument against the hormonal theory is that if same-sex attractions or gender dysphoria originated from the prenatal hormonal environment, there would be a higher concordance rate for same-sex attractions among identical twins who shared the same hormonal environment in the womb.[86] A 9.8 percent concordance rate among identical twins suggests that the prenatal hormonal environment does not contribute significantly to the development of same-sex attractions.

## Closing Thoughts

Despite decades of research investigating the potential influence of genetics, brain structure, and prenatal hormones, scientists have yet to identify a definitive biological origin for same-sex attractions and transgender feelings. In their meta-analysis of the latest biological, psychological, and social-science research on sexuality and gender, Mayer and McHugh note, "The understanding of sexual orientation as an innate, biologically fixed property of human beings—the idea that people are 'born that way'—is not supported by scientific evidence."[87]

While biological factors may play a minor role, research indicates that same-sex attractions remain subject to change over time, a concept known as sexual fluidity. Conversely, opposite-sex attractions remain relatively stable.[88] This suggests that environmental factors affect the development and fluctuation of same-sex attractions. Psychologist and researcher Stanton Jones offers a similar conclusion:

> Recent studies show that familial, cultural, and other environmental factors contribute to same-sex attraction. Broken families, absent fathers, older mothers, and being born and living in urban settings all are associated with homosexual experience or attraction. Even that most despised of hypothesized causal contributors, childhood sexual abuse, has recently received significant empirical validation as a partial contributor from a sophisticated thirty-year longitudinal study published in the *Archives of Sexual Behavior*. Of course, these variables at most partially determine later homosexual experience, and most children who experienced any or all of these still grow up heterosexual, but the effects are nonetheless real.[89]

In the next chapter, we will look at environmental factors that can affect our sexuality and consider some examples of how same-sex attractions may develop.

## DISCUSSION QUESTIONS

1. Summarize what the latest research reveals regarding the existence of a "gay gene."
2. How does the concept of neuroplasticity conflict with the argument that one is born gay/trans?
3. What is the strongest argument against the theory of prenatal hormonal influences as a determinant of same-sex attractions?
4. Do you think researchers will find a biological origin to same-sex attractions or gender dysphoria? Why or why not?

6

# HOW SAME-SEX ATTRACTIONS DEVELOP

According to a recent Gallup poll, the number of adults who identify as LGBTQ has doubled over the past decade, from 3.5 percent in 2012 to 7.1 percent in 2022. The poll reveals that those twenty-five and under are driving the numbers higher, as Gen Z-ers are adopting LGBTQ identities at an alarming rate.[90] In fact, Barna reports that nearly 40 percent of eighteen- to twenty-four-year-olds identify as LGBTQ.[91] What accounts for the increased prevalence?

It could be that our permissive culture makes it easier for people to self-identify as LGBTQ, resulting in more people coming out of the closet. Yet the increase is not consistent across generations, indicating that something unique is happening among youth. Barna suggests the increase has more to do with peer acceptance than with sexual desires. Their poll didn't ask about sexual attractions but rather how someone "identifies," which fits into a larger narrative:

> Millennials are a group that has trouble creating lasting, meaningful relationships. . . . If their sense is that some of the people they want to be friends with—and a group they want to be accepted by—is LGBTQ, then they'll identify with them. It's about image, belonging and acceptance.[92]

It appears the surge in LGBTQ-identified youth is linked to peer approval and social contagion instead of an increase in those who genuinely experience disordered sexual desires. The astronomical rise of rapid-onset gender dysphoria (ROGD) among teen girls certainly fits into that narrative (more on that in the next chapter), as does the increase of girls identifying as bisexual or even asexual (not attracted to either sex). Teen girls are in the phase of learning what sexual desire is, and in today's overly sexed, LGBTQ-saturated culture they can sometimes confuse natural admiration of a beautiful woman or emotional closeness with a female peer with sexual desire. They may have no awareness that they are simply confused and pressured into adopting an identity that makes them feel special.

Social contagion aside, there are three developmental influences that we commonly see among those who experience genuine same-sex attractions: 1) gender nonconformity, 2) adverse family dynamics, or 3) childhood sexual abuse. Those influences were common among the case studies in my dissertation research, and I often see them in regard to the young women I counsel. They are part of my own story as well.

This is not to say that these three factors are the only ones that may contribute to sexual brokenness. But they are among the most common influences we see in research and practical experience. I will first summarize the research and then share examples of how developmental factors might play out in real life.

## 1. Gender Nonconformity

Gender nonconformity refers to not fitting into a cultural gender stereotype, such as "boys like sports" and "girls like to play with dolls." Psychologist Gerard van den Aardweg notes the correlation between gender nonconformity and homosexuality:

> The efforts of the last few decades to find evidence to support a biological theory have made it more doubtful than ever that such evidence will be found. In contrast, many studies have shown that the most significant factor which correlates with homosexuality is "gender nonconformity" or same-sex peer isolation.[93]

According to the theory of gender nonconformity, a child's personality temperament or biological characteristics may conflict with cultural gender stereotypes, negatively affecting a child's self-perception. For example, a gender-nonconforming boy may have a sensitive temperament, be more in touch with his emotions, and enjoy music, theater, art, or cooking with his mom/sisters instead of playing sports with other boys. In addition to his sensitive personality, he may have physical traits typically considered less masculine, like having a slight build, high cheekbones, long eye lashes, a higher voice, or being unable to grow a beard. A gender-nonconforming girl may have a bold temperament, tough exterior, high aptitude in math/science, and she may be athletically inclined, preferring to play football with the boys instead of dolls with the girls. She may also have physical traits considered less feminine like a bigger body build, a deeper voice, a square jaw, or more body hair than a typical female.[94]

Because of cultural stereotypes, gender-nonconforming children often feel "different" than their peers, unable to connect with their own gender in meaningful ways. Their sense of isolation is often compounded by peers who call them names such as *sissy, fag, dyke,* or *butch*. The psychological trauma of such teasing may lead gender-nonconforming children to question their masculinity or femininity. Consequently, they may grow up feeling like there's something deficient about their sexuality and that they'll never be "a man among men" or "a woman among women." Their same-sex peers seem like an exotic species, leaving them with a longing to fit in—to become whole where they perceive themselves lacking. Because of the interrelatedness of spirit, soul, and body, the psychological trauma of being "different" registers in the soul (mind/emotions), which can affect a child's psychosexual development involving the body's response to sexual stimuli. Remember, the brain and sexuality are inextricably linked.

To develop a stable sense of their own sexuality, children need meaningful connection with members of the same sex. We see this play out regularly as young boys build a treehouse with the universal sign above the door: "No girls allowed." Why? Because girls have "cooties"! As children progress into adolescence, they typically grow out of the boys-only/girls-only clubs and enter the mysterious stage in which they discover that those who once had cooties are now quite intriguing. That's all a normal part of our psychosexual development.

Gender-nonconforming children, however, sometimes find themselves stuck at the "cooties stage" because they were never able to complete the developmental milestone of identifying meaningfully with their own gender. As a result, they may feel like their own gender remains foreign to them. When their hormones kick in, their longing for same-sex acceptance can become confused with their God-given sex drive, resulting in attractions to the same sex. In the words of psychologist Darryl Bem, "The exotic becomes erotic."[95]

Because opposites attract, gender-nonconforming males may find themselves especially attracted to stereotypically masculine men, and gender-nonconforming females may find themselves attracted to stereotypically feminine women. In this case, same-sex attractions (SSA) stem from a legitimate desire to connect meaningfully with the same sex. This unmet need becomes confused with God-given sexual desires that would ordinarily develop toward the opposite sex when a child feels secure as a boy among boys or as a girl among girls.

## 2. Adverse Family Dynamics

Large-scale, longitudinal studies over the past forty years reveal that those with SSA tend to have experienced higher rates of adverse family dynamics such as:

- parental separation/divorce
- domestic violence
- parental neglect
- parental criminal activity
- physical and psychological abuse
- living apart from the same-sex parent (especially during the first six years of life)
- boys who have never met their father
- girls whose mother died during adolescence[96]

It comes as no surprise that children who lack meaningful connection with parents experience greater challenges in life. This is not to say that every child who grew up in a broken family will struggle with their sexuality, but many do. By God's design, every child is meant to have a father and a mother. Fathers invite their sons into the world of men and affirm their daughters as distinct from, yet cherished by, men. Mothers invite their daughters into the world of women and affirm their sons as distinct from, yet respected by, women. When

God's design for the family is disrupted for whatever reason, children pay the highest price, because they need healthy investment from both a father and a mother to develop security in their sexuality.

If a disruption with the same-sex parent occurs, and no substitute mother/father figure steps in, children may grow up with a deficit for same-sex love that affects their psychosexual development. This disruption may be extreme, like the physical loss of a parent through death or divorce, or an emotional disconnect due to substance abuse, or physical abuse. In some cases, this could be as minor as a subtle difference in personality temperament, whereby the same-sex parent doesn't know how to bond in a way that the child feels an emotional connection. I have counseled many individuals who have grown up with a well-meaning parent who simply wasn't able to connect in a way that felt meaningful to them. There was no malice on the part of the parent. They did everything they could to love well, but a child's *perception* of an emotional disconnect trumps a parent's *best intentions.*

Of course, the devil does everything he can to fuel the child's misperception. One man grew up thinking his father loved his athletic brother more because his brother bonded with their father through sports. Later in life, he discovered his assumption was simply a misperception fueled by the enemy. *But for children, perception trumps reality.* Children are incredible recorders of history but terrible interpreters of reality.

When children with a same-sex love deficit become teenagers, that emotional deficit can become confused with their God-given sex drive so that their attractions fixate on the same sex instead of the opposite sex.[97] Similar to the phenomenon of gender nonconformity, children with a same-sex love deficit become trapped in a pattern of arrested emotional development, unable to bond with the opposite sex until they first find security in same-sex connection.

In this situation, the root of SSA is not a sexual issue but rather an emotional-relational deficit that becomes sexualized. It can *feel* like one is "born that way" because, in this case, SSA is a subconscious response to trauma, not a conscious choice to rebel. Again, spirit, soul, and body work in tandem so that the brain and sexuality are inextricably linked. We cannot divorce the emotional-relational deficits in our soul (mind/emotions/will) from our psychosexual development (mind/body).

Consequently, we can't fault those who find themselves involuntarily attracted to the same sex. The attraction itself is not a sin, though meditating or acting upon it is. Rather, the disordered desire signals an unmet yearning in the soul that is manifesting in a sexual way.[98] Elizabeth Moberly calls the urge for erotic same-sex love the "reparative drive."[99] In other words, it's a subconscious attempt to "repair," or satisfy, an unmet God-given yearning for same-sex love by bonding sexually with a member of the same sex. Yet a physical substitute cannot satisfy an emotional-relational deficit. The same principle lies at the root of any addictive behavior: We look to created things (food, sex, drugs, fame, money, achievements, etc.) instead of our Creator to satisfy the yearning in our soul (Romans 1:25).

## 3. Childhood Sexual Abuse

Not surprisingly, sexual abuse can impact a child's psychosexual development. Research indicates that "compared to heterosexuals, non-heterosexuals are about two to three times as likely to have experienced childhood sexual abuse."[100]

To understand how childhood sexual abuse (CSA) can affect a child, consider a young girl who is sexually abused by a male perpetrator. She may conclude that men are not safe and vow never to be vulnerable with a man ever again. Because the brain and sexuality are inextricably linked, the little girl cannot isolate the trauma in her soul from her psychosexual development. Consequently, she may find men emotionally or sexually unsafe and instead gravitate toward relationships with women to meet her emotional and sexual desires. Sometimes female CSA victims begin to dress androgynously or gain weight as a subconscious wall of protection to insulate them from the gaze of men. However, we all respond to trauma in different ways, so not every girl who is molested will develop SSA. Some women respond in the opposite manner, becoming promiscuous with men so that they are always the aggressor and never again the victim.

If a boy is sexually molested by a male perpetrator, he can become confused, thinking, "Why did he choose me and not some other boy? There must be something deficient about my masculinity. And why did my body respond that way? Does that mean I'm gay?" The enemy will gladly answer "Yes" to that question. Child molesters know how to groom their prey and often target the gender-nonconforming boy who already feels disconnected from his own father and longs for male affirmation. The evil one knows how to capitalize on our vulnerabilities. But we all respond to trauma differently. Not every boy who is sexually molested develops SSA, but many do.[101]

In addition to the emotional trauma of CSA, biological factors may come into play as well. The chemicals released during orgasm (vasopressin in men and oxytocin in women) serve as powerful bonding agents.[102] If a child's first pleasurable sexual experience occurs with someone of the same sex, the associated chemical release may influence his or her desire to bond with the same sex from that point forward—to say nothing of the demonic influences that may reinforce illicit desires. The chemical release in the brain may also explain why exposure to homosexual pornography at a young age can have devastating effects.[103]

## Practical Examples

Human sexuality is complicated, so not every child who experiences gender nonconformity, adverse family dynamics, or sexual abuse develops SSA. For some, peer pressure, exposure to gay pornography, or sexual experimentation open the door for sexual struggles. It has been said, "There's many a way to SSA."[104] It's not always a cut-and-dried process, which is why we need the Holy Spirit to discern what may have contributed to disordered sexual desires.

However, in both my practical ministry experience and dissertation research, gender nonconformity, adverse family dynamics, and childhood sexual abuse are some of the most common developmental influences. In my thirty case studies, 100 percent of the participants experienced at least one of those influences. The vast majority (93 percent) experienced at least two, and almost half (47 percent) experienced all three. At the same time, we can't say that there's a singular "cause" of SSA. It's most often a combination of factors, which may include our personality temperament, physical traits, life experiences, fallen nature, and demonic influences that capitalize on our vulnerabilities.

Below are two examples of how a combination of factors contribute to the development of SSA:

> John is the youngest of two sons. His older brother is athletic and "manly," just like their dad. John, on the other hand, is sensitive and in touch with his emotions, doesn't have an athletic bone in his body, and excels at art, music, writing, and cooking. Due to their similar personality temperaments, John's dad seems to connect more easily with John's brother, while John connects more easily with his mother. John's peers tease him, calling him a "sissy" and a "fag," confirming John's perception that he doesn't

fit in with boys and will never be able to measure up to his dad or his brother as a real "man among men." John's lack of emotional connection with his dad leaves him with a longing in his heart for male affection, making him vulnerable to inappropriate attention from an older man who takes advantage of him sexually. John wonders why the predator chose him instead of the athletic boys and why his body responded positively to sexual touch from another male. He concludes that he must be gay.

Jill is an only child, and her father is an alcoholic who is verbally and physically abusive to her mother. Jill sees men as unsafe and her mother as weak and concludes that she never wants to be like her mom. Unbeknownst to her parents, an older male cousin sexually abused Jill over the course of several years, reinforcing Jill's perception that men are not safe. Jill vows that she will never make herself vulnerable with a man. As she reaches puberty, Jill finds herself attracted to women who exhibit a strength she saw lacking in her own mother, and she develops a deep emotional connection with women. Finding safety in the arms of other women, Jill concludes that she must be a lesbian.

As illustrated in these examples, there is no one factor that "causes" someone to be gay. Most often it's a unique blend of environmental influences interacting with one's personality temperament and biological traits. Additional factors are demonic influences that seek to destroy our sexuality because it images God. This complicated mixture could explain why one identical twin experiences SSA while the other doesn't. Consider these examples:

> Perhaps the sexual abuse of one twin but not the co-twin; perhaps reactions to perceived parental preference of one twin above the other; maybe one twin is exposed to gay pornography and develops a habit, but his co-twin does not; maybe one male twin misinterprets his intense envy and admiration of confident, popular boys and wonders if he is gay; perhaps one is persistently unlucky with girls, unlike his co-twin, and seriously questions whether he may be gay; one might be the target of denigrating sexual innuendo from other males, but not the co-twin; a slightly gender-atypical physical feature may sometimes be taken obsessively to heart by one child, but not another.[105]

As illustrated above, two children with shared DNA could be raised in a similar environment yet experience different outcomes. No two children respond in the same way. I have a friend who was sexually abused by her father, and she never struggled with her sexuality, but she has other issues stemming from abuse. Another friend was also sexually abused by her father, and she ended up becoming a lesbian. We all break in different ways based on our varying personality temperaments, biological traits, peer influence, support systems, and other factors that may be involved.

Last, some women find themselves in a lesbian relationship somewhat by surprise. Teen girls, for example, can become emotionally dependent on their best friend, and the relationship may turn sexual without their ever having intended that to happen. The same can happen when a married woman, discontented with her husband, finds emotional solace in a girlfriend, and their relationship turns sexual. Such scenarios may be more common among women because they approach sex differently than men. For women, the emotional attraction usually comes first, followed by the physical. For men, usually physical attraction comes first, followed by the emotional. Consequently, some men become aware of disordered sexual desires from an early age, while some women may not discover disordered sexual desires until later in life.

The bottom line is that there is no singular formula as to how same-sex attractions develop. However, it can be helpful to investigate the potential impact of environmental influences including, but not limited to, gender nonconformity, adverse family dynamics, or childhood sexual abuse.

The next chapter will look at how transgender desires develop.

## DISCUSSION QUESTIONS

1. Explain how gender nonconformity may contribute to the development of same-sex attractions.
2. Explain how adverse family dynamics may contribute to the development of same-sex attractions.
3. Explain how childhood sexual abuse may contribute to the development of same-sex attractions.
4. If you or someone you know experiences same-sex attractions, did any of the environmental influences mentioned in this chapter resonate with you? Why or why not?
5. What else do you think may influence the development of same-sex attractions?

7

# HOW TRANSGENDER DESIRES DEVELOP

Those who develop transgender desires, clinically known as *gender dysphoria*,[106] often experience some of the same environmental factors mentioned in the previous chapter. However, not all transgender experiences are the same.[107] Some people experience both gender dysphoria and same-sex attractions; others experience gender dysphoria but remain attracted to the opposite sex. The former is more common with women, the latter more common among men. It helps to understand the three categories of transgender desires: traditional gender dysphoria, autogynephilia, and rapid-onset gender dysphoria.[108]

## 1. Traditional Gender Dysphoria

Traditional gender dysphoria involves same-sex attractions in addition to gender dysphoria. The technical term would be homophilic (*homo* = same; *philia* = love) gender dysphoria.[109]

Those with traditional (homophilic) gender dysphoria are attracted to the same sex but don't necessarily consider themselves gay. They feel, rather, like a member of the opposite sex trapped in the wrong body, as was my experience. They are typically gender-nonconforming kids who don't fit in with gender stereotypes and identify more with the opposite sex than with their own. They may also experience other factors that contribute to the development of same-sex attractions, such as childhood sexual abuse or adverse family dynamics, that prevent them from bonding with their biological sex.

Traditional gender dysphoria likely has roots in early childhood. Most children become aware of the differences between males and females around age two. By age three, they can identify themselves as a boy or a girl (known as "gender identity"). By age five, they begin to develop a stable sense of their own gender identity (known as "gender stability"). By age seven, they understand that their gender identity cannot change, even if they wear clothes of the opposite sex (known as "gender consistency").[110] Statistically, 80 to 95 percent of children who experience childhood gender dysphoria eventually find resolve as they go through natural puberty, making it unwise to reinforce a child's false gender identity through social transition (identifying socially as the opposite sex, changing their name/pronouns), taking puberty blockers (which can lead to sterilization), or undergoing "gender affirmation" surgery (removing the breasts or mutilating the genitalia).[111]

Some who experience traditional gender dysphoria recall feeling like the opposite sex as early as age three, indicating a wound in the soul that occurred prior to establishing a stable sense of gender identity. Sometimes that wound comes from a parent who was hoping for a child of the opposite sex, and the child perceives that he or she was not wanted. In other cases, the child may be jealous of a sibling of the other sex, contributing to gender insecurity. Others may see their same-sex parent as weak and undesirable and determine that it's more desirable to be the opposite sex. As with same-sex attractions, there is no standard formula since each child responds differently to environmental influences. Usually, a combination of factors is at play.

Traditional (homophilic) gender dysphoria is essentially an intensified form of homosexuality that manifests not only in attractions to the same sex but in a complete rejection of one's physical body, to the point of believing one *is* the opposite sex. Those with homophilic gender dysphoria tend to "transition" earlier in life, using hormones or surgery to appear like the opposite sex. Boys who want to transition often feel that they're better at being feminine than masculine. In that sense, transitioning becomes a subconscious remedy for a boy failing at manhood. Sometimes girls who have been sexually abused at an early age seek refuge in becoming a boy—i.e., someone who cannot be violated like they were. In that sense, transitioning becomes a subconscious place of protection from male violation.

## 2. Autogynephilia

Autogynephilia (*auto* = self; *gyne* = female; *philia* = love) refers to a man who becomes sexually aroused at the thought of himself as a woman.[112] Years ago, we used the term *transvestite* (*trans* = across; *vestite* = clothing), or cross-dresser. In contrast to males with traditional (homophilic) gender dysphoria, who are typically effeminate and sexually attracted to males, autogynephilic men are typically masculine and sexually attracted to women. They often choose stereotypically masculine careers. Many of them marry and father children, but end up transitioning later in life, much to the surprise of others—as did Bruce Jenner. Autogynephilic men differ from drag queens, who are usually effeminate gay men dressing up as women to entertain others. The autogynephilic man remains attracted to women, yet in his private life he experiences a sexual high from dressing as a woman and thinking of himself as a female.

Autogynephilia does not appear to have a counterpart in female sexuality.[113] Most women who experience transgender desires also experience same-sex attractions, although there are rare exceptions.[114] Researchers speculate as to why some men develop autogynephilia. One theory refers to "erotic target location error," where the male finds himself attracted to the feminine within himself and feminine objects instead of being attracted to a female partner.[115]

Jerry Leach, a former autogynephilic man, describes his own journey of never being affirmed by his father and secretly dressing in women's clothing to quell his anxiety when his affirming mother became unavailable.[116] His was a case of symbolic confusion, receiving comfort from articles of clothing that represented his absent mother with whom he desperately longed to connect. Jerry notes that when an autogynephilic man first starts cross-dressing as an adult, he tends to choose outdated clothing, unaware that he gravitates toward styles his mother used to wear. Interestingly, Bruce Jenner's "Call Me Caitlyn" cover photo on *Vogue* magazine features him dressed in an outfit like Marilyn Monroe would wear. Marilyn was born in 1926, the same year as Bruce's mother.[117]

Walt Heyer, a former autogynephilic man who transitioned and lived as Laura for eight years, shares how his grandmother used to secretly dress him up as a girl when he was four years old. Walt recalls his grandmother's excitement at seeing him as a girl. He felt deeply loved and affirmed in the purple chiffon dress she made for him. After two years of cross-dressing in secret at his grandmother's house, Walt sneaked the dress home and hid it in his bottom drawer, hoping to put the dress on again in private to experience the same feelings of love and affirmation. When his parents discovered that his grandma was cross-dressing him, they forbade further visits with her. Later, Walt was sexually molested by his uncle and physically abused by his father, resulting in extreme gender confusion.[118]

In his book *Flight Toward Woman*, Jerry Leach lists several factors that he found to be common to men who experience autogynephilia, including:

- Parents who wished for a female child. (Jerry's mother expressed disappointment that he was not a girl who would one day take over her beauty shop; Walt's grandmother dressed him as a girl.)
- Boys who long to connect with their affirming mother (or mother figure), who suddenly becomes unavailable through separation, death, or circumstances beyond her control—such as returning to work or devoting attention to an ill sibling. The boy connects with feminine objects in her absence (like Walt's obsession with the purple chiffon dress after forced separation from his grandmother). Sometimes boys find comfort in wearing their absent mother's intimate apparel because it's worn closest to her skin.
- Boys who experience rejection from male figures, making their mother's world seem more desirable. The rejection can be real (like Walt being sexually and physically abused) or perceived (the son who feels distant from a father who must work long hours to provide for the family, or the father appears to favor another sibling who is more like the father).
- Parents who favor their daughter, provoking jealousy in their son.[119]

Though we see some factors more frequently than others, there is no set formula as to how gender dysphoria develops in children. As with same-sex attractions, it often results from a combination of factors, including a child's personality temperament, physical traits, life experiences, fallen nature, and demonic influences that capitalize on vulnerabilities to distort a child's sexuality.

## 3. Rapid-Onset Gender Dysphoria

In 2018, Lisa Littman published a study analyzing a phenomenon she calls rapid-onset gender dysphoria (ROGD), which occurs predominantly among teenage girls who previously showed no signs of gender nonconformity.[120] Littman's study suggests that ROGD may result from social contagion via social media or teens in the same peer group coming out as transgender around the same time.

In her book *Irreversible Damage: The Transgender Craze Seducing our Daughters*, journalist Abigail Shrier expounds on the phenomenon of ROGD, noting the influence of social media platforms such as Tumblr, Instagram, Reddit, TikTok, and YouTube, which convince teen girls who don't feel like they fit in that they are, in fact, transgender. Just ten years ago, gender dysphoria affected a tiny minority of the population (less than 0.01 percent),[121] most of them boys. In the last decade, the demographics shifted, and now adolescent girls are in the majority,[122] with the United Kingdom reporting a 4,000 percent increase in girls seeking to transition.[123] What happened?

The invention of the iPhone in 2007.

Shrier notes that anorexia, self-harm, depression, suicide, and ROGD have all increased among teens over the past decade, corresponding to the time when teenagers became attached to their smartphones, succumbing to virtual reality rather than experiencing real relationships. Girls are especially vulnerable to the pitfalls of social media—a seemingly flawless world with perfect poses in the happiest moments of life. Many teens spend hours alone on social media, feeling like their selfie pictures will never measure up to the beauty of other girls, and they feel left out when they see friends posting pictures together without them. It can appear that everyone's life is perfect—except theirs.

With the help of social media, teen girls in the throes of puberty who are feeling socially isolated and uncomfortable with their developing bodies may become convinced that their social awkwardness and body discomfort must mean they were meant to be a boy. Further conflating the matter, society pressures girls to live up to the air-brushed, super-model image. Add to the mix exposure to violent porn that makes sexual intercourse seem unsafe, and it's a recipe for disaster. ROGD is wholly different from the gender-nonconforming girl who has felt like a boy trapped in a girl's body since age three. It typically begins with girls embracing alternative sexual identities, such as "nonbinary" (identifying as neither male nor female) and progressing toward embracing a transgender persona.

Littman suggests that ROGD may be a maladaptive coping mechanism in response to mental health issues.[124] Those with ROGD have higher rates of mental health problems, including depression, self-harm, and even mild forms of autism.[125] Shrier describes the ROGD phenomenon as follows: A girl who is already grappling with depression and poor self-image finds comfort in binding her breasts to hide her developing body and prevent guys from gawking at her. When she "comes out" on social media as nonbinary or trans, she receives a showering of affirmation like she has never experienced before. This brings further comfort and encouragement to her heart and shields her from future peer rejection now that she is part of an "oppressed minority," which our culture celebrates. Transitioning represents a fresh start, a new beginning, a new identity, a counterfeit "born again" experience—supposedly leaving her mental health issues behind. When she begins testosterone ("T") injections, her anxiety may lessen in response to the natural euphoric effect of T, convincing her that transitioning is indeed the cure for her anxiety and depression.[126] Additionally, testosterone stops her menstrual cycle, redistributes fat, and gives her a sense of boldness in social situations, further convincing her that transitioning will solve all her problems. What doctors won't tell her is that injecting cross-sex hormones can lead to infertility and increased risk for cancer and cardiovascular disease, among other maladies.[127]

Sadly, if you search YouTube for "detransitioners," you will find scores of young women living with the permanent effects of double mastectomies, sterilization, male-sounding voices, and five-o'-clock shadows. Our vulnerable daughters are paying the highest price for the glorification of all things LGBTQ. ROGD is a social contagion spreading rapidly among teen girls, much the same way eating disorders and cutting became popular in previous generations. Some of the girls who succumb to ROGD may have been considered "tomboys" in previous generations. But today's LGBTQ-affirming culture has erased the concept of a tomboy, offering transitioning to look/act like a male as the only alternative to not being a "girly girl."

## A Word to Parents

If your child struggles with his or her sexuality, these last two chapters were probably difficult to read. I urge you not to blame yourself or walk in condemnation. God is not looking to assign blame but to bring about redemption. Adam and Eve had a perfect Father and still fell into sin. My parents, who have been married over fifty years, had the best of intentions. They did everything they could to love me well and provide a stable home. When I was in my mid-twenties, I told them about my struggles, and they battled with thoughts like, "What did we do wrong? How could we not have known? What could we have done differently?"

The fact that you may be entertaining such questions demonstrates that your heart has always been for your child's best interest and welfare. That's the parental instinct God put in you. No caring parent sets out to harm their child or derail his or her sexuality. While family dynamics can play a role in your child's psychosexual development, it's important to remember that parenting is not the only factor at play. You must also take into consideration surrounding circumstances, your child's personality temperament, and outside influences (like peer influence, social media contagion, and porn) in combination with your child's fallen response to real or perceived pain—not to mention the fact that a very real spiritual enemy wants to steal, kill, and destroy your child's sacred sexuality.

There may have been influences that were beyond your ability to change, such as illness, death, divorce, an abusive spouse, the complexity of adoption, the demands of a job to provide for your family, and a myriad of other possibilities beyond your control. Despite your best efforts, if your child *perceives* something as hurtful, their perception trumps your loving intention. As mentioned previously, children are marvelous recorders of history but terrible interpreters of reality.

You are not responsible for how your children perceive reality or for the choices they make as a result. It doesn't all boil down to the relationship with a parent. So, don't walk in condemnation. The same devil who seeks to destroy your child's sexuality also seeks to discourage you and get you to walk in condemnation instead of praying for your child.

At the same time, if the Lord shows you areas where you need to repent, then humble yourself before the Lord, receive His merciful forgiveness, and, if you feel led, meet face-to-face with your child, and ask them to consider forgiving you. Sometimes healing can happen when we are honest about our sin with those whom we have hurt.

But even if the Lord shows you some areas where you missed it, don't believe the lie that "It's all my fault." Some of the dynamics in the relationship with your child may not have been ideal (as is true with every parent/child relationship), but there are still other factors at work. Your child's sinful choices do not negate the positive influence you have had on their life. If your child chooses bitterness and unforgiveness in response to pain, they open a door that gives the enemy a foothold to influence them, and that's beyond your control.

So, if your child is struggling, resist the enemy's trap of making it all about you and how you've failed as a parent. Remember, the evil one is the enemy—not you, not your child, not even the fallen culture in which we live. The devil is the one who seeks to kill, steal, and destroy. But God can redeem anything. Come into agreement with the Lord against the real enemy behind your child's struggles. Your child needs you to stand *with* them and fight *for* them against a common enemy.

Perhaps you are reading this book because your child just confessed their struggles to you. If so, you may find it helpful to connect with other parents who are walking a similar path. I highly recommend the affiliate ministries listed on the Restored Hope Network website.[128] I also recommend Joe Dallas's book *When Homosexuality Hits Home*.[129] Joe offers sage advice to parents as a former gay man, seasoned counselor, and father of two sons. For transgender matters, I recommend Help4Families[130] and Walt Heyer's ministry.[131]

Finally, I recommend the following Pure Passion Media documentaries available for free on YouTube:

- *Such Were Some of You*[132]—stories of twenty-nine ex-gay men and women
- *How Do You Like Me Now? When a Child, Parent, Spouse or Sibling Says They're Gay*[133]—stories of how families respond to LGBTQ loved ones, based on Joe's book *When Homosexuality Hits Home: What to Do When a Loved One Says, "I'm Gay"*
- *TranZformed: Finding Peace with Your God-Given Gender*[134]—stories of 15 former transgender individuals, including yours truly

The above videos highlight the process of transformation, which is the topic of the next few chapters.

## DISCUSSION QUESTIONS

1. Describe the development of gender identity between ages two and seven and how a disruption in that process may lead to traditional (homophilic) gender dysphoria.
2. What is autogynephilia and how might it develop?
3. What is rapid-onset gender dysphoria, and why is it so prevalent among teenage girls today?
4. How would you encourage a parent who is feeling like they failed because their child struggles with their sexuality?

8

# HOW TRANSFORMATION HAPPENS: THEOLOGICALLY SPEAKING

The lie that people are born gay/trans and can't change has been repeated so many times that, as of this writing, more than twenty states have banned so-called "conversion therapy" for minors.[135] The end game is to make it illegal for all ages, as has already happened in Canada, where violators face a potential five-year prison sentence.[136] "Conversion therapy" is a pejorative term created by pro-gay activists to imply that religious workers, counselors, and therapists impose their will upon innocent LGBTQ-identified people, forcing them to change (i.e., convert). "Conversion therapists" are accused of using unorthodox methods like shaming, electroshock therapy, and aversion techniques (like shoving someone's hand in ice water each time they experience an unwanted attraction).[137]

Coercion wasn't part of my journey of transformation, and neither I nor my colleagues who are slandered as "conversion therapists" would ever endorse such practices. Coercion has nothing to do with biblical transformation.[138]

Sadly, some well-meaning parents have forced their LGBTQ-identified children into talk therapy against their children's will. I do not recommend that for reasons I will expound upon in the next few chapters. There are some LGBTQ-identified individuals who tried to change, but after a while concluded that they could not and, therefore, changed their theology to match their subjective experience. That gave way to a new breed of believers who identify as "celibate gay Christians" and accommodate transgender identities among believers.[139] Yet Scripture makes no concession for fallen desires dictating our identity. Rather, sinners who turn from sin and surrender to Christ have a new identity:

> Or do you not know that wrongdoers will not inherit the kingdom of God? Do not be deceived: Neither the sexually immoral nor idolaters nor adulterers nor men who have sex with men nor thieves nor the greedy nor drunkards nor slanderers nor swindlers will inherit the kingdom of God. *And that is what some of you were*. But you were washed, you were sanctified, you were justified in the name of the Lord Jesus Christ and by the Spirit of our God. (1 Corinthians 6:9–11; italics mine)

Consider the sins listed above. Do you know anyone who used to be addicted to porn but is now free? Do you know anyone who used to be an adulterer but is now faithful to their spouse? Do you know anyone who used to be greedy but is now a sacrificial giver? Do you know anyone who used to be an alcoholic but no longer lives as a drunkard? Of course, you do—because the expectation of Scripture is that everyone who comes to Christ experiences continual transformation as they surrender each area of life to Him.

Homoerotic behavior is included in the same list, indicating the same kind of transformation is possible: "that is what some of you were." As I noted in chapter 4, the Apostle Paul doesn't say, "that is what some of you used to *do*." Salvation involves more than a mere change in behavior; it involves a change in identity that marks new life in Christ so that our sinful desires no longer dictate our actions, much less determine our identity. In other words, transformation is a natural byproduct of salvation. Each day we surrender to Jesus, we walk further away from who we used to be and are continually conformed to the image of Christ (Romans 8:29; 2 Corinthians 3:18).

And yet, some in the body of Christ have caved to cultural pressure and consider LGBTQ feelings a fixed and immutable part of one's identity. As I stated in chapter 3, "sexual orientation" and "gender identity" are false constructs the world invented to explain sexual brokenness from a fallen human perspective. From a biblical perspective, there is no such thing as sexual orientation or gender identity, but rather deceitful desires that arise from the old self. When one's sexual attractions or gender identity do not align with one's God-given biological sex, that is an indicator of disordered desires in the soul (mind, emotions, will). God cares about the whole person (spirit, soul, and body) and delights in healing our soul so that we can be reconciled to His design for our sexuality.

Rather than embracing fallen desires as our identity (i.e., identifying as a "gay Christian" or adopting a transgender identity), Scripture urges us to "put off your old self, which is being corrupted by its deceitful desires; to be made new in the attitude of your minds; and to put on the new self, created to be like God in true righteousness and holiness" (Ephesians 4:22–24). This is what the Bible calls sanctification, which is a lifelong process for the believer.

Paul refers to sanctification as involving our entire tripart being: "May God himself, the God of peace, sanctify you through and through. May your whole spirit, soul and body be kept blameless at the coming of our Lord Jesus Christ" (1 Thessalonians 5:23). Scripturally speaking, we aren't talking about "sexual orientation change," but rather sanctification of the soul (mind, emotions, will) that brings our entire tripart being into alignment with God's design.

## The Process of Sanctification

Let's look more closely at each verse in Ephesians 4:22–24, which outlines a three-phase process of sanctification incorporating body, soul, and spirit.

### 1. "Put off your old self, which is being corrupted by its deceitful desires." [body]

The first phase in the sanctification process addresses the body and its associated desires. Paul notes in Ephesians 4:22 that our corrupted, fallen desires are *deceitful*—they're lying to us! We need to align with God's Word and call same-sex attractions and gender dysphoria what they really are: disordered desires *based on lies*. Certainly, the feelings are real. I'm not saying that same-sex attractions or gender dysphoria are figments of the imagination. But remember that our spirit, soul, and body are inextricably linked. This means that whatever we dwell on in our mind (soul) can affect our body, *including* our sexual responses. Therefore, to see a change in our bodily desires, we must address the lies that afflict the soul (mind, emotions, will). We need to repent for our sinful behavior and renounce the lies that have held us captive. That leads to phase two.

### 2. "Be made new in the attitude of your minds." [soul]

This phase addresses the soul (mind, emotions, will). Bringing our minds into alignment with the Word is the key to transformation. If we identify as a gay/trans Christian, we are coming into agreement with a lie from the pit of hell, and we will remain stuck in the old self instead of stepping into the new. Transformation happens when we renew our minds according to God's will:

> Do not conform to the pattern of this world [believing you were born gay/trans], but be transformed by the

> renewing of your mind [understanding that same-sex attractions and gender dysphoria are deceitful desires arising from the old self]. Then you will be able to test and approve what God's will is—his good, pleasing and perfect will [created in His image as male or female and designed to be attracted to the opposite sex]. (Romans 12:2)

Renewing the mind also involves replacing lies that may have contributed to the development of same-sex attractions and gender dysphoria. For example, a gender-nonconforming child might believe the lie, "You're not truly a man among men or a woman among women because you don't fit the cultural stereotype." Those who did not connect emotionally with their same-sex parent might subconsciously believe the lie that connecting sexually with a person of the same sex will complete them. Boys who have been sexually abused might believe the lie that they're gay because their body responded to pleasure or because the abuser chose them instead of the jock they admire. Girls who have been abused might believe men are not safe and vow that they will never be vulnerable with a man again. Remember neuroplasticity? As we replace lies with truth, we forge new pathways that not only change the way we think but also affect the way we feel—which then influences the way we behave.

In addition to ministering to the *mind* by replacing lies with truth, I will explain in a later chapter how inner healing can bring freedom from the *emotional* pain that accompanies those lies as we engage our *will* to repent and forgive. In that sense, being made new in the attitude of our minds addresses all three parts of the soul (mind, emotions, and will).

### 3. "Put on the new self, created to be like God in true righteousness and holiness." [spirit]

This phase addresses the spirit (the new self in Christ). Putting on the new self does not refer to legalistic behavior modification but rather to stepping into who God already created us to be inwardly, which will eventually manifest outwardly in our soul and body. I will explain in a future chapter how inner healing plays a part in helping us to live from the new self instead of the old self.

Progressive sanctification means our fallen desires remain subject to change as the Spirit continues to conform us to the image of Christ. We are "being transformed into his image with ever-increasing glory" (2 Corinthians 3:18) and are "being renewed in knowledge in the image of [our] Creator" (Colossians 3:10). Paul attested to the experience of ongoing sanctification in his own life:

> Not that I have already obtained all this, or have already arrived at my goal, but I press on to take hold of that for which Christ Jesus took hold of me. Brothers and sisters, I do not consider myself yet to have taken hold of it. But one thing I do: Forgetting

> what is behind and straining toward what is ahead, I press on toward the goal to win the prize for which God has called me heavenward in Christ Jesus. (Philippians 3:12–14)

Rather than focusing on the old self and how to integrate our fallen desires into our Christian identity (à la "gay/trans Christian" ideology), sanctification means putting off our deceitful desires with their associated false identities and choosing to align our mind with who God created us to be. We clothe ourselves with the Lord Jesus Christ and do not even consider how to gratify the desires of the flesh (Romans 13:14). As we continue to put off the old and put on the new, we create new neural pathways that transform our thinking, which eventually affects our emotions and will, conforming them to God's design for our sexuality.

## Behavior, Beliefs, Identity, Desire

Another way of looking at the sanctification process is to consider how change happens at the level of behavior, beliefs, identity, and desire. Most overcomers[140] are fixated on changing their desires (same-sex attractions or gender dysphoria) as their primary goal. But a change in desires typically doesn't happen until we change our behavior (put off the old self), change our beliefs (be made new in the attitude of our minds), and adopt our new identity (put on the new self).

For the overcomer, this looks like repenting for acting out (i.e., sexual fantasy, pornography, or acting out with another person); renewing the mind with Scripture (understanding same-sex attractions and gender dysphoria as disordered desires contrary to God's design); and embracing our identity in Christ as a dearly loved child created by God to be content in the body He gave us, with attractions to the opposite sex. As we persist in repenting, renewing the mind, and embracing our new identity as a beloved child of God, we begin to experience desires that align with the new self, "created to be like God in true righteousness and holiness" (Ephesians 4:24).[141] Mind you, I'm summarizing in a few sentences a process that can take years to walk out. The upcoming chapters describe that process in more detail.

## What About Temptation?

Some mistake transformation to mean that a person can never be tempted in that area again. But progressive sanctification doesn't eliminate temptation. As long as we live in this fallen world, we will experience temptation. Even Jesus was tempted, yet his temptations didn't dictate His identity or compel Him to sin (Hebrews 4:15). Temptation can lead to sin if we meditate on it (James 1:13–15), but temptation itself is not a sin. The Bible commands us to flee from temptation, not to repent for it (1 Corinthians 6:18, 10:13; 2 Timothy 2:22). The fact that we are tempted doesn't say anything about us, except that we live in a fallen world and have an enemy who wants to lure us away from who we truly are in Christ.

Thus, the goal of the Christian life is not to experience freedom from temptation but to know Jesus and become like Him. As we grow in intimacy with Christ and are conformed to His image, we discover over time that although we may on occasion experience a former temptation, the old life doesn't have a hold on us like it used to. In other words, while we may be tempted to sin, we are no longer *mastered by* nor *defined by* sin (Romans 6:14).

The medical world describes change in terms of frequency, duration, and intensity of symptoms. The same can be said of how transformation happens in the soul. As we experience healing in our soul, we notice that the frequency, duration, and intensity of temptation begins to diminish over time. That's because we are building new neural pathways as we renew our mind with God's truth. For some, the temptations eventually disappear. Others may notice increased vulnerability to temptation during times of stress.

Transformation in this area is no different than in other areas, such as porn addiction, alcoholism, binge eating, or substance abuse. Just because a person experiences a former temptation doesn't mean they haven't been transformed. Sometimes temptation functions like a breadcrumb trail, revealing lies and wounds in the soul that God wants to address, resulting in further transformation as we yield to God's pruning work in our lives (more on that in a future chapter). The goal is not freedom from temptation itself but becoming conformed to the image of Christ, even in the context of temptation.

## Sanctification over the Long Haul

Progressive sanctification occurs over time, which is not what this microwave, fast-food, instant-gratification generation wants to hear. We're talking about a lifelong journey, continually pressing on toward the goal to win the prize for which we have been called heavenward in Christ Jesus. The tendency is to give up, conforming to the pattern of this world and allowing our desires to define and defeat us so that we concede to things like adopting a "celibate gay/trans Christian" identity instead of making our goal to be transformed into His image.

As one who has been on this journey since 1994—the most difficult part being the first eleven years—I can understand why people give up. Transformation can be messy. And painful. And slow. That's because we're often dealing with deeply engrained neural pathways in the natural realm, in addition to demonic forces in the spiritual realm.

It can be an especially difficult road for those who have been involved in unhealthy, emotionally dependent relationships or enslaved to sexual addictions such as porn, compulsive masturbation, or acting out with others. Overcoming sexual addiction involves the added dimension of withdrawal from the incredibly powerful high of relieving sexual urges. It feels like death to deny our flesh what it craves in order to finally face the emotional pain held at bay through self-medicating behaviors. But freedom won't come until we turn from sinful coping mechanisms and face our pain in the presence of Jesus. Only then can He heal the wounds in our soul that fuel our disordered desires.

As we continually die to self, renew our mind, and put on the new self, we eventually develop new neural pathways, and new desires emerge to replace the old. But before we experience new desires, there's a tension in the journey where we must embrace the objective truth of who we are in Christ, even when our subjective feelings seem to contradict that. The Bible refers to that tension as the "faith and patience" through which we inherit what God has promised (Hebrews 6:12).

I discovered in that season of tension that faith is believing God's Word is true, even when our feelings make it seem like nothing will ever change. I was tempted to give up multiple times, but as I continued to cry out to God, He responded by giving me grace to believe His Word over my subjective feelings. The Lord placed a supernatural seed of faith in my spirit to believe that nothing was impossible and that He would eventually conform me to His design for my sexuality.

Though death to self is painful, the good news of the gospel is that resurrection follows crucifixion. The old way of life that we give up pales in comparison to the new life Christ has for us. On the other side, we discover that God loves to fulfill His promise that "he satisfies the thirsty and fills the hungry with good things" (Psalm 107:9). God has indeed satisfied my thirst for feminine love and resolved my gender identity confusion. I no longer hunger for that forbidden fruit as a false substitute for His love. And as God satisfied my hunger and thirst, attractions to men began to emerge. The next three chapters offer practical insights as to how that kind of transformation happens.

## DISCUSSION QUESTIONS

1. Theologically speaking, there is no such thing as a homosexual orientation or a transgender identity. How does the Bible describe those desires?
2. Instead of "sexual orientation change," what does the Bible call the transformation process?
3. Give an example in your life in which you've experienced the three-phase process of sanctification mentioned in Ephesians 4:22–24.
4. Why might transformation in the area of sexuality be more difficult for some than others?
5. How would you respond to someone who equates transformation with the removal of all temptation?

9

# HOW TRANSFORMATION HAPPENS: PRACTICAL APPLICATION

As we turn toward practical application, remember that transformation is not a one-time event but a lifelong journey of being conformed to the image of Christ. He who began a good work in us will carry it on to completion until the day of Christ Jesus (Philippians 1:6). As we behold the Lord, spending time in His presence and yielding to the power of His Spirit in us, we are transformed into His image with ever-increasing glory (2 Corinthians 3:18). That means there's no end to God's transforming power to restore us to His original design for our sexuality—no matter how we may have been marred by sin and brokenness. There's always more transformation available in Jesus. Always. We don't have to settle for less. What great news!

What follows in the next few chapters are common components of transformation I saw at work among those who participated in my dissertation research. Reflecting on my own journey, I saw the same components at work in my life as well. While there's no formula for transformation, some of the principles here are universal to transformation, whether one deals with sexual brokenness or any other bondage.

## Why Some Experience Greater Degrees of Transformation

Before I share the key components of transformation, keep in mind that there can be individual factors that influence the degree of transformation one experiences. For example, some are more committed to the journey than others. Some have better support systems. Some have acted out with hundreds of partners, resulting in deeply embedded neural pathways that need to be rerouted over time. Others have never acted on their compulsions outside of pornography or self-gratification and may experience change more quickly. Some have additional components of abuse or adverse family dynamics they need to work through.

The bottom line is that everyone is different, and multiple factors can affect the journey of transformation and how long it takes for one individual versus another to see tangible change. The focus is not how long it takes to change but rather keeping our eyes fixed on Jesus and being continually transformed into His image.

The concepts in this chapter apply to same-sex attractions and traditional (homophilic) gender dysphoria. I will address the transformation process for autogynephilia and rapid-onset gender dysphoria in a future chapter.

## Keys to Transformation

### 1. Transformation happens through intimacy with Christ.

The key to transformation is first and foremost intimacy with Jesus. I cannot stress that enough. My goal was not to be free as much as it was to be *His*—whether or not my desires ever changed. Transformation came as a byproduct of intimacy with Jesus. As I surrendered everything and sought Him with all my heart, He began to expose the lies I believed and the wounds of rejection that had become lodged in my soul. It was like a mystery being unraveled. As the Lord showed me the reasons for my disordered desires, He gave me hope and expectation for resolution. Even so, my end goal was not to discover all the reasons why my sexuality became derailed; it was to know Christ. As my friend David Kyle Foster says, "Knowing *why* helps, but knowing *Him* is what heals."[142]

One of the greatest pitfalls is making change itself an idol. If the overcomer makes attractions to the opposite sex their primary goal, they'll be utterly disappointed when that idol lets them down. As one of my research participants said, "Change isn't a process; it's a Person: Jesus Christ." The overcomer must fix their eyes on the Author and Finisher of their faith (Hebrews 12:2), lest they become fixated on their perceived lack of progress. The attitude of the overcomer needs to be like that of Shadrach, Meshach, and Abednego, who, when threatened to be thrown into a furnace for not bowing down to Nebuchadnezzar's idol, responded:

> If we are thrown into the blazing furnace, the God we serve is able to deliver us from it, and he will deliver us from Your Majesty's hand. But even if he does not, we want you to know, Your Majesty, that we will not serve your gods or worship the image of gold you have set up. (Daniel 3:17–18)

It's that kind of attitude that precipitates change: "God is going to deliver me, and even if He doesn't, I will honor God's Word and seek Him with all my heart. I won't bow my knee to the enemy, embrace a gay/trans identity, or concede that transformation isn't possible." Those who exercise that kind of tenacity tend to experience the greatest degree of change.

Encourage the overcomer to make intimacy with Jesus their primary focus:

- Teach the overcomer how to commune with Jesus through the Word and prayer. Daily intake of the Word grounds them in truth, fuels their faith, and guards them against deception, discouragement, and unbelief.
- Teach the overcomer how to discern God's voice from their own flesh, the world, and the evil one, so that they can hold fast to God's objective Word rather than succumb to subjective feelings.

- Demonstrate how to journal and write down significant insights from the Word so that the overcomer can remember them and pray them back regularly.
- Teach the overcomer how to deny the flesh through fasting and prayer, whereby they feed their spirit and grow in intimacy with Jesus.
- Pray for the overcomer to be baptized in the Holy Spirit so that they can pray in the Spirit as much as possible, releasing their burdens to the Lord and experiencing Spirit-to-spirit intimacy.[143]
- Connect the overcomer to other believers who meet regularly to study the Word, pray, memorize Scripture, and support one another in the faith. It doesn't matter whether those believers struggle with sexual brokenness. In fact, one of the most helpful insights for overcomers is to see that their struggles are no different from those of any other believer who must learn how to die to self and be continually conformed to the image of Christ.
- Encourage the overcomer to find a place to serve so that they don't grow overly introspective and self-absorbed.

Overall, encourage overcomers to follow Jesus for the sake of Jesus—not because of what Jesus can give them. Help them get to the point where they seek to know Jesus and to make Him known, regardless of whether their subjective desires ever change. Again, change happens as a byproduct of intimacy, not from seeking change as the primary goal.

The Apostle Paul's passionate words in Philippians 3:10–11, quoted here from the Classic Edition of the Amplified Bible, encapsulate the goal of knowing Jesus:

> [For my determined purpose is] that I may know Him [that I may progressively become more deeply and intimately acquainted with Him, perceiving and recognizing and understanding the wonders of His Person more strongly and more clearly], and that I may in that same way come to know the power outflowing from His resurrection [which it exerts over believers], and that I may so share His sufferings as to be continually transformed [in spirit into His likeness even] to His death, [in the hope]
>
> That if possible I may attain to the [spiritual and moral] resurrection [that lifts me] out from among the dead [even while in the body].

### 2. Transformation does not happen by force.

Well-meaning family and friends often refer their LGBTQ-identified loved one to a counselor or prayer minister, hoping that they can "fix" their loved one. However, if the individual isn't motivated to seek intimacy with Jesus and to surrender every area of their life to His Lordship, change is unlikely to happen. In the same way that you can't force the gospel on someone who doesn't want it, you can't force transformation on someone who isn't seeking transformation through

Jesus. Forcing the matter may unwittingly bias them against transformation, because they won't likely experience change and will therefore conclude, "I already tried that, and it didn't work." Only someone who is seeking Jesus for the sake of Jesus will be able to persevere through the ongoing journey of transformation.

### 3. Transformation happens through holistic surrender.

Some try to make a deal with God by saying that they will give up homoerotic behavior *if God will take their attractions away.* Thus, they hold their morality for ransom and dictate to God their terms of surrender. But the attitude of the overcomer must be that they will follow God whether or not their desires ever change—because their goal is not just a change in attractions but to know Jesus and become as surrendered to Him as possible.

Surrendering to Christ's Lordship means the overcomer is willing to follow James 5:16: "Confess your sins to each other and pray for each other so that you may be healed." This applies to confessing and repenting (turning away from sin and toward Christ) in the areas of behaviors, beliefs, and identity.

Behaviors include things like acting out sexually with another person, in addition to secret sins such as pornography use, compulsive masturbation, fantasy, and emotional dependency.[144] Those who struggle with their sexuality often engage in secret sin as a form of self-medication, so that they don't have to face the pain in their soul at the root of their addictive behavior. Unless the overcomer is willing to bring secret sin into the light, breaking the power of the enemy to energize that sin, they will remain in bondage and forfeit the transformation that could be theirs in Christ. It's humbling—even humiliating—to confess our sins to others, but the way of the kingdom is that God gives grace to the humble and opposes the proud (James 4:6). Humbling ourselves is how we submit to God and receive His grace (the power and the desire to do His will). Only then can we resist the devil, and he will flee from us (James 4:7).

When an overcomer confesses their secret sin to you, be sure to affirm them for their honesty and let them know that their confession doesn't change your opinion of them. Most overcomers have deep wounds of rejection, so it's important to acknowledge the courage it took for them to risk rejection by confessing everything to you. They need to know it's safe to bring secret sin into the light, and that neither you nor God condemns them (Romans 8:1). Your reaction can help them see that God loves them even though they have sinned (Romans 5:8) and that there's hope for transformation as they turn from sin and receive God's love and grace to change.

The repentant overcomer will need accountability (i.e., an internet filter, mentor, or support group) to help them break sinful habits and end emotionally dependent relationships. This can be a painful process, as the overcomer detoxes from addictive behaviors and emotional dependency that used to mask the pain they were once afraid to face. Renewing the mind and building new neural pathways takes time, and withdrawing from sexual addictions and emotionally dependent relationships can be overwhelming. It's not uncommon for overcomers to lapse back into familiar sin when they become overwhelmed. This requires much grace and patience on the part of the leader seeking to help the overcomer.

The overcomer's goal should not be legalistic perfection, but rather paving a new way of life that involves confession, turning away from sin, and renewing the mind to receive the Father's love—especially when they fail. Help the overcomer *run to* the Father instead of *running away from* Him. The pastoral leader plays an important role of helping the overcomer experience the Father's compassion, even if they stumble along the way, so the repentant overcomer understands that it is God's grace (the power and desire to do His will)—not their own self-effort—that will transform them (Titus 2:11–14).

This is where a change in beliefs and identity come into play. The overcomer must renew their mind to see God as He really is, a gracious and compassionate Father who has paid our debt in full and longs to draw near to us as we draw near to Him. Otherwise, the overcomer will remain in bondage, leaning on secret sin and emotionally dependent relationships to alleviate the pain of perceived rejection from God and others. Many overcomers operate in performance orientation, believing their self-worth is based on their perfect behavior. Consequently, they have difficulty believing God loves them when they fail. They likewise have difficulty receiving God's power and desire to do His will because they are used to relying upon themselves.

Finally, the overcomer needs to understand that their identity is rooted in Christ. God sees them as a dearly loved son or daughter whose disordered desires remain subject to change as they are continually conformed to Christ's image. Adopting a gay/trans identity is a form of unbelief, turning disordered desires into an idol that has the power to dictate an overcomer's identity and determine their destiny. If the overcomer believes they were born that way and cannot change, they will bear the fruit of that belief. Surrendering to Christ's Lordship means the overcomer repents for wrong beliefs and surrenders to what God's Word says rather than following their subjective feelings or cultural trends. Without first surrendering to Christ in the areas of behavior, beliefs, and identity, an eventual change in desires is unlikely.

### 4. Transformation happens over time.

The overcomer needs to understand transformation as a lifelong journey, not a one-time event. I was hoping for the latter and that God would instantly "cure" me of my sexual brokenness in response to an altar call: I'd get slain in the Spirit, fall to the floor sexually broken, and rise anew, content in a female body and attracted to men. Ta-da!

If only transformation were that easy. But that's not generally how progressive sanctification happens. Disordered sexual desires don't develop overnight, and they typically don't resolve overnight.

Sanctification is a lifelong journey that involves continual growth and transformation as we repent of sin, draw near to God, and become conformed to the image of Christ. We can't put a timeline on transformation or give God an ultimatum that we will only stay on the path of sanctification for "X" amount of time. Some go back to the old life or concede to an unscriptural "gay Christian" identity because they didn't see the amount of change they had hoped for in a certain period of time, revealing that they had made change itself—not the Lord—their primary goal.

### 5. Transformation happens one layer at a time.

Rather than a one-time event that occurs within a prescribed time frame, the transformation process is much like peeling back the layers of an onion, one by one. This is true of any issue we seek to overcome, not just LGBTQ feelings. We would much prefer that God put a Ginsu knife to the whole onion and cut through every layer simultaneously. But realistically, we wouldn't be able to handle that much truth at once.

The Lord knows what we can bear and will not overwhelm us in the process. He determines how many layers of the onion need to come off and when. Sometimes He peels back a few layers at once. Sometimes He waits months or even years before we are ready to face another layer. He is not slow in keeping His promise to transform us—although sometimes

He doesn't move as quickly as we think He should. The timing varies based on our level of surrender, our willingness to face the pain behind each layer, and the number of layers. For example, a teenage boy who grew up in a stable home and has never acted on his attractions may not have nearly as many layers to work through as the middle-aged man who grew up without a father, was sexually molested multiple times, and has had hundreds of same-sex partners.

Overcomers often become results-oriented, thinking God can't be pleased with them until they've worked through all their layers. The cross says differently: "But God demonstrates his own love for us in this: while we were still sinners, Christ died for us" (Romans 5:8). This is one of the greatest revelations the overcomer needs to comprehend. God is not uptight about their brokenness. He knew what He was getting into when He sacrificed all on the cross. He's not in a rush to see tangible results like we are because He knows transformation happens from the inside out, as a byproduct of intimacy with Him. His focus is on relationship, sharing every moment of the journey with us as He conforms us to the image of Christ.

As much as I wanted to experience change in an instant, I'm grateful that God didn't answer my prayer because I would have missed out on divine encounters along the way. Through those encounters, I experienced the Father's love on such a deep level that my relationship with Him became more intimate than it could have been if we had not shared those moments together. He didn't just change my outward appearance or reform my external behavior; He transformed my heart to long for Him and become more like Him. In the end, I discovered that my greatest problem wasn't sexual at all. It was my sinful responses to wounds of rejection that lay at the root of my disordered desires.

As I neared the eleven-year mark in my own journey and despaired of how long it was taking, the Lord revealed that His strategy with me was similar to that of the Israelites going into the Promised Land. The Lord didn't drive out all their enemies in one year, lest the land became desolate and the wild animals too numerous (Exodus 23:29–30; Deuteronomy 7:22). It is through faith and patience that we inherit what He promised (Hebrews 6:12). God was more concerned about my relationship with Him and conforming me to the image of Christ than He was with instantly removing my disordered desires. He was sanctifying me through and through—spirit, soul, and body (1 Thessalonians 5:23). Progressive sanctification takes time, trust in God's goodness, and perseverance in the Word. There is no shortcut, as much as we would like one.

Peeling an onion can be messy, stinky, and bring tears to your eyes. Yet onions (if you like them) enhance the flavor and aroma of the dish you're making. Similarly, the Father isn't afraid of our mess, our stinkiness, or our tears. If we focus on sharing every moment of the journey with Him rather than "arriving" at a final destination, we will discover that He takes the very thing we despise most and uses it to draw us closer to

Him and transform us. The scars from our past will become a fragrant aroma that brings life.

### 6. Transformation happens at the root.

As discussed in previous chapters, there are often developmental deficiencies and accompanying wounds in the soul that contribute to sexual brokenness. The most common developmental influences include gender nonconformity, childhood sexual abuse, or adverse family dynamics. When puberty hits, unmet needs for same-sex attachment can become sexualized, manifesting as attractions to the same sex. If we focus only on changing the outward sexual behavior but fail to address the emotional-relational deficits that fuel the attractions, the overcomer may eventually return to old coping mechanisms, as the emotional thirst in their soul combined with their God-given bodily sex drive remains difficult to resist.

Therefore, don't just deal with the fruit (i.e., homoerotic behavior, gay porn, or emotionally dependent relationships); trace the bad fruit back to the bad root (lies, bitterness, unforgiveness, and wounds of rejection that contribute to same-sex detachments or fear of the opposite sex). Ask the Holy Spirit to reveal the roots of bad fruit and to replace lies with truth, bringing healing to the wounded soul.

That said, the roots are not the same for every person. Each person's unique personality temperament and life experiences will affect the way they perceive God, themselves, members of the opposite sex, and members of the same sex. That's why we need the Holy Spirit and His gifts (words of knowledge, words of wisdom, discernment of spirits, etc.) to reveal the unique ways the enemy sought to derail the overcomer's sexuality.

### 7. Transformation happens when we understand temptation.

The tendency for the overcomer is to become fearful of same-sex attractions and run away from them. While I don't encourage meditating on tempting desires, I do encourage overcomers to become curious about their patterns of temptation, as many times those patterns can function as proverbial breadcrumbs that lead us to root lies and wounds in the soul that God wants to heal.[145]

The participants in my research noticed three patterns regarding temptation: 1) Sometimes temptation is simply the enemy luring us into familiar patterns of the old self, and we resist by dismissing the thought and declaring the truth: "That's not who I am in Christ." 2) Sometimes temptation is not coming from within but from a spirit of lust operating through someone else. We resist by thanking God for spiritual discernment and praying for the other individual the way we would want someone to pray for us. 3) Sometimes temptation gives us clues to roots of bitterness our hearts have formed in response to wounds of rejection (Hebrews 12:14–15). Resolving those roots can lead to further healing.

For example, one of my greatest desires as a child was to be held by a nurturing mother figure. That legitimate, unmet desire became sexualized in junior high, and the evil one was all too happy to offer illegitimate ways to satisfy it. Part of the transformation process was to follow that breadcrumb trail, which led to a primary bitter root: rejecting my own mom and her best efforts to nurture me. In chapter 11, I will explain how God healed that wound.

Normal development involves children not only being held by a same-sex grown up but learning to admire their qualities and seeking to emulate them. But if for some reason a child fails to bond meaningfully with the same sex, normal same-sex admiration can become sexualized, resulting in same-sex attractions, as it did for me.

Encourage the overcomer not to fear their attractions but rather to approach them with curiosity: "What, specifically, am I attracted to?" Answers may range from physical traits to character qualities to spiritual gifts. Oftentimes the overcomer is attracted to qualities in another person that they deem lacking in themselves. In that sense, homosexual desire is a drive toward oneness to feel complete, whereas heterosexual desire is the drive toward relational oneness with a person created to be your sexual *complement*.

As a child, I needed meaningful connection with my mom to help me feel complete. In short, I needed to feel secure in who Mom was, which would have enabled me to feel secure in who I was. But because I rejected the world of woman and didn't bond with Mom, I never developed a secure sense of who I was. I subconsciously began searching for other women to "complete" me. Leanne Payne refers to this as the "cannibalism complex" in her book *The Broken Image: Restoring Personal Wholeness through Healing Prayer*. Payne compares the driving force behind same-sex attractions to that of cannibals, who choose their victims based on the admirable traits they hope to acquire when they ingest their victim. For instance, to become brave, cannibals would consume the heart of a brave warrior. To become strong, they would consume his muscles.

Similarly, the person who experiences same-sex attractions subconsciously desires to become one with a person of the same sex whom they greatly admire. They choose partners with admirable traits that they want or may even already have but do not feel secure in. Drinking in nurture from such partners is an attempt to imbibe that security and gain a stronger sense of self. It is again an expression of Romans 1:25: looking to created things to satisfy our needs rather than to our Creator who can meet those needs in legitimate ways.

In my own experience, I was sexually attracted to strong, competent women who served as spiritual leaders yet were feminine in the way they lived out their calling. I was captivated by the wholeness in their femininity. After reading Payne's book, I realized the same qualities I admired in those women were already latent within me, though I didn't see it. I asked God to help me become secure in those qualities so that I didn't seek to bond with those in someone else. In that sense, the origin of my disordered desires was not sexual but relational. I simply didn't know who I was. Transformation involved discovering the uniqueness of my God-given identity and developing security in that. I needed other believers—males and females in my spiritual family—to affirm those qualities in me, thus solidifying my understanding of who God created me to be.

The intangible qualities were easier for me to embrace than the physical qualities. However, I noticed a marked difference in my physical attractions as I began to embrace the physical qualities I admired in Pastor Nan: her bold, red lipstick; stylish hair; unique jewelry; and fragrant perfume. I started incorporating what I admired—experimenting with bold lipstick, growing out my hair, wearing rings and perfume. I changed my style of dress from androgynous clothes to fitted shirts that were distinctly more feminine.

At first it felt uncomfortable and awkward, seeking to discover my identity as a woman at age thirty instead of thirteen. But embracing in myself the qualities I admired in confident women was an essential part of my transformation process. After years of emotional healing, God had brought me to a point where I genuinely wanted to embrace femininity in myself. I wasn't putting on a costume and pretending anymore. He showed me how my same-sex attractions were simply a breadcrumb trail revealing the disconnect with my own identity as a woman. To this day, I wear the same bold, red lipstick; rings; and Pastor Nan's perfume as a confident expression of my own femininity.

Another example involves a research participant who felt a sexual attraction to a man he saw running with his shirt off. When he surrendered that attraction to the Lord, the Holy Spirit revealed that the root of his disordered desire was not sexual but emotional, namely jealousy. He wanted to *be* that young man—slim, tall, and attractive, with ripped muscles—rather than a 5'8" middle-aged man with a potbelly, average looks, and zero athletic ability. The key to transformation was not fixating on the temptation and becoming discouraged but rather to discover what lay at the root of the attraction (jealousy and insecurity) and ask the Lord to help him become secure in his own manhood.

### 8. Transformation happens through redemptive relationships and inner healing prayer.

The linchpins of transformation are redemptive relationships and inner healing prayer. If either aspect is lacking, the process can fall short of transformation, resulting in mere behavior modification that fails to produce lasting change. Because redemptive relationships and inner healing are so crucial, I've made that the focus of the next two chapters.

## DISCUSSION QUESTIONS

1. Why is experiencing opposite-sex attraction not the primary goal of transformation?
2. What happens if you try to force transformation on someone?

3. How is surrender to Christ's Lordship essential to transformation?
4. How is the transformation process like peeling back the layers of an onion?
5. Explain why same-sex attractions, at their root, are not a sexual issue.
6. How can temptation offer clues for transformation?

10

# REDEMPTIVE RELATIONSHIPS: ADDRESSING THE FRUIT

Transformation doesn't occur in a vacuum. God uses the body of Christ. In short, we get hurt in relationship, and we get healed in relationship. The principles from the previous chapter will prove ineffective apart from the context of a loving faith community where the overcomer can work through arrested emotional-relational development. The following relationships are crucial toward that end.

## Christian Counseling

Christian counseling can help the overcomer discover lies and identify dysfunctional relationships that may have contributed to the development of disordered sexual desires. Counseling might be a first step, but it is not the last step; and it mustn't happen in isolation from other relationships.

I met with multiple counselors in my own healing journey. Some were local, but the most helpful was a nonlocal man who had himself come out of a transgender background and counseled me over the phone. He was the first person I ever talked to who understood my pain, and his story gave me hope that God could help me. Overcomers need that kind of hope, hearing testimonies from others who have experienced transformation.

A word of caution: It's crucial to find a counselor who believes in transformation and doesn't concede to accommodation or mortification (addressed in chapter 12). Contact the Restored Hope Network for referrals.[146]

## Spiritual Family

Overcomers often feel orphaned and battle intense loneliness. The good news is that God sets the lonely in families (Psalm 68:6), and He can use spiritual fathers/mothers and brothers/sisters to model healthy relationships that foster spiritual, emotional, and relational healing. In that sense, the body of Christ functions as God's hands and feet to manifest His love and bring healing.

Thus, it is imperative that the overcomer commit to a healthy local fellowship and develop relationships across generations. Healing comes through sharing life together in person, not virtually. I benefited from both peers and spiritual parents God used in my journey, including Pastor Russ and Pastor Nan, who loved me through some of my darkest hours.

Each time I move to a different city, I ask the Lord to connect me with spiritual family to help me stay healthy. I continue to meet regularly with other believers today, including a spiritual mom from my local church.

### Affirming Same-Sex Relationships

Some overcomers feel ostracized because they don't fit gender stereotypes. They need peers who are secure in their own sexuality to affirm them in their unique personality temperament and interests as "a man among men" or as "a woman among women"—especially if they don't fit cultural norms. It helps overcomers to know that their struggles are not much different from those of other men/women. We all struggle with root issues of insecurity, rejection, jealousy, unforgiveness, and so forth. No temptation has overtaken us except what is common to humanity (1 Corinthians 10:13).

Don't be threatened if an overcomer finds themselves sexually attracted to you. It's common for them to be attracted to people who are secure in their own sexuality, because same-sex attractions are not a sexual issue. Disordered sexual desires are fruit from a deeper root, which is typically an emotional/relational deficit that has become sexualized. The Lord can use you to demonstrate healthy relating and to support overcomers as they discover who they are and gain confidence in their God-given identity.

That said, I don't recommend your being the only person reaching out to an overcomer, as emotional dependency can result. I suggest that at least three same-sex friends (none of whom struggle with same-sex attractions themselves) offer simultaneous support. The healing process can be intense, and there will be times that the three of you need to "tag team" when one of you gets drained.

Remember, overcomers are working through arrested emotional development, and it might get messy as unmet emotional needs surface. The fallen instinct of the overcomer is to look to created things rather than to the Creator (Romans 1:25), which may manifest as latching on to a physical person to meet a thirst in the soul that only God himself can fill. Working as a team assures the overcomer that there are always multiple options for help, making them less likely to become emotionally dependent on one person and encouraging them to turn toward the Lord.

In my own experience, Pastor Nan, Sherilyn, and Emily teamed up to help me. All of them were happily married and unfazed by my attractions. I often became overly fixated on Pastor Nan and experienced separation anxiety when we parted ways. I was jealous when she gave her attention to others instead of to me. It was a relief for Nan to have Sherilyn and Emily available to step in when she couldn't take any more of Linda. (I was a pitiful handful!) Healthy relating to Sherilyn and Emily helped me discover how to meet emotional-relational needs in a nonsexual way, as I wasn't attracted to them like I was to Pastor Nan.

## Platonic Opposite-Sex Relationships

The overcomer also needs opposite-sex peers who can affirm them as a "man distinct from, yet respected by, women" or as a "woman distinct from, yet cherished by, men." Again, I recommend at least three opposite-sex peers who are aware of the overcomer's struggles and can make intentional efforts to affirm them in their sexuality. Women need to know that men are safe and that their femininity is a blessing. Men need to know that women will not ridicule them, but rather respect them as masculine men even though they may not fit the cultural male stereotype.

In my own experience, Sean, Tata, and Bob knew about my struggles and came alongside to affirm me as a woman distinct from, yet cherished by, men. They intentionally treated me like a woman instead of one of the guys and gave me consistent support and encouragement, which helped me realize that men are safe.

## Pastoral Care

I recommend that overcomers work with their pastoral leader to decide which same-sex and opposite-sex peers they can privately invite to walk alongside them in their journey. I don't recommend that an overcomer "come out" to an entire local congregation for the same reason I wouldn't recommend someone having sexual problems in their marriage to "come out" to the church. The overcomer needs a safe place to find pastoral care while they are in a vulnerable state. By inviting only those who are part of the solution to come alongside the overcomer, you offer a layer of protection from the schemes of the enemy to disrupt the transformation process, including undue temptation or potential seduction from someone else in the congregation who has similar struggles but is not submitted to Christ's Lordship.

Additionally, coming out publicly not only mirrors the world's way of embracing LGBTQ as an identity, but it also produces undue pressure on the overcomer to impress others who are "watching" and the potential for others to heap condemnation on the overcomer if they fall. Just like a vulnerable seed needs to be planted deep in the earth to protect it from harsh elements, so the vulnerable overcomer needs a season of protected hiddenness where it's safe to heal and grow.

In the future, there will be a time for the overcomer to share their testimony, but it's of utmost importance for them to have a season to develop intimacy with the Lord and not let their sexual struggles define their identity. Transformation will come as a byproduct of seeking the Lord and allowing Him to deal with root issues in His timing. If we short-circuit that process and catapult the overcomer into the limelight before they have resolved root issues and had their freedom tested over time, they won't be able to withstand the spiritual warfare that comes at them when they share their story publicly. Seek the Holy Spirit for His wisdom on matters of timing.

## Wholesome, Nonsexual Touch

Many overcomers long for physical touch. Some didn't receive healthy touch from their same-sex parent, so when their hormones kicked in at puberty, same-sex touch became unintentionally sexualized. Or, in some cases the overcomer was molested as a child, and thus they associate same-sex touch with sex.

Look for ways to affirm the overcomer with wholesome, nonsexual touch by considering the hurting little boy or little girl who is longing for same-sex connection. While we don't want to feed sexual fantasies, there are ways we can offer nonsexual, affirming gestures that help normalize same-sex touch: a pat on the back, a squeeze on the shoulder, a gentle touch on the forearm, a non-sensual hug. I caution against prolonged, full-body hugs and holding that can feed sexual fantasies and prompt the overcomer to fixate on you instead of the Lord. But wholesome, nonsexual hugs are entirely appropriate. Follow the promptings of the Holy Spirit.

One of the best things you can do is connect the overcomer to a local church where they are likely to find spiritual parents (people literally old enough to be their parents) who can offer non-sensual, fatherly/motherly hugs. I used to crave touch so badly, and it helped to have safe people whom God could use to meet that need in a legitimate, nonsexual way.

## Closing Thoughts

While counseling, healthy relationships, and affirming touch are essential to maturing past arrested emotional development, redemptive relationships alone do not resolve the root to the fruit. Resolution happens through encounters with the Father's love that bring healing to the soul. Some call healing of the soul "inner healing" (as opposed to physical healing), which I address in the next chapter.

## DISCUSSION QUESTIONS

1. Why are redemptive relationships an integral part of the healing process?
2. How can Christian counseling be helpful to the overcomer?
3. How do affirming same-sex relationships meet a need for the overcomer?
4. How do platonic opposite-sex relationships meet a need for the overcomer?
5. What are the potential pitfalls of being the only person reaching out to an overcomer?

11

# INNER HEALING: RESOLVING THE ROOT

Some reject inner healing because it sounds New Age, or they've had negative experiences with flaky inner healing/deliverance ministries that aren't grounded on God's Word. But what I'm talking about is rooted in Scripture. Jesus healed people physically, but he also came to heal the brokenhearted and set the oppressed free (Luke 4:18–19; Isaiah 61:1–2).

While physical healing may manifest instantly, healing of the soul tends to be more of a process that aligns with progressive sanctification of spirit, soul, and body (1 Thessalonians 5:23). The soul can become wounded through painful life experiences, especially rejection and trauma. The enemy capitalizes on those vulnerable moments to sow lies in the soul. If we believe the lie with our heart, it will affect our emotions and influence our will. What results is a vicious cycle: We begin to think, feel, and act in ways that keep us in bondage. But Jesus came to set the captive free! When we know God's truth in our innermost being, His truth sets us free (John 8:32; Psalm 51:6, NKJV). And as we embrace the truth and face our pain in the presence of our heavenly Father, He comforts us with His love so that we can comfort others with the comfort we ourselves receive from God (2 Corinthians 1:3–4).[147]

Scripture reveals spiritual laws at work that keep us in a vicious cycle of bondage. For example, if we harbor bitterness toward our parents, life will not go well for us (Ephesians 6:2–3; Deuteronomy 5:16). If we judge and condemn others, we will experience multiplied judgment in return (Matthew 7:1–2, Luke 6:37–38). If we refuse to forgive others from our heart, we will experience torment in our soul (Matthew 18:21–35). If we let the sun go down on our anger, we give the devil a foothold, or a place of influence, in our lives (Ephesians 4:26–27).

Inner healing stops the vicious cycle by addressing unresolved roots of bitterness, judgment, and unforgiveness that open doors for the evil one to keep our souls in bondage. Coming out of agreement with demonic lies and repenting for our wrong responses to pain (bitterness, judgment, unforgiveness, etc.) breaks the power of the enemy to influence us in that area. Think of bitterness and unforgiveness like "hooks" on the soul where the enemy can grab hold. When we release forgiveness and bless those who have hurt us, the hooks are removed, and the enemy can no longer get a grip in that area of our lives.

That's not to say that a Christian can be possessed by a demon. Once we are in Christ, the Holy Spirit indwells our spirit, and we are God's possession (Ephesians 1:14). But when we operate in bitterness and unforgiveness, we open a door to the enemy to influence our thinking, feeling, and reacting. The evil one will retain that foothold (oppressing the soul) until we repent for our sinful responses, come out of agreement with his lies, and receive God's truth to replace the lies.

If you are unfamiliar with inner healing, I recommend the book *Transforming the Inner Man*, which is the first of a four-book series authored by inner-healing pioneers John and Paula Sandford. I also recommend *Deliverance and Inner Healing* by John Sandford and Mark Sandford. This is an area where the body of Christ needs to grow—not just to address LGBTQ, but every area of life. So many believers are trapped in cycles of sin, unable to find lasting freedom because they address only the fruit (outward behavior) and ignore the root (sinful reactions to wounds in the soul). If you are a pastor, consider asking one of your leaders to get trained in inner healing and disciple others so that your congregation is equipped to heal the brokenhearted and set the captives free, no matter what their bondage. There are many in the body of Christ who offer inner-healing training. I personally recommend Elijah Rain Ministries and Elijah House Ministries.[148]

## The Basics of Inner Healing

Here are some basic inner healing principles and examples:

### 1. Seek God's timing.

I don't recommend skipping straight to inner healing as the proverbial silver bullet. Although my greatest breakthroughs came through inner healing, I first needed to have a stable relationship with the Lord so that my focus was knowing Jesus, not seeking a quick fix to change my attractions. In addition to stability with the Lord, I needed to be established in redemptive relationships so that I had the necessary support system to face the pain in my soul.

I also benefited from basic counseling to help me understand how my disordered desires were related to bitter reactions to wounds in my soul. The Lord brought me to a point of desperation where I was finally ready to confess whatever He told me to confess, forgive whomever He told me to forgive, and repent from whatever He asked me to repent. The repentance part was the most difficult for me because I saw myself as a victim, innocent of any wrongdoing. The Lord showed me that even though I may have been hurt, I didn't respond with the love of Jesus toward those who had hurt me. And for that I needed to repent, turning my heart away from my selfish desire for vengeance and forgiving and blessing my offenders in the same way that God had forgiven me.

Unless the overcomer is grounded in the Word, connected with the body, and has reached a point where they are willing to confess, forgive, and repent, it would not be wise to engage in inner healing. Otherwise, you risk stirring up a hornet's nest, and the overcomer will not have the support system with the Lord or His people to stay the course. That may unwittingly immunize the overcomer against inner healing because they may think, "I tried that, but it didn't work." Move slowly and ask the Holy Spirit to show you when the overcomer is ready to face the pain in their soul through inner-healing prayer.

### 2. Look for "hooks."

Satan typically uses trauma and wounds of rejection as "hooks" to influence the soul. Sometimes the hooks are obvious, like childhood sexual abuse, being teased about gender nonconformity, or overt rejection from a parent. But sometimes the hooks are not as obvious, and we need the Holy Spirit to reveal where bitterness and unforgiveness remain buried in the heart.[149]

For example, a nonathletic son may judge his father because he feels like his father loves his athletic brother more than him. The reality is that the father and brother are similarly gifted and find it easy to connect over a common interest. The father has no ill will toward the nonathletic son and loves him just as much; he simply may not know that he's not bonding with his son in a way that's meaningful to the son. Or he may not know *how* to bond with him. Despite the father's best intentions, the enemy uses perceived rejection, jealousy, and a bitter-root judgment (Hebrews 12:14–15) to plant the lie in the son's heart that there's something deficient about his masculinity. In that case, the son needs to repent for his sinful response to his father's best intentions and renounce the enemy's lie about his masculinity.

Another example would be a five-year-old girl who was sexually molested by an older male cousin. In response to that painful, violating experience, she holds unforgiveness toward her cousin and makes a bitter-root judgment that men are not safe. She vows that she will never let a man hurt her again by allowing him to get close to her. That bitter-root judgment will remain lodged in her soul as she enters puberty, and she may find that she doesn't experience attractions to men because of the core lie that men are unsafe. She may also have poor relationships with men in general because of the bitterness in her soul. In her case, she needs to forgive her cousin, repent for her bitterness, and renounce the lie that all men are unsafe. It may be helpful to review the developmental influences mentioned in chapters 6 and 7 as you ask the Holy Spirit to reveal potential hooks and roots of bitterness. There are usually multiple hooks, not just one.

Sometimes the Holy Spirit waits to reveal deeper roots until we are ready to face the pain. For years, I had asked the Lord what was at the root of my desire to be a man. I didn't get a clear answer until I was in my thirties and came across my mom's pregnancy journal and read where she had written that she had wanted a son. That was news to me. I always knew my parents were thrilled to have two daughters, and they never verbalized that I should have been a boy. In fact, Mom had forgotten she ever felt that way until I showed her the journal in her own handwriting.

I didn't think my mom's pregnancy journal held any significance until my prayer counselor, Mark, sensed the Spirit leading us to pray about my experience in the womb. That was a bit of a stretch for me. I mean, I know God is outside of time and all that but going back to the womb sounded wacky. I followed Mark's lead, but I didn't expect anything to happen, as I'm a rather analytical person and not given to dramatic experiences.

As soon as Mark asked the Lord what I was feeling in the womb, I was suddenly gripped with a sense of frustration: I couldn't be the boy that Mom wanted me to be because God created me to be a girl, and yet I believed I wouldn't be loved unless I were a boy. Mark suggested I release forgiveness toward my mom in the event there was anything in her spirit that unknowingly communicated rejection toward me. That didn't make sense to my mind, because I knew my mom loved me and did her best to mother me well. But in faith, I released forgiveness from my spirit and said aloud, as if my mom were in the room, "Mom, if there was anything in your spirit that wanted me to be a boy, I forgive you the same way Christ has forgiven me. I won't hold that against you."

That ended up being a huge turning point in my healing journey. Were it not for the Holy Spirit, I would never have known my spirit perceived rejection in the womb and responded by rejecting Mom in return. The gifts of the Spirit are essential to the inner-healing process.

This example is just one hook the Lord showed us. After exposing the root, the Holy Spirit revealed multiple ways the enemy had reinforced that lie throughout my childhood and early adult years. For instance, I didn't understand sarcasm as a child, so when Dad made sarcastic comments toward Mom, it felt threatening to my sensitive heart. I decided it wasn't safe to be like Mom, lest Dad make fun of me. As a result, I formed a bitter-root judgment toward Mom and sought to become just like Dad because I wanted his affirmation. Additionally, I remember watching *Little House on the Prairie* as a family. My mom and sister Nancy would cry at the end of almost every episode. Dad was uncomfortable with tears (I never saw him cry until he was in his eighties), so to break the tension he would always make a sarcastic comment, like "Somebody get the Kleenex!" I came to believe the lie that it wasn't safe to cry. I formed a bitter-root judgment toward crying women, stuffed down my emotions, and tried to be tough, like Dad. My dad, of course, had no idea how those dynamics affected me, and there was no ill will in his heart. But the enemy took advantage of my sensitive heart to reinforce the lie that it was better to be like Dad than to be like Mom.

There were more hooks like that than I could count. We needed the Holy Spirit to guide us to each one so that I could repent for my sinful responses and choose to forgive and bless my offender the same way Jesus has forgiven and blessed me. It didn't matter whether or not the person meant to hurt me. As with my parents, my perception of rejection trumped the fact that they never intended to reject me. Again, for the child, perception trumps reality.

Roots of rejection are more readily obvious when the offender has malicious intent. But regardless of whether the wound is perceived or real, the overcomer must forgive. Forgiveness does not mean that what the offender did was OK or that the overcomer must be restored to relationship with someone who is untrustworthy or dangerous (such as a molester or violent person); it simply means the overcomer exercises their will to forgive the other person the same way that Christ has forgiven them, regardless of whether the face-to-face relationship is ever restored.

### 3. Expose the lies.

The enemy takes advantage of painful experiences to plant lies in our soul. In my case, my sensitive spirit picked up on Mom's unspoken desire to have a son and interpreted that as rejection. The enemy took advantage of that perceived rejection to persuade me that I wouldn't be loved as a girl, that I must be a boy to be loved. That's where the lie, "It's superior to be a man," became lodged in my soul.

When addressing painful experiences that the enemy used as a hook, ask the Holy Spirit what lie the overcomer believed as a result. Then, wait on the Lord in silence. Resist the temptation to answer on the Lord's behalf; let Him speak directly to the person's heart. I'm not talking about an audible voice, but the still, small voice of God that sometimes feels like your own thoughts. When we create space for the Lord to speak, He can do more in a moment than we can do in a lifetime. Encourage the overcomer to verbalize the first impression that comes to their heart when you wait on the Lord.

I'm assuming that you as a leader are familiar with the way God speaks to our spirit. If the overcomer is not familiar with listening for God's voice, sometimes it helps to use this example: Ask them to state their full name in their mind without speaking. In the same way that they can "hear" themselves stating their full name in their mind, God's voice comes as a thought that we "hear" in our spirit, as opposed to our physical ears. Obviously, we need to test every subjective impression against the Word of God and reject anything that violates His Word.

#### 4. Replace lies with truth.

Once you've identified a lie, have the overcomer renounce the lie in prayer. Then ask the Lord for His healing word. Encourage the overcomer not to overanalyze but share the first impression that comes. They may sense the Lord speaking to their heart, or it may come as a picture in their mind's eye. Again, resist the temptation to speak on the Lord's behalf; one word or picture directly from Him is infinitely more powerful than something coming indirectly out of your mouth.

Once the overcomer reports what the Lord shares with them, have them pray it back to the Lord and thank Him for the truth. It helps to have someone taking notes while you pray so the overcomer has a record of what the Lord said. Or you can record the session on a smartphone so the overcomer can take notes later. Encourage the overcomer to affirm the truth in prayer on a regular basis, standing their ground against the enemy (Ephesians 6:10–18).

In my case, I subconsciously believed the lie that I was rejected because I wasn't a boy. Once the lie was exposed, we asked the Lord what He had to say about it. Again, I wasn't expecting to hear anything, but as we waited in silence, the Father spoke into my spirit, "They may have wanted a son, but I have veto power. You have full permission to be the woman I created you to be."

That was September 26, 2005, and I have not had a compelling desire to be a man since that day! That doesn't mean the enemy didn't try to tempt me after that—he did—but the "hook" was gone. As I continued to affirm the truth in prayer, the lie lost its hold over me. To this day, I have zero desire to be a man, and I'm not tempted to visit men's restrooms and pretend to use a urinal. My lifelong transgender desires were resolved when I repented for my own sinful response to perceived rejection and heard directly from God who He created me to be.

I tried for years to pound Genesis 1 into my head, reminding myself that God called His creation "very good." I prayed aloud, "It's good to be a woman!" And while that was somewhat helpful in renewing my mind, I couldn't receive the fullness of God's truth due to the wall of bitterness and unforgiveness in my soul that started in the womb and was reinforced throughout my life. I had given the devil a foothold and wasn't able to find freedom until the Lord revealed the wound of rejection and its associated lie. As I came out of agreement with the enemy, repented for my sinful response, and released forgiveness from my heart, Jesus's healing word penetrated my deepest being and transformed my life forever.

### 5. Renounce inner vows.

Another aspect of inner healing is identifying any inner vows the overcomer may have made in response to painful experiences. An inner vow is a promise or determination we make in the flesh to keep from ever being hurt again. Sometimes these are made consciously, but often children simply act them out, never putting them into words.

For example, I made an inner vow that I would never cry or show emotion because I deemed emotions to be weak and womanly. Mom cried, and Dad didn't, so I vowed I would be like Dad instead of Mom. I aligned my will with the enemy in a vain attempt to deny who God created me to be as a woman. As the Holy Spirit made me aware of inner vows I had made, I renounced them and thanked God for who He made me to be as a woman, aligning my will with His.

Two weeks after I renounced the inner vow that I wouldn't cry or show emotion, the Holy Spirit brought to mind painful memories from the past thirty-two years. One by one, He showed me each memory and encouraged me to release the pain I had stuffed down for decades. I cried for three hours straight. I felt the Father draw near and hold me, as if He were holding my heart. He showed me there was a place for the pain to go—up and out of me and into the cross. Jesus didn't just die for the sins I committed; He also died for the sins committed against me, and He invites me to release my pain to Him and find comfort in His heart. That day was a huge step in connecting with my God-given emotions, and I continue to grow in that area.

### 6. Address demonic forces when necessary.

Along with inner healing comes deliverance from demonic influences. Again, a believer's spirit cannot be possessed by a demon because a believer belongs to God. However, a believer can be oppressed in their soul (mind, emotions, and will) when they open a door to the evil one through bitterness and unforgiveness (Ephesians 4:26–27).

The key to deliverance, then, is repenting for unforgiveness associated with painful experiences in the past. Once the overcomer repents for their sinful responses to pain and forgives and blesses their offender from their heart, the enemy loses his foothold. Some demonic entities leave quietly on their own once their power is broken. However, often there are demons that must be confronted directly and sent away in Jesus's name.

For example, when I was meeting with Mark, I felt a cold presence to my left and something around my neck. I freaked out and prayed silently to the Lord, "If this is what I think it is, please tell Mark so we can get rid of it." No sooner had I finished praying silently than Mark said, "The Lord is showing me there's a spirit of compulsion that wraps itself around your neck like a noose and pulls you away to your demise. We send that away in the name of the Lord."

Boom! I literally *felt* that demonic spirit leave my side!

I told Mark what had happened, and he acknowledged that sometimes we can feel the oppression of demons who have had particularly strong influence over our lives. I didn't know it at the time, but in that moment, I was instantly set free from decades of sexual addiction, including compulsive masturbation and the sexual fetish for urinals. My unrepentant sexual sin had left the door open for a spirit of compulsion to enslave me. But as the Lord exposed the root lies behind my compulsions, I yielded to Jesus, forgave those who hurt me, and repented for my wrong responses to pain—and the enemy lost his grip. Mark could send the demon away without incident. That doesn't mean the enemy quit trying to tempt me in that area, but from that point forward I had a fresh fear of the Lord, a desire for purity, and Holy Spirit power to resist temptation like never before.

About a week after that deliverance, I felt some old temptations luring while I was talking to a woman. I panicked, thinking I wasn't free. Then the Holy Spirit spoke to my heart: "Discern. Where is it coming from?" I realized at that moment that although the temptation felt similar, it was coming from the *outside* trying to get in instead of from the *inside*. I easily resisted the temptation with the thought, "That's not who I am anymore," and moved on.

The enemy tried the same tactic multiple times, and sometimes the oppression was so heavy that I needed to call an intercessor to agree with me until it lifted. But as I continued to take my stand and pave new neural pathways in my mind, it became increasingly easier to dismiss the schemes of the enemy and move on. The devil doesn't give up easily, so we need to be aware of his tactics to send seducing spirits to lure us back into our old ways.

Dealing with the demonic is much like dealing with flies swarming around a garbage can. You have two options to get rid of them: swat in vain, attempting to kill every last fly, or get rid of the garbage. Inner-healing prayer gets rid of the garbage in our soul (lies, bitterness, unforgiveness, etc.), so there's no more garbage (or "hooks") to attract the enemy.

## Persevere in the Journey

Some of the examples I shared in this chapter may make it sound like inner-healing prayer and deliverance offer instantaneous results, but that's only because I'm summarizing years of experience in a few pages. While I did have a few experiences that brought immediate change, most of my transformation journey was a process that occurred slowly over time. The examples I share in this chapter were preceded by *eleven years* of pursuing intimacy with Jesus and experiencing measures of healing through redemptive relationships, Christian counseling, and inner-healing prayer sessions. Most of it seemed rather ordinary, though eventually the cumulative effects were extraordinary. Instantaneous breakthroughs were an exception to the rule, not the norm. If we seek God in the ordinary, the extraordinary will come. The overcomer needs to understand that transformation is a journey that requires perseverance and patience for the long haul and that there is always more freedom possible in Jesus. Never give up or settle for less than wholeness in Christ.

## Resolving Autogynephilia and ROGD

The principles I mentioned in the last few chapters apply to autogynephilia and rapid-onset gender dysphoria (ROGD) as well. However, with autogynephilia, you will need to seek the Lord regarding where the fixation with womanhood began. It may have to do with the parents' desire for an opposite-sex child, an affirming mother who was unavailable for whatever reason, a family member who cross-dressed the child and affirmed them as the opposite sex, a root of jealousy based on the parents favoring their daughter over their son, or something else that the Holy Spirit reveals. It is likely a combination of factors and not just one source.

ROGD does not necessarily share the same origins as traditional gender dysphoria, so you will need to seek the Lord regarding root issues that may be contributing to the teen's susceptibility to social contagion, which may also be contributing to anxiety and depression. ROGD is usually more about finding affirmation and feeling celebrated than it is about disordered sexual desires. Thus, teen girls need moms or female mentors who can help them process common adolescent challenges like not feeling like they fit in, being uncomfortable with their developing bodies, or navigating troubles at home. I highly recommend the book *Desist,*

*Detrans & Detox: Getting Your Child Out of the Gender Cult.* Author Maria Keffler explains common factors that contribute to ROGD and gives sound advice to parents navigating ROGD with their daughter.

Additionally, therapist Lisa Marchiano has written some blogs offering practical advice to parents.[150] Though her advice does not come from a Christian perspective, she does offer some helpful guidance regarding boundaries and how parents should respond to a child with ROGD. She encourages parents to express genuine interest, ask lots of questions, and invite heart-to-heart discussion—being careful not to shame their child while not being afraid to set loving boundaries. You can support your child without affirming their self-diagnosis of a false identity. Get them help for any underlying mental health issues, and limit their internet and smartphone use by encouraging them to engage in other activities that build relationships. Spend more time together as a family and make it a priority to do things with them that they love—without involving smartphones.

## Two Commonalities

There is no one formula that can predict who will develop same-sex attractions or gender confusion. Contributing factors will differ from person to person based on their unique life experiences, personality temperament, and other variables. However, I have noticed two commonalities among those who experience disordered sexual desires: They are often deeply sensitive people, and they have a profound wound of rejection.

You may not think the butch lesbian or the woman who transitions to live like a man is deeply sensitive, but often under the tough exterior is a deeply sensitive woman who is keenly attuned to the spiritual realm. Similarly, behind the flair of the flamboyant gay man or the man who transitions to live like a woman, there is often a deeply sensitive man who is keenly attuned to others' hearts. Their gift of sensitivity may be why they respond differently to trauma; or it may be that the evil one sees their gift and targets them because he knows that people who are attuned to the Lord and attuned to others are a threat to his kingdom.

Second, because of their sensitivity, they often feel rejection deeply. Whether real or perceived, rejection often lies at the root of disordered sexual desire.[151] Same-sex attractions are essentially a primal cry for love, indicating that some form of rejection occurred during the developmental years. It could have been as seemingly mild as being teased for gender nonconformity or as painful as overt sexual abuse. Both are destructive to the sensitive child. It was likely a combination of factors that repeatedly reinforced the message of rejection. Interestingly, it's the root of rejection that fuels the pride movement, insisting that others not only accept LGBTQ behavior, but affirm and celebrate it.

Those who have been gender dysphoric from their earliest memory often have wounds of rejection that happened before age five, when stable gender identity forms (see chapter 7). Those with ROGD often have wounds of rejection that make them susceptible to anxiety, depression, and social contagion. The enemy capitalizes on rejection and lures the wounded soul to alleviate their emotional pain through false forms of comfort like emotionally dependent relationships and sexual addictions. That's why mere behavior modification doesn't set us free. It takes redemptive relationships, inner healing, and deliverance to address the root wound of rejection. That's also why intimacy with our heavenly Father is key. The lies we believe in reaction to wounds of rejection (such as "God doesn't love me" or "God isn't there for me") skew our view of God. Thus, those struggling with their sexuality need a revelation of our heavenly Father's love and acceptance. That's why it's so important that the overcomer spend regular time in the Word and praying in the Spirit (Romans 8:26-27; 1 Corinthians 14:14–15; Ephesians 6:18; Jude 20–21).

## Transformation Is an Ongoing Process

Again, transformation is not a one-time event but rather a journey that the Lord faithfully shares with us. The diagram below illustrates the journey of transformation as an ongoing cycle that begins with recognizing deceitful desires (rather than adopting a gay orientation), submitting those deceitful desires to Christ's Lordship in the context of Christian community (redemptive relationships), pursuing greater intimacy with the Lord (prayer, Word, baptism in the Holy Spirit), facing the pain behind wounds of rejection in the presence of the Father (inner healing/deliverance), and remaining open to continued growth and healing, as the Holy Spirit reveals another layer to start the cycle again.

### The Process of Transformation

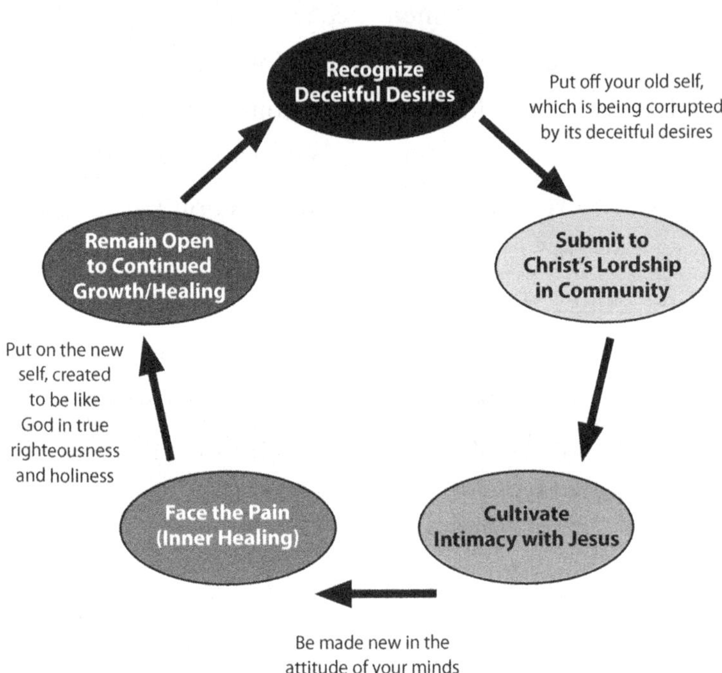


I lost count of how many times I've personally cycled through the above process—and it continues even now. Though I don't struggle with my sexuality anymore, I continue to discover ways that past hurts affect my present relationships; and I continually need to put off the old self, be renewed in my mind, and put on the new self. That's why it's called "progressive sanctification": a lifelong journey of walking with Jesus and becoming more and more like Him.

## Further Resources

For more guidance, I highly recommend resources by David Kyle Foster, a former gay prostitute who experienced profound transformation. Foster wrote three e-books available for free online: 1) "What the Bible Says About Homosexuality and Restoration," 2) Primary Causes for Sexual Identity Confusion: Homosexuality/Bisexuality," and 3) "A Healing Path for the Homosexual and Bisexual."[152] I also recommend Foster's book *Transformed into His Image: Hidden Steps on the Journey of Christlikeness* for overcomers and *Sexual Healing Reference Edition: A Biblical Guide to Finding Freedom from Every Major Area of Sexual Sin and Brokenness* for pastors and lay leaders.

Additionally, Foster's article "The Truth About the Transgender Movement" specifies what to look for to resolve transgender desires, such as addressing childhood sexual abuse or other trauma that brought about gender confusion, correcting lies about one's gender, forgiving parents who may have wanted the opposite-sex child, forgiving a male-hating mother or female-hating father, addressing childhood peer humiliation, and renouncing the rejection of one's biological sex.[153] Again, there's no singular formula that applies universally since the root issues differ from person to person. However, the above resources should give you a good place to start as you seek the Holy Spirit for guidance.

Below is a summary of the last few chapters:

*Keys to transformation:*

- Transformation happens through intimacy with Christ.
- Transformation does not happen by force.

- Transformation happens through holistic surrender.
- Transformation happens over time.
- Transformation happens one layer at a time.
- Transformation happens at the root.
- Transformation happens when we understand temptation.
- Transformation happens through redemptive relationships and inner healing prayer.

*Redemptive relationships include:*

- Christian counseling
- Spiritual family
- Affirming same-sex relationships
- Platonic opposite-sex relationships
- Pastoral care
- Wholesome, nonsexual touch

*Inner-healing prayer includes:*

- Seeking God's timing
- Looking for "hooks"
- Exposing lies
- Replacing lies with truth
- Renouncing inner vows
- Addressing demonic forces when necessary

*Hindrances to transformation:*

- Focusing on change in attractions rather than on intimacy with Jesus
- Refusing to submit secret sin to Christ's Lordship

- Embracing a gay/trans identity
- Ignoring the potential role of developmental influences and wounds of rejection
- Refusing to face the pain associated with wounds of rejection
- Refusing to persevere in the lifelong process of progressive sanctification
- Rejecting inner-healing prayer and the gifts of the Spirit

See appendixes for quick guides on how to respond to someone seeking help for unwanted same-sex attractions, traditional gender dysphoria, or rapid-onset gender dysphoria.

## DISCUSSION QUESTIONS

1. How do "hooks" on the soul form, and how do you get rid of them?
2. Why is it important to seek God's timing for inner healing?
3. What's the difference between behavior modification and transformation?
4. How is the process of resolving ROGD different from that of traditional gender dysphoria?
5. What are the two commonalities among those who experience same-sex attractions and gender dysphoria? Have you seen that to be true in your own observation?
6. Take a look at the Quick Guides in the appendixes. Which one do you find most helpful, and why?

12

# THE FIVE STREAMS: DIFFERING RESPONSES TO LGBTQ

Many pastoral leaders seeking guidance on LGBTQ matters turn to the internet to find the most popular books, podcasts, videos, etc., on the subject. They may come across a resource that seems biblically orthodox because it prohibits homoerotic behavior. However, not every resource that holds to a biblical sexual ethic contends for transformation. In fact, some subtly teach against it. Due to today's rapidly shifting culture, the deception can be difficult to discern.

Thirty years ago, there were basically two Christian responses to LGBTQ: those who held to a biblical sexual ethic and those who held to pro-gay revisionist theology to justify homoerotic behavior. (I'm using the term *Christian* loosely in this chapter. Some who claim to be Christians adhere to teaching contrary to Scripture.) As secular culture shifted over the past three decades to normalize all things LGBTQ,

Christian culture shifted as well, resulting in five differing responses to LGBTQ.

I call the five responses "streams" (rather than "categories" or "lanes") because there can be some overlap between one response and another, just as in nature streams sometimes run into each other. The five streams are not original to me; they are an expansion of a four-part paradigm that emerged in the 1990s using the terms *Side A*, *Side B*, *Side Y*, and *Side X* to compare differing approaches to LGBTQ.[154] In 2017, Portland Fellowship reworked the original paradigm into the categories of revel, resist, renounce, and rebuild.[155]

I've added a fifth stream to include a worldview absent from the original paradigm. Rather than using the letters A, B, Y, or X, I name the five streams according to their predominant response to LGBTQ: *condemnation, affirmation, accommodation, mortification,* and *transformation.* Each stream arrives at a different conclusion based on its premise in two areas: 1) theological beliefs regarding homoerotic behavior, and 2) beliefs regarding the origin of same-sex attractions (SSA) and transgender feelings (i.e., do such desires originate out of the spirit, soul, or body?). In short, the approach a leader takes toward Scripture and their beliefs about the origins of LGBTQ feelings will determine their pastoral response.[156] This is one of the most important chapters of this book, integrating concepts from previous chapters and equipping pastoral leaders to vet resources through the lens of transformation.

In this chapter, I will outline each of the five streams, beginning with *condemnation* and moving toward *transformation*, describing how each approach arrives at its pastoral response. I will explain the impact each stream has on the overcomer, assess its strengths and weaknesses, and give examples of its most popular proponents. I conclude with a chart outlining all five streams in a side-by-side comparison.

## Condemnation

The condemnation stream believes that God hates all LGBTQ-identified people, considering them beyond redemption.

**Theological premise:** Condemnation proponents misapply the concept of *abomination* (see chapter 4), which leads to their belief that God literally hates LGBTQ-identified people. They make no distinction between those who experience unwanted SSA and transgender feelings versus those who act on their desires. They take verses like Psalm 11:5 out of context, categorizing LGBTQ-identified people as spiritual rebels who deserve God's wrath. In addition, they are in favor of enforcing the Levitical law of capital punishment for homosexual acts (Leviticus 20:13).

**Origin: (Spirit)** Those who adopt an LGBTQ identity are seen as spiritual rebels whom God condemns. It is entirely a spiritual issue with no consideration of soul/body (i.e., how wounds in the soul may affect one's psychosexual development or bodily desires).

**Pastoral care:** No pastoral care is available for people whom God considers beyond redemption and deserving of death.

**Impact on the overcomer:** Guilt, shame, condemnation, and alienation from God.

**Strengths and weaknesses:** The only potential strength of this perspective is that its adherents desire to stay true to God's Word. Their misapplication of Scripture, however, skews God's character and distorts the gospel, causing irreparable harm.

**Proponents:** The most infamous condemnation proponents are members of a group who call themselves Westboro Baptist Church. You may have seen pictures of them holding atrocious picket signs saying, for example, "God hates fags" or "Fags die, God laughs."[157] Their website address is literally godhatesfags.com, and their home page once touted: "'God hates fags' . . . is a profound theological statement, which the world needs to hear more than it needs oxygen, water and bread."[158] Westboro changed its web design in 2019, but their messaging remains the same. Other condemnation proponents are listed in this endnote[159] and in the chart at the end of this chapter.

Sadly, condemnation proponents have gained widespread media coverage, leading people to believe that their views represent most Christians. When I interviewed LGBTQ-identified college students for my research and told them I was a Christian, most of them assumed I aligned with the condemnation stream. When I realized that, I apologized for how Jesus and the gospel had been grossly misrepresented to them, and I let them know I was not coming from that perspective.

## Affirmation

The affirmation stream believes that God affirms gay partnerships and marriage. This position was originally called "Side A" (A = Affirming).

**Theological premise**: In direct contrast to condemnation, affirmation proponents contend that God affirms gay partnerships/marriage. They follow pro-gay revisionist theology, including the popular argument that scholars mistranslated the Greek word in 1 Corinthians 6:9 as "homosexual" (see chapter 4). In short, the affirmation approach attempts to syncretize[160] (or sync) contemporary culture with the gospel, suggesting that we need to update the Bible to align with the modern concepts of sexual orientation and gender dysphoria.

**Origin: (Body)** Same-sex attractions and transgender desires are inborn and immutable. God created people that way, making it entirely a biological (body) issue.

**Pastoral care:** Affirmation proponents endorse the modern constructs of gender identity, gender expression, biological sex, and sexual orientation (see chapter 3), insisting that a person can fall anywhere on each of those spectrums based on inborn determinants. Because they believe people are born gay/trans and cannot change, affirmation proponents consider it cruel to suggest that transformation is possible. They malign the message of transformation as "conversion therapy," a pejorative term created by pro-gay activists to dismiss those who contend for transformation as religious extremists or cruel therapists, as described in chapter 8.

**Impact on the overcomer:** The individual may feel affirmed by affirmation proponents, but those who persist in unrepentant homoerotic behavior will not inherit the kingdom of God (1 Corinthians 6:9–11).

**Strengths and weaknesses:** In contrast to the condemnation stream, a strength of the affirmation approach is its emphasis on God's love. As Christ followers, we ought to love LGBTQ-identified people as fellow human beings made in the image of God. However, the Bible never affirms homoerotic behavior, much less gay "marriage." To insist otherwise, one must revise the Scriptures, resulting in syncretism (i.e., merging fallen human desires and culture with Christian beliefs). Affirmation proponents elevate the second-greatest commandment (to love our neighbor) over the first and greatest commandment (to love God, including His Word).

**Proponents:** One of the most prominent affirmation proponents is Matthew Vines, author of *God and the Gay Christian* and founder of The Reformation Project, which promotes LGBTQ inclusion in the church.[161] Other well-known proponents are author and HGTV star Jen Hatmaker, musicians Ray Bolz, Jennifer Knapp, and Vicki Beeching, sociologist and pastor Tony Campolo, and academics James Brownson and David Gushee.

A common characteristic among affirmation proponents is that either they or a loved one came out as gay and tried to change their attractions but couldn't. Consequently, it seems callous to insist that they or their loved one is in the wrong. Therefore, they change their theology to match their subjective experience in an attempt to reconcile Scripture with full affirmation of their LGBTQ-identified loved one.

## Accommodation

The accommodation stream is so named because its proponents accommodate a "gay Christian" identity yet abstain from homoerotic behavior. They consider their attractions a unique cross they must bear. Singles identify as "celibate gay Christians," while those who marry the opposite sex yet still experience same-sex attractions refer to themselves as gay Christians in a "mixed-orientation marriage." This stream is known as "Side B" (in contrast to "Side A").

**Theological premise:** Accommodation proponents reject the condemnation and affirmation streams, seeking to find a middle ground where Christians can be honest about their ongoing same-sex attractions while still following a biblical sexual ethic. To that end, they embrace a "celibate gay Christian" identity, which is a more subtle form of syncretism that seeks to integrate Christianity with LGBTQ culture and the idea that our sexual desires determine our identity.

Instead of relying solely on Scripture, accommodation proponents tend to bolster their position by referring to their subjective experience or quotes from noted Christian authors.[162] Additionally, they embrace a view of God's sovereignty in which healing (whether physical or emotional) only happens if God wills it. Therefore, the individual cannot contend for nor expect a change in their sexual desires in this life. As one proponent says,

> Since God has providentially refrained from changing people's sexual orientations, then He is the one who has chosen not to change their identity. That's why gay Christians (properly understood) still call themselves gay. Why are we taking issue with them, when all they have done is read the hand of Providence and bend the knee—sometimes bitterly, sometimes tearfully—to God's sovereign will over their lives?[163]

In that sense, the "celibate gay Christian" is considered a noble martyr who bears the unique cross of dying daily to their attractions in order to submit to the sovereign will of God not to heal them.

**Origin: (Body/disability)** Accommodation proponents consider SSA to be inborn and immutable, not because God created people gay but because we live in a fallen world. In that sense, SSA is akin to a physical disability that's beyond healing unless God does a creative miracle. It's not a temptation to overcome, or a developmental issue to work through, but rather an inborn "orientation" that's resistant to change.

**Pastoral care:** Accommodation proponents reframe SSA as an inherent identity that can be redeemed as a gift from God. One proponent reframes SSA as the unique ability to appreciate beauty in the same sex.[164] Another reframes SSA as a calling: "How might my being gay itself constitute a call, and how might it be the very means by which I discover new ways to love God and others?"[165] Another proponent reframes his gay orientation as a redemptive fulfillment of God's plan for his life:

> But what if there's goodness hiding within the ruins? What if the calling to gay Christian celibacy is more than just a failure of straightness? What if God dreamed it for me, wove it into the fabric of my being as he knit me together and sang life into me? Is it possible for me to continue pursuing wholeness in Christ even if I stop praying to be straight?[166]

Like the affirmation stream, accommodation proponents refer to transformation as "conversion therapy," since the presumed "disability" of "sexual orientation" cannot change. If

SSA is an inborn disability beyond healing, there's no need for inner-healing prayer or the gifts of the Spirit to reveal potential developmental influences that may have affected their psychosexual development. Thus, pastoral care for this stream consists of helping "gay Christians" cope this side of heaven. They champion abstinence while also encouraging "spiritual friendships," a formal commitment between members of the same sex to ease the loneliness of lifelong singleness.[167]

Many of the leaders in the accommodation stream grew up in the church and recount stories of having been hurt by church leaders who didn't know how to respond when they confided in them about their SSA. To that end, accommodation proponents are on a mission to train the church how to welcome LGBTQ-identified people in the same way they wish they had been accepted growing up.

**Impact on the overcomer:** A "celibate gay Christian" identity fixates on fallen desires, keeping the believer enslaved to sinful impulses with no hope for change. It is essentially a mindset of unbelief that cuts against any expectation for transformation. Because the accommodation approach disregards developmental influences that may contribute to SSA, the struggler[168] may be left with unhealed wounds in the soul that intensify their longings to bond sexually with members of the same sex.

For example, one proponent explains his devastation when his roommate got engaged, which felt like a deep betrayal:

> I started to cry. I clenched my fists and swallowed and gritted my teeth, imploring myself to stop. I didn't want him to see how difficult this was, how I felt as though I'd lost all equilibrium, how I'd never felt so unsteady and sad and bereft. But I couldn't stop, and I hid my face in my hands and kept crying. My body was heaving, and I thought, *I've heard people talking about "heaving sobs" and this is what they feel like. This is what it's like when the floodgates inside are opened up and your body is kind of swept along in the tide of it . . .* At some point, we both stood up, and my friend gave me a long hug, cradling my still-shaking upper body in his arms, and I put my wet face on his shoulder, and he said, "I'm not walking away from you. I'm not leaving. You're not losing me." The next day I stayed in bed, unable to summon the energy to leave the apartment.[169]

This response indicates an unhealthy degree of emotional dependency that prevents the proponent from entering into the joy of his friend's engagement. The accommodation approach does not explore unresolved wounds in the soul that may be at the root of such dependency since it stems from the unfortunate "disability" of a "gay orientation." This results in continued anguish with no hope of reprieve, reinforcing the idea that change remains impossible.

**Strengths and weaknesses:** Accommodation proponents' compassion for those who experience unwanted SSA and their unwavering commitment to celibacy are commendable. However, their approach results in a form of godliness that denies the power of God to transform (2 Timothy 3:5). They hold fast to the scriptural prohibition of homoerotic behavior, yet they accommodate their fallen sexual desires as their identity.

Identifying as a "gay Christian" conflicts with Scripture and introduces unnecessary confusion. The term *gay* has political and moral implications, reframing sinful impulses in a positive way. It enshrines the old self as an idol that must not be crucified but rather justified. Further, the accommodation stream aligns with pro-gay political ideology, introducing terms such as *sexual minorities, heteronormativity, straight privilege,* and *mixed-orientation marriage.*

Identifying ourselves by our temptations conflicts with Scripture. We are no longer slaves to sin, much less identified by it (Romans 6:14). To that end, a "gay Christian" identity acts as a barrier to further transformation, as it communicates, "This is who I am; I cannot change"—which unwittingly reinforces the LGBTQ born-gay-can't-change narrative instead of the new-creation-in-Christ reality. The accommodation stream is quite popular among Millennials and Gen Z, as they are prone to elevate subjective feelings over the objective truth of God's Word.

Further, accommodation proponents appropriate a victim mentality. They see themselves as noble martyrs who pay a greater sacrifice than the average Christian because they must wage war on two fronts: dying daily to illicit sexual impulses while also being attacked by the church for embracing a gay identity. As one author says, "It's hard to avoid the conclusion that Christianity expects more from gay people than it does from straight people."[170]

The "gay Christian" identity creates an "us vs. them" dichotomy among believers, which perpetuates a victim mindset. Rather than repenting of sinful impulses and an over-identification with the world, "celibate gay Christians" call upon the church at large to repent for oppressing "celibate gay Christians." They accuse the church of idolizing the nuclear family because it makes them feel left out.[171] As a single person, I can empathize with sometimes feeling left out, but it's a step too far to say that esteeming marriage is idolatry. Hebrews 13:4 says, "Let marriage be held in honor among all." God himself designed earthly marriage to image the message of the gospel, ultimately fulfilled in the marriage of Christ and the church (Ephesians 5:31–32). That's a glorious mystery to behold, not an idol to be shunned.

Ironically, in decrying the idolization of the nuclear family, accommodation proponents fail to see how they've enshrined their own sexual impulses as an idol that dictates their identity and determines their destiny. They focus on the price they must pay to follow Jesus as "gay Christians" rather than the price Jesus paid to redeem His Bride from the old self. Even more ironic, their solution to ease the loneliness of celibacy is to enter a lifelong "spiritual friendship" covenant with the same sex, which parallels a gay marriage—only without the sex.[172] Such partnerships feed emotional codependency, which can fuel sexual attractions and distract the overcomer from facing the pain in their soul at the root of their sexual confusion.

**Proponents:** Some of the leading proponents of the accommodation stream are authors Preston Sprinkle (*A People to Be Loved* and *Embodied*, and president of The Center for Faith, Sexuality & Gender), Greg Coles (*Single, Gay, Christian*), Wesley Hill (*Washed and Waiting* and *Spiritual Friendship*), Christian psychologist Mark Yarhouse (*Costly Obedience: What We Can Learn from the Celibate Gay Christian Community* and *Understanding Gender Dysphoria*), and Nate Collins (*All But Invisible* and founder of the Revoice movement).

As of this writing, Preston Sprinkle is the most popular accommodation proponent. While he adheres to the prohibition of homoerotic behavior, Sprinkle endorses a "gay Christian" identity and is an outspoken critic of those who contend for transformation. He doesn't believe real change is possible,[173] and he's against all forms of "conversion therapy."[174] Sprinkle discounts environmental influences that may affect one's psychosexual development and ridicules those who contend for transformation as those who attempt to (unsuccessfully) "pray away the gay."[175] His message echoes that of pro-gay activists who dismiss transformation. Ironically, Sprinkle gives credence to the potential role of developmental influences contributing to gender dysphoria,[176] yet he refuses to give credence to developmental influences contributing to same-sex attractions and the potential for change. The video in this endnote best summarizes Sprinkles views in his own words.[177]

Sprinkle is a strong supporter of Revoice, a movement pioneered in 2018 with the mission of "supporting, encouraging, and empowering gay, lesbian, same-sex attracted, and other LGBT Christians so they can flourish while observing the historic, Christian doctrine of marriage and sexuality."[178] Interestingly, Revoice removed the "T" and any reference to "transgender Christians," presumably because it's more difficult to defend biblically a transgender identity which defies obvious biology. Still, their annual conference syncretizes Christianity with LGBTQ culture, as illustrated by the 2018 elective entitled "Redeeming Queer Culture: An Adventure," answering the questions, "What does queer culture (and specifically, queer literature and theory) have to offer us who follow Christ? What queer treasure, honor, and glory will be brought into the New Jerusalem at the end of time (Revelation 21:24–26)?"[179] Christian psychologist Mark Yarhouse also has ties to Revoice, having spoken at their 2019 conference on his book, *Costly Obedience: What We Can Learn from the Celibate Gay Christian Community,* and writing favorably about the Revoice movement in his blog.[180]

The 2022 Revoice conference pushed the transgender envelope, using *they/them* pronouns to introduce Lesli Hudson-Reynolds,[181] a female speaker who wore a t-shirt with the words *Imago Dei* in transgender flag colors.[182] Sprinkle dedicated his book *Embodied* to Lesli and describes "them" as a mentor, someone he turns to for prayer and encouragement.[183]

Additionally, the 2022 Revoice conference featured affinity groups based on identities such as bisexuals/pansexuals, asexuals/aromantics, women "assigned female at birth," mixed-orientation marriages, and celibate partnerships.[184] It's not difficult to see why the Revoice movement finds greater affinity with the LGBTQ community than with Christians who contend for mortification or transformation.

All in all, accommodation proponents do well to exercise compassion for those who experience SSA while holding to a biblical sexual ethic, but they fall into syncretism by integrating a gay identity, embracing LGBTQ culture, and discounting the potential influence of wounds in the soul that may contribute to disordered sexual desires.[185]

## Mortification

The mortification stream renounces a gay identity and urges believers to mortify (or kill) sin, including homoerotic desires and behavior. This approach is traditionally known as "Side Y."

**Theological premise:** Mortification proponents believe SSA results from the fall and that sinful desires must be mortified, as Paul talks about in Romans 8:13 and Colossians 3:5: "Put to death, therefore, whatever belongs to your earthly nature: sexual immorality, impurity, lust, evil desires and greed, which is idolatry." Mortification proponents often come from a Reformed/Calvinist perspective that discounts healing and the gifts of the Spirit and emphasizes God's sovereignty and His ability to use our struggles for our good and His glory.

**Origin: (Spirit)** Same-sex attractions are part of humanity's sin nature, resulting from the fall.

**Pastoral care:** Mortification proponents emphasize repentance, which includes renouncing a gay identity and dying to sinful impulses by replacing those desires with spiritual disciplines (Bible reading, prayer, Scripture memory, devotional reading, etc.). They don't anticipate a change in their attractions, but rather a change in behavior and identity that may or may not result in a change of attractions. Their main emphasis is faithfulness to the Lord despite one's attractions.

Because mortification proponents view SSA as a spiritual effect of the fall, they oppose the idea of investigating developmental influences in the soul, dismissing it as Freudian psychology that removes responsibility from the sinner to repent.[186] As a result, mortification proponents typically don't engage in inner healing to address soul wounds, but instead offer *nouthetic* counseling (now called *biblical* counseling), which relies entirely on scriptural exhortation to effect change.[187] They label the transformation approach "conversion therapy," and distinguish themselves from that approach by noting that they follow the Bible, not secular psychology, and that the goal is not heterosexuality but "holy sexuality."[188]

**Impact on the overcomer:** The mortification approach encourages change in behavior and identity without expectation of change in desires. Disregarding potential developmental influences may result in unresolved wounds in the soul that contribute to ongoing SSA and the belief that their desires can never change; they can only be resisted.

For example, one proponent acknowledges the draw he sometimes feels toward a same-sex friend:

> One of the features of my own experience has been a tendency towards emotional over-dependency on particular friends. Over the years it has happened a number of times. Things with a good friend can be chugging along quite normally and quite happily, and then—almost out of the blue—I can feel a deep tug towards them; a profound need to be around them, to know their approval and affection. Left unchecked, this would quickly grow and grow. And before I know it, this person has become very close to being the centre of my life. It's what the Bible calls idolatry, and it is unbearable. It creates deep yearnings that cannot be fulfilled, and it can put a terrible burden on the friendship.[189]

The mortification approach recommends keeping such desires in check, so they don't grow into idolatry. This contrasts with the accommodation stream that encourages "spiritual friendships" without consideration of the idolatry involved.

While mortification proponents do well to avoid emotional dependency, there's no exploration as to why the pattern of such dependency occurs; it's considered part of the fall and nothing more. Therefore, the only option is to repent and avoid such relationships without considering how unresolved wounds in the soul may contribute to repeated patterns of emotional dependency.

**Strengths and weaknesses:** The strength of the mortification approach is that it holds firmly to a biblical sexual ethic, emphasizing repentance for homoerotic behavior and renouncing a gay identity. It also promotes a high view of Scripture and encourages spiritual disciplines that aid in spiritual growth and behavioral change.[190]

The weakness of the mortification approach is that while it emphasizes repentance, it does not consider how developmental influences and wounds in the soul may play a crucial role in repentance and healing. The purpose of investigating developmental influences is not merely to understand *how* SSA came about, but also to reveal *sinful reactions* to past pain (bitterness, unforgiveness, inner vows). The overcomer needs to repent not just for outward behavior but for attitudes of the heart that fuel sin and keep the overcomer in bondage. As prayer counselor Mark Sandford says,

> The reason we look at developmental influences is *in order to repent* of our reactions to developmental influences—reactions that became permanent

> motivating factors that incline us toward sinning. In inner healing, we do not blame developmental factors, as some contend, nor do we just understand them. We *repent* of our sinful reactions to developmental influences, just as we repent of sinful homosexual actions that are motivated by such roots.[191]

**Proponents:** The most popular proponents of the mortification stream are Christopher Yuan (*Holy Sexuality*), Rosaria Butterfield (*The Secret Thoughts of an Unlikely Convert*), Jackie Hill Perry (*Gay Girl, Good God*), Rachel Gilson (*Born Again This Way*), Sam Allberry (*Is God Anti-Gay?*), and Denny Burk and Health Lambert (*Transforming Homosexuality*)—all of whom have written for The Gospel Coalition.

(Note: Gilson's messaging fits into the mortification stream, yet she associates with the accommodation stream, having spoken at Revoice conferences.[192] Similarly, Jackie Hill Perry associates with the accommodation stream, speaking at Preston Sprinkle's conferences, and appearing on his podcast and video series.[193] These are examples of how streams sometimes overlap.)

Mortification proponents emphasize repentance for sin yet oppose the exploration of developmental influences that may contribute to SSA. For example, Yuan contends that "homosexuality isn't a psychological disorder or a developmental problem. To think that way is a futile, human-centered attempt to erase the reality of original sin."[194]

Butterfield criticizes those who consider developmental influences as having a low view of sin, stating, "Often they look at homosexuality as a behavior to be modified rather than a sin to be mortified."[195] Butterfield has been especially outspoken against reparative therapy (a psychological method of investigating developmental influences that may contribute to same-sex attractions or gender insecurity), characterizing it as "a modern version of the prosperity gospel. Name it. Claim it. Pray the gay away."[196] (Note: In 2022, Butterfield recanted her statement, saying, "This ranks among the most misguided words I have written as a Christian."[197] Though she still holds fast to the mortification perspective, Butterfield is now open to counseling and change-allowing therapy.)

Gilson calls reparative therapy a false gospel that aims to "create" heterosexuality and

> makes promises God does not and is not even scientifically valid, let alone biblically valid. It blames same-sex attraction on various environmental factors—even on the person who doesn't want those attractions—leading to an endless search for *why* instead of equipping to fight the *what.*[198]

That leads to an inordinate waste of time, says Gilson, "trying to figure out what causes same-sex attraction, as if we could reverse the effects of the fall through human tactics."[199]

Jackie Hill Perry concurs:

> In a spiritual sense, [reparative therapy] doesn't work because it's a human attempt to fix a spiritual problem. We experience sinful temptation because of our sin nature that we have inherited from Adam. Reparative therapy doesn't even think of homosexuality in those terms.[200]

Living Out, founded by Sam Allberry, at one point stated that sexual orientation is an immutable characteristic of the fall that cannot be transformed, only subdued:

> We believe it is essential to help people accept themselves as they are, just as God accepts us as we are. This will include accepting our sexual orientation. . . . We believe that attempting to change someone's sexual orientation sends a number of potentially damaging messages.[201]

Some mortification proponents like Burk and Lambert contend that the very temptation of same-sex attractions is in and of itself sin.[202] Consequently, the struggler must repent for even having same-sex attractions.[203] Those who hold this view tend to come from a strict Calvinist perspective that emphasizes humanity's total depravity and discounts the potential role of developmental influences that can shape one's sexual desires.

Mortification proponents emphasize the gospel and dying to self with no anticipation of a change in sexual attractions. As Yuan says, the opposite of homosexuality is not heterosexuality but rather "holy sexuality," which he defines as "chastity in singleness and faithfulness in marriage."[204] Jackie Hill Perry says, likewise, that "heterosexuality isn't a fruit of the Spirit."[205] While Perry's statement is technically true, it's misleading because it conflates the unscriptural concept of "sexual orientation" with the fruit of the Spirit and presupposes that God does not delight to restore our disordered desires to His original design for our sexuality.

Overall, the mortification approach is biblically sound, encouraging believers to renounce a gay identity and repent from homoerotic behavior. However, it stops short of the transformation approach in that it does not take into consideration sinful reactions to developmental influences that may underlie SSA compulsions. It's unfortunate that some mortification proponents publicly disparage the transformation approach, as both streams share similar theological and moral convictions.

## Transformation

Similar to mortification, the transformation approach prohibits homoerotic behavior and renounces a gay identity. It differs from mortification in that it traces the origin of SSA to both the sin nature *and* developmental influences that result from living in a fallen world. In that sense, transformation is holistic, affecting the spirit and the soul (mind, emotions, will), which, in turn, affects the body—including one's sexual desires. This approach is known as "Side X" (as in ex-gay).[206]

**Theological premise:** In addition to repentance, the transformation approach emphasizes holistic sanctification involving spirit, soul, and body (1 Thessalonians 5:23) that progresses over the lifetime of the believer. It considers how potential environmental influences (i.e., childhood sexual abuse, teasing because of gender nonconformity, adverse family dynamics, or other childhood experiences) may have contributed to wounds in the soul that manifest as disordered sexual desires. In contrast to accommodation and mortification, transformation proponents often come from denominational perspectives that emphasize individual free will and remain open to the gifts of the Holy Spirit.[207]

**Origin: (Spirit, Soul, Body)** SSA results from the fall (spirit) and wounds in the soul (mind, emotions, will) which can impact sexual desires (body). Like those of the mortification stream, transformation proponents reject the notion of sexual orientation because it implies an inborn, immutable state of being resistant to change. Instead, they view SSA as deceitful desires that remain subject to change as the believer puts off the old self, renews the mind, and puts on the new self.

**Pastoral care:** The transformation process is twofold: 1) redemptive relationships to meet same-sex emotional/relational deficits in legitimate ways, and 2) counseling or inner-healing prayer to address sinful reactions to wounds in the soul that contribute to disordered sexual desires. In some cases, the roots of disordered desires are not readily obvious, and the gifts of the Spirit are needed to reveal where lies became lodged in the soul during painful childhood experiences. This holistic approach incorporates the spirit (releasing forgiveness, renouncing lies), the soul (renewing the mind with truth), and the body (disordered sexual desires can change when the roots to those desires are dissolved).

**Impact on the overcomer:** The overcomer finds hope, knowing that if there's a *reason* for their disordered desires, there's a *resolution*. They were not born gay; their God-given sexuality became derailed through painful life experiences, and Jesus can bring healing and restoration through the process of progressive sanctification. Transformation is not a one-time event but rather a lifetime trajectory of being continually conformed to the image of Christ (2 Corinthians 3:18).

**Strengths and weaknesses:** The strength of the transformation approach is that it is biblically sound and holistic (ministering to spirit, soul, and body), and it also aligns with truths revealed through scientific research like sexual fluidity and neuroplasticity (see chapter 5). Additionally, for those who come from a Pentecostal perspective, as I do, it integrates the distinctives of Holy Spirit baptism and the gifts of the Spirit (word of knowledge, discernment of spirits, diving healing, etc.) and aligns with the Assemblies of God position paper on homosexuality.[208]

The greatest weakness of the transformation approach is the tendency for overcomers to make attractions to the opposite sex their primary goal. As mentioned in chapter 9, knowing Jesus and becoming increasingly surrendered to Him is the goal. Change happens as a byproduct of surrender and progressive sanctification, which means it doesn't necessarily happen all at once. It's not like flipping a light switch and going from gay to straight; it's more like a dial that turns slowly over time. In my case, it was eleven years before I saw significant change in my desires; and it was several years after that, as I continued to repent, renew my mind, and experience deeper healing for wounds in my soul, that attractions to the opposite sex began to emerge. Some may fail to persevere and conclude that change isn't really possible and then accuse transformation proponents of offering them a false hope.

Another weakness of the transformation approach is the potential for creating a pecking order based on the degree of change one has experienced, implying that those who still experience same-sex attractions are somehow inferior. The goal is not the degree of change in comparison to another, but rather pursuing Jesus, becoming increasingly surrendered to Him and remaining open to continued growth and healing. There is always more in Jesus. In the words of one of my case-study participants, "My goal wasn't to become straight; it was to become whole."

Some think transformation means a person reaches the point where all temptation disappears. While temptation may decrease over time as the overcomer builds new neural pathways, there is no guarantee that the overcomer will never be tempted again. The Bible doesn't promise that for any sin struggle. In fact, temptation can play a crucial role in the healing process, as discussed in chapter 9. The more healed we become, the less appealing our fleshly ways of coping become. There are some for whom temptation becomes a nonissue, while others may continue to experience temptation on occasion. In short, temptation may not disappear, but there's a difference between being *tempted to sin* and being *dominated by sin.*

Another downside associated with the transformation approach is that pro-gay advocates use relapse examples to argue that change never truly happens. While it's true that some do relapse, that's not because change is impossible, but because the process of transformation is messy, involving a person's free will and associated vulnerabilities. Overcomers may experience a measure of freedom and then relapse during times of stress. Some may not only relapse but give up entirely and return to their old ways.

Does that mean change is impossible? Imagine if we applied the same reasoning to the possibility of finding freedom from drugs, alcohol, gluttony, greed, or any other life-controlling behavior. Change is a process of growth that involves failures along the way to overcoming. "The godly may trip seven times, but they will get up again. But one disaster is enough to overthrow the wicked" (Proverbs 24:16, NLT). I stumbled many times in my own journey, but by God's grace I got up again each time, and I continue in progressive sanctification and ongoing transformation. Just because some give up doesn't mean change is impossible.

Still, pro-gay advocates work diligently to perpetuate the lie that transformation ministries fail more than they succeed. They often quote Alan Chambers, the former president of Exodus International, who said, "The majority of people that I have met—and I would say the majority, meaning 99.9% of them—have not experienced a change in their orientation."[209] Chambers had no empirical data to back up his statement. He simply made up the statistic, and yet pro-gay advocates repeat it so often that even well-meaning Christians think it's true. Few are aware that Chambers drove Exodus International into the ground by promoting a hyper-grace heresy that requires no repentance for sin nor expectation of a transformed life in Christ.[210]

The greatest liability of the transformation approach is that pro-gay advocates mischaracterize it as "conversion therapy," eliciting images of shock therapy, aversion techniques, and other forms of coercion. Unfortunately, some have used strange practices, including "holding therapy,"[211] promoting the use of straight porn,[212] or stripping naked with members of the same sex.[213] Aside from being outright wacky and immoral, none of those techniques work, as physical stimulation arouses the struggler sexually but does not address unmet emotional/relational needs in the soul. Sadly, strange practices like those gain media attention, leading the general public to believe that's what transformation proponents do.

Making matters worse, pro-gay advocates proliferate fabricated stories of "conversion therapy torture" to bolster public outrage. Most people accept such heart-wrenching stories at face value, but further investigation reveals the hoax behind it all.[214] The most notable liar is Sam Brinton, who testified of his own "conversion therapy" abuse before the United Nations Committee Against Torture, urging them to ban "conversion therapy" worldwide. Despite the publicity Brinton receives, he's such a prolific liar that even the most anti-ex-gay activist won't use his testimony to advance the cause because Brinton can't provide facts to verify his story.[215] In fact, there's an entire website (SamBrintonHoax.com) dedicated to exposing Brinton's deception. In 2022, Brinton made national headlines when he was fired from the US Department of Energy for stealing baggage claim luggage full of women's apparel.[216]

In response to pro-gay activists' outrage against so-called "conversion therapy," companies are now banning transformational resources. For example, Amazon has banned certain books that contend for transformation,[217] Facebook deleted the Restored Hope Network's ministry page,[218] and the Living Hope app was deleted from the Apple, Google, Microsoft, and Amazon platforms.[219] There is a concerted effort to cancel transformational resources, making them difficult to find in online searches.

Last, some Christians are skeptical of transformation due to negative experiences with flaky deliverance ministries. While there are often demonic influences involved, it's not as simple as casting out a demon of homosexuality. Demonic spirits gain influence through wounds in the soul, so if we don't deal with associated bitterness, unforgiveness, and lies embedded in the mind, the demonic influence will remain. In other words, you can't cast out disordered sexual desires. Those are merely fruit of deeper roots in the soul that God wants to resolve through redemptive relationships and inner healing.

**Proponents:** Transformation proponents include authors such as Joe Dallas (*Desires in Conflict*),[220] Andrew Comiskey (*Pursuing Sexual Wholeness*), Leanne Payne (*The Broken Image*), and Anne Paulk (*Restoring Sexual Identity*)[221]; Pure Passion Media,[222] which produces training videos, testimonies, and documentaries on transformation; and organizations such as ReStory Ministries,[223] Restored Hope Network,[224] Portland Fellowship,[225] and the Changed Movement.[226]

## Why Transformation?

Transformation encompasses positives from each stream: it holds uncompromisingly to a biblical sexual ethic, it affirms God's love for those who experience disordered sexual desires, and it offers compassion for overcomers while also encouraging them to repent from homoerotic behavior and renounce a gay identity. Additionally, it involves holistic, progressive sanctification, aligning with Romans 12:1–2, not being conformed to the pattern of this world (born-gay-can't-change) but rather being transformed by the renewing of the mind (dying to deceitful desires, forgiving those who have hurt us, resolving childhood trauma, etc.) so that we will be able to test and approve what God's will is (conformed to the image of Christ and restored to God's original design for our sexuality).

Not surprisingly, the transformation stream has come under the most scrutiny, while the accommodation stream is gaining in popularity. As a result, droves of young believers have become defiled against the message of transformation. When I first heard testimonies of transformation, it resonated with my spirit that freedom is possible, and I thought to myself, "How did you get there, and what can I learn from your experience?" Today's LGBTQ-affirming culture elicits the opposite response: "Change is impossible, and anyone who says they've experienced change is lying." Starting from that position of unbelief makes transformation unlikely.

## Streams Can Merge

I mentioned that I call the five perspectives "streams" because, just as in nature, one stream can run into another. Some people move through a progression in the streams as they grow in Christ: starting in affirmation, moving to accommodation, then to mortification, and on to transformation. In my own experience, I started in the mortification stream, as I was adamantly opposed to Holy Spirit baptism and anything associated with spiritual gifts. After I got baptized in the Holy Spirit, I became open to further transformation through inner healing.

My purpose in outlining the five streams and sharing my Pentecostal experience is not to cause division but to explain why believers approach LGBTQ from different perspectives. Despite our differences in approach, the streams that hold to a biblical sexual ethic will likely need to pull together in the days to come to oppose "conversion therapy" bans that seek to silence believers who contend for God's design for sexuality.[227]

The following chart summarizes the five streams.

# The 5 Streams: Differing Responses to LGBTQ

| Stream | Condemnation | Affirmation | Accommodation | Mortification | Transformation |
|---|---|---|---|---|---|
| **Approach to Same-Sex Attraction (SSA)** | God condemns all gay people as beyond redemption | God affirms gay partnerships/ marriage | Accommodates a "celibate gay Christian" identity as a unique cross to bear | Mortify (kill) sin by renouncing gay identity and repenting of homoerotic behavior | Mortification + address wounds in the soul that may contribute to sexual brokenness |
| **Original Side** | (N/A) | Side A | Side B | Side Y | Side X |
| **Theological Premise** | God hates sinners (Ps. 11:5); gay people deserve the death penalty (misapply Lev. 18:22, 20:13; Prov. 6:16-19) | Revisionist pro-gay theology justifies homoerotic behavior; a good tree cannot bear bad fruit (Mt. 7:18) | Follows a biblical sexual ethic, but desires & identity do not change; fallen desires determine identity | Follows a biblical sexual ethic; God gives us power to mortify sinful impulses (Rom. 8:13; Col. 3:5) | Follows a biblical sexual ethic; God heals and transforms spirit, soul, and body (1 Thess. 5:23; 1 Cor. 6:9-11; Rom. 12:1-2; Eph. 4:22-24) |
| **Origin of SSA (spirit, soul, body)** | Spirit:<br>People choose to be gay out of sheer spiritual rebellion against God | Body:<br>God created people gay (so the Scriptures need to be updated) | Body:<br>SSA is inborn & immutable because of the Fall (similar to an inborn physical disability) | Spirit:<br>Primarily a sin nature issue; result of the Fall | Spirit, Soul, & Body:<br>Both a sin nature (spirit) and developmental issue (soul) that can affect sexual desires (body) |
| **Pastoral Care** | No redemption possible for people God hates | No need to repent for inborn, God-given sexual orientation; malign transformation as "conversion therapy" | SSA reframed as a gift from God; promote "spiritual friendships" to ease loneliness; malign transformation as "conversion therapy" | Emphasize repentance & spiritual disciplines; some malign transformation as "conversion therapy" and/or "secular psychology" | Healing and restoration through the body of Christ, counseling/talk therapy, and inner healing prayer; open to gifts of the Spirit |
| **Outcome for the overcomer** | Guilt, shame, condemnation, and alienation from God | Those who persist in unrepentant homoerotic behavior will not inherit the Kingdom of God (1 Cor. 6:9-11) | Fixating on fallen desires, instead of putting off the old self (Eph. 4:22), results in continued enslavement to sin (Rom. 6:14) | Ongoing battle to kill sinful impulses while discounting wounds in the soul that may contribute to gender insecurity and desires to bond with the same sex | Progressive sanctification that remains open to the Holy Spirit healing wounds in the soul that may contribute to gender insecurity and desires to bond with the same sex |
| **Proponents** | **WESTBORO BAPTIST CHURCH**<br><br>**Pastor Steven Anderson -** Faithful Word Baptist, AZ<br>**Pastor Patrick Boyle –** Revival Baptist Church, FL<br>**Pastor Roger Jimenez -** Verity Baptist Church, CA<br>**Pastor Kevin Swanson -** Reformation Church, CO | **REFORMATION PROJECT**<br>**Q CHRISTIAN FELLOWSHIP**<br><br>**James Brownson**<br>*Bible, Gender, Sexuality*<br>**David Gushee**<br>*Changing Our Mind*<br>**Justin Lee**<br>*Torn*<br>**Matthew Vines**<br>*God and the Gay Christian* | **REVOICE.ORG**<br>**POSTURE SHIFT**<br><br>**Greg Coles**<br>*Single Gay and Christian*<br>**Nate Collins**<br>*All But Invisible*<br>**Wesley Hill**<br>*Washed and Waiting*<br>**Preston Sprinkle**<br>*Embodied; People to Be Loved*<br>**Mark Yarhouse**<br>*Costly Obedience* | **THE GOSPEL COALITION**<br><br>**Sam Allberry**<br>*Is God Anti-Gay?*<br>**Rosaria Butterfield**<br>*The Secret Thoughts of an Unlikely Convert*<br>**Becket Cook**<br>*A Change of Affections*<br>**Jackie Hill Perry**<br>*Gay Girl, Good God*<br>**Christopher Yuan**<br>*Holy Sexuality* | **RESTORY MINISTRIES**<br>**RESTORED HOPE NETWORK**<br>**HELP4FAMILIES.ORG**<br>**PORTLANDFELLOWSHIP.COM**<br>**MASTERINGLIFE.ORG**<br>**CHANGED MOVEMENT**<br><br>**Anne Paulk**<br>*Restoring Sexual Identity*<br>**Joe Dallas**<br>*Desires in Conflict*<br>**Linda Seiler**<br>*Trans-Formation* |

## DISCUSSION QUESTIONS

1. Which of the five streams resonates with you the most and why?
2. What value do you see in identifying different streams of Christian thought?
3. Have you read any of the authors listed in the five-streams chart at the end of the chapter? If so, what did you glean from their book that aligns with their stream? Did you notice anything that does not align with the stream in which the book is listed? (Remember, some streams overlap.)
4. Which stream do you think gives the overcomer the most hope? Why?

13

# SPIRITUAL WARFARE: WHAT'S FUELING THE CULTURAL SHIFT?

Just ten short years ago, only a minority of states supported same-sex marriage,[228] and no one had ever heard of Caitlyn Jenner—much less knew what a "preferred pronoun" was. Now the Olympics allows biological men to compete against women,[229] libraries promote "Drag Queen Story Hour,"[230] the American Medical Association wants to eliminate sex designations on birth certificates,[231] Hershey's International Women's Day ad campaign features a biological male identifying as a woman,[232] women are referred to as "people who menstruate"[233] and birthing persons,[234] breastfeeding is also called chestfeeding,[235] and anyone who speaks out against the madness is threatened with cancellation.[236] What we are witnessing is the effect of demonic strongholds gaining increasing momentum. In this chapter, I will explain the nature of demonic strongholds, offer examples of strongholds at work, and suggest how we should respond as believers.

## The Nature of Demonic Strongholds

"The Spirit clearly says that in later times some will abandon the faith and follow deceiving spirits and things taught by demons" (1 Timothy 4:1). The lunacy of what we're seeing today is not of human origin; it is fueled by "deceiving spirits and things taught by demons." And the greater the number of people who believe the lies, the greater the demonic influence grows.

Some thought the legalization of same-sex marriage would end the cultural controversy over LGBTQ rights. Yet on the heels of the Supreme Court marriage ruling came the push to normalize transgender rights, first among adults and now among children. The absurdity of it all grows with each passing day. It may appear to some to be about civil rights for LGBTQ-identified people, but the ultimate motive of the evil one behind it all is to destroy the very concept of male and female altogether. That's why "nonbinary" and "gender-fluid" identities are among the most popular today, blurring the lines of God's sacred design for our sexuality. We are battling demonic strongholds that we can only overcome with spiritual weapons.

> For though we live in the world, we do not wage war as the world does. The weapons we fight with are not the weapons of the world. On the contrary, they have divine power to demolish strongholds. We demolish arguments and every pretension that sets itself up against the knowledge of God, and we take captive every thought to make it obedient to Christ. (2 Corinthians 10:3–5)

Scripture defines strongholds as "arguments and every pretension [unjustified claim] that sets itself up against the knowledge of God." In short, whatever God is *for*, a stronghold will automatically be *against*. And it need not be logical. In fact, a stronghold cannot be logical, because no one can oppose the God of truth and operate in logic. That's why, in response to cultural conundrums like biological males competing against female athletes, Christians look at each other in disbelief, saying, "Doesn't anyone see how *illogical* this is?"

No, they don't. Why? Because "the god of this age has blinded the minds of unbelievers, so that they cannot see the light of the gospel that displays the glory of Christ, who is the image of God" (2 Corinthians 4:4). Those who oppose God have been blinded by the enemy's deception so that they can't discern the truth. Instead of operating out of reason, they argue out of carnal emotion, unaware of how illogical their beliefs are. That's why it is called "deception." When someone is deceived, they don't know it.

We need to remember that principalities and demons are the real enemy—not human beings, political figures, the LGBTQ community, or the media. "For our struggle is not against flesh and blood, but against the rulers, against the authorities, against the powers of this dark world and against the spiritual forces of evil in the heavenly realms" (Ephesians 6:12). Therefore, the only way we can win the spiritual battle is by using spiritual weapons. We can't use human logic to reason a deceived person out of a demonic stronghold. Strongholds don't respond to logic; they respond to spiritual weapons—namely, the Word of God and prayer.

### How Strongholds Work

Strongholds begin by subtly influencing people's mindsets to accept the enemy's lie. As more people begin to believe the lie, the stronghold gains momentum. That's what we've seen happen over the past three decades with the normalization—and now glorification—of all things LGBTQ. None of it is based on logic or science; it's based on a subtle lie of the enemy that gains greater and greater influence as more people believe the lie and succumb to deception.

If we don't recognize the spiritual forces behind the normalization of LGBTQ, we can unwittingly energize the very stronghold we say we oppose. For example, we are now encouraged to list our "preferred pronouns" (i.e., he/him/his; she/her/hers; or as some individuals in the LGBTQ community prefer: they/them/theirs), reinforcing the idea that people can choose whatever sex they want to be, despite our Creator's design. Some well-meaning Christians comply, thinking they are expressing love toward the LGBTQ community. However, when we bow the knee to the normalization of LGBTQ, we give the stronghold greater power. Yes, we want to be compassionate and love LGBTQ-identified people as fellow human beings made in the image of God. But what we *don't* want to do is elevate the second-greatest commandment (to love our neighbor) above the first and greatest commandment to love God with all our heart, soul, mind, and strength (Matthew 22:37–39). We cannot please people and serve God at the same time. As Paul stated so simply,

> Am I now trying to win the approval of human beings, or of God? Or am I trying to please people? If I were still trying to please people, I would not be a servant of Christ. (Galatians 1:10)

## The Stronghold of Tolerance

One of the demonic strongholds that paved the way for the normalization of LGBTQ is the stronghold of "tolerance,"[237] leading to today's concepts of diversity, equity, and inclusion (commonly referred to as DEI). In his book *The Intolerance of Tolerance*, theologian D. A. Carson explains how the definition of "tolerance" has shifted in Western culture. Years ago, we believed in absolute truth and embraced the idea that it is our duty to pursue truth. We tried to persuade others with reason instead of coercion. In that context, the free exchange of competing ideas caused truth to rise to the forefront. Opposing ideas were a means of discovering truth. We embraced the sentiment behind Voltaire's adage: "I disapprove of what you say, but I will defend to the death your right to say it."[238]

But the understanding of tolerance has changed to mean something wholly different today. Under the new definition of "tolerance"—which is the hallmark of political correctness—truth is relative rather than absolute.[239] If there is no absolute truth, then everyone's subjective truth must be considered of equal value: "What is true for you may not be true for me." If all ideas are equal, then you cannot direct disagreement toward an idea, as if one idea were superior to another. The only remaining option is to attack the person who holds the idea.[240] That's how we arrived at the point where disagreement is interpreted as hatred: "If you disagree with me, you hate me."

For example, if you state publicly that you believe same-sex marriage is immoral, you're accused of being a homophobe. Never mind that the use of the term *homophobe* is inherently illogical, as technically it implies someone has a phobia (or irrational fear) of gay-identified people—which is wholly different from disagreeing with a moral position. You can disagree with someone's moral choices and still love them as a person. No irrational fear or hatred is involved.

The subtle scheme of the enemy is to move the argument out of the realm of morality and into the realm of civil rights. If homosexuality is a moral issue, you can objectively oppose same-sex marriage based on your deeply held religious convictions. However, as soon as homosexuality is framed as a civil rights issue, anyone who opposes same-sex marriage becomes the equivalent of the Ku Klux Klan. Disagreement is now interpreted as denigration. Truth and love are pitted against one another as mutually exclusive. That, of course, contradicts the Word of God, which instructs us to speak the truth in love (Ephesians 4:15).

At its core, the stronghold of tolerance is an outright attack against the supremacy of God and His Word, raising the age-old question: "Did God really say . . . ?" Once the Word of God is discredited, our ideas become superior to God's ideas, elevating humans above God. The priority becomes pleasing people so as not to offend them, rather than loving God and honoring His Word so that we may love others with His love.

## The Stronghold of Intimidation

Closely linked to the stronghold of tolerance is the stronghold of intimidation. The stronghold of tolerance intolerantly demands us to normalize all things LGBTQ, lest we be labeled a hater. The stronghold of intimidation pressures us not only to affirm all things LGBTQ but to participate in the celebration—or be canceled. This is what fuels cancel culture: Anyone who attempts to expose the irrationality behind a demonic stronghold must be silenced. For those who cannot discern the truth—much less refute the rational logic behind the truth—vilifying and silencing the opposition is the only option.

The imposition of the banning of so-called "conversion therapy" is a prime example of the stronghold of intimidation in operation. LGBTQ activists coined the term *conversion therapy* as a scare tactic, implying that people like me use religious dogma and aversive techniques to change someone's presumably inborn, immutable sexual orientation.[241] The term *conversion therapy* itself is an oxymoron. *Conversion* is a religious term for the experience which, in the context of Christianity, happens the instant one places faith in Christ. *Therapy* is a medical term which implies a process that occurs over time. Therefore, banning conversion therapy equates to banning an "instant process." LGBTQ activists coined the term to silence both religious practitioners and licensed therapists who pose a threat to exposing their deception.

As noted in chapter 8, more than twenty states have passed laws banning licensed therapists from practicing conversion therapy on minors.[242] The ultimate goal of pro-gay activists is to ban conversion therapy in all states for all ages, effectively silencing anyone who wants to help those with unwanted same-sex attractions and gender dysphoria. Never mind that there's no scientific evidence that such desires are inborn or immutable, nor can activists name a single therapist today who practices electroshock therapy to treat homosexuality. But then again, strongholds aren't logical. The opposition demands that those who don't conform to the LGBTQ narrative must be silenced—period.

## The Stronghold of Pride

It's no mistake that the LGBTQ movement embraces "pride" as its main descriptor. Pride is the root of sin, exalting oneself over God. That's why God opposes the proud (James 4:6). And that's precisely why the evil one uses "gay pride" and the rainbow, God's covenant symbol never to flood the earth again, as an "in your face" attitude toward God.

Consider the pervasiveness of the stronghold behind gay pride. No other sin in our culture has an entire month dedicated to its celebration, featuring community parades and enticing corporations to go the extra mile to promote LGBTQ as a virtue signal. Imagine if we did the same thing to celebrate drug addiction, adultery, incest, or pedophilia. We've grown so numb to LGBTQ that we're not even shocked by our culture's admiration of what the Bible calls an abomination.

## How Should Believers Respond?

As we see our culture shifting, we need to focus our efforts on the real enemy and defeating his demonic schemes. We demolish strongholds by taking every thought captive (2 Corinthians 10:5) and replacing lies with truth. The more we give in to lies, the more we energize the demonic stronghold in operation. That's why it's so important to renew our mind daily with the Word and to speak out when others try to coerce us into agreeing with a known lie.

Before we speak out, however, we must realize that we can't argue someone out of a stronghold. Remember, strongholds don't respond to human logic, nor do they respond to carnal efforts to persuade others. Everything we say and do must first be backed by prayer, the Word, and spiritual discernment. As Oswald Chambers said, "Prayer does not equip us for greater works—prayer is the greater work."[243]

Before we rise up in word and deed, we must be on our knees, aligning with God's spiritual power that enables us to defeat a spiritual enemy. The enemy knows how to outwit you and me. But if we seek the Lord, He will grant us wisdom to confound the wise, and we can defeat the spiritual enemy. The evil one is gaining ground quickly because Christians continually cave to intimidation rather than seeking God for divine wisdom and Holy-Spirit boldness. May we be like Paul, who operated in the Spirit's power: "My message and my preaching were not with wise and persuasive words, but with a demonstration of the Spirit's power, so that your faith might not rest on human wisdom, but on God's power" (1 Corinthians 2:4–5).

Before we speak out publicly or have a conversation with someone who disagrees with our biblical worldview on sexuality, we must pray first for their hearts to be receptive to the truth. Ask God to soften their heart and remove the blinders of the enemy so they can discern truth. Pray for the Holy Spirit to bring deep conviction. Ask the Lord for words of wisdom to expose lies and for grace to respond in the opposite spirit. When others come at us with vitriol, it's easy to respond in kind with anger. But a gentle answer turns away wrath (Proverbs 15:1), and humility disarms the stronghold of pride (James 4:6). God will give us wisdom from heaven (James 3:17) when we first pray through the conversation in the secret place.

Finally, remember that no matter how compassionately we come across, we may still be hated. Even Jesus, the most compassionate, loving person in the universe, was hated. Jesus

Himself said, "If the world hates you, keep in mind that it hated me first. . . . 'They hated me without reason'" (John 15:18, 25). It made no sense for the world to hate the very One who came to save them, but that is the illogical nature of a stronghold. Like our Savior, we must be willing to endure irrational hatred, forgiving those who persecute us and asking the Lord to open their eyes to the truth in the same way that He opened our eyes. To those with believing hearts, our message will be the fragrant aroma of Christ. But to those who are entrenched in unbelief, we will be the stench of death (2 Corinthians 2:15–16).

May we be like the disciples in the book of Acts who responded to irrational hatred and cancellation by seeking God for spiritual strength and boldness. Instead of complaining about persecution or looking for ways to blend in with their culture, the disciples lifted their voices in prayer, asking God to

> Consider their threats and enable your servants to speak your word with great boldness. Stretch out your hand to heal and perform signs and wonders through the name of your holy servant Jesus. (Acts 4:29–30)

May we respond in like kind:

> Lord, consider the enemy's threat of cancellation and empower us to speak Your truth with even greater boldness, with even greater love—and use us as agents of healing!

I believe the body of Christ is at a crucial turning point, and if we begin to respond in prayer both individually and corporately, we will operate in Holy–Spirit discernment and boldness that will overturn the powers of darkness and usher in the greatest awakening we have ever seen. The darker our culture gets, the brighter the gospel will shine in contrast!

## DISCUSSION QUESTIONS

1. A stronghold, by definition, *cannot* be logical, because you cannot oppose the God of truth and operate in logic. What evidence do you see of illogical arguments against God's design for sexuality?
2. What evidence do you see of the spirit of tolerance infiltrating the body of Christ?
3. How have you experienced the spirit of intimidation regarding the topic of LGBTQ?
4. If it isn't possible to argue someone out of a spiritual stronghold, how should a believer respond when interacting with someone who has come under the influence of a spiritual stronghold?
5. Think of someone in your sphere of influence who is under the influence of a spiritual stronghold. Take some time to pray for that person, applying the concepts at the end of this chapter.

14

# HOW TO ENGAGE LGBTQ-IDENTIFIED FRIENDS AND LOVED ONES

Ministering to those with *unwanted* same-sex attractions and gender dysphoria is one thing. But it's an entirely different conversation when it comes to friends and loved ones who willfully embrace an LGBTQ identity. Christians are widely considered *homophobes* and *transphobes* based on the mistaken notion that "if you disagree with me, you hate me" (addressed in chapter 13).

Nothing could be further from the truth. Loving someone doesn't mean you agree with everything they think, say, and do. Imagine if we applied that standard to God. It would be impossible for Him to love us because many things we think, say, and do are far from agreement with His standards. To love someone means to value them as a person, whether we agree with them on everything or not. We love others in their brokenness, the same way God loves us in our brokenness.

What follows are six practical tips to engage with LGBTQ-identified friends and loved ones. I'm choosing my terms carefully. I'm using the word "engage" because our approach needs to be interactive—engaging our friends and loved ones in life-giving, *two-way* dialogue—not dogmatically preaching *at* them. I also use the descriptor "LGBTQ-identified" to accurately reflect reality. Scripturally and scientifically speaking, there's no such thing as a "gay person" or "trans person," as if those labels represent inborn characteristics that cannot change. People adopt an LGBTQ identity because they've been deceived into thinking that their disordered sexual desires or gender insecurity dictate their identity and determine their destiny. It may sound like I'm splitting hairs, but it's important to reinforce biblical truth and see our friends and loved ones from God's perspective. That helps us to pray with expectation and not succumb to the hopeless, inaccurate belief of born-that-way-can't-change.

This chapter merely scratches the surface. For an entire book on the subject, consider reading Joe Dallas's *Speaking of Homosexuality: Discussing the Issues with Kindness and Clarity*. If you're a parent seeking guidance on how to talk to your child who embraces an LGBTQ identity, I highly recommend Joe Dallas's *When Homosexuality Hits Home: What to Do When a Loved One Says, "I'm Gay."* If you have a prodigal child, consider finding a support group with other parents who have faced the same trial. The Restored Hope Network can connect you with online parent groups.

## Six Tips to Engage with LGBTQ-identified Friends and Loved Ones

### 1. Focus on connecting them to Christ, not on changing their views about sexuality.

The greatest problem for our LGBTQ-identified friends and loved ones is not their broken sexuality; it's the fact that they're disconnected from their Savior. Make Jesus and the gospel the focus—not getting your loved ones to change their views on sexuality. If you persuade them to adopt a biblical position on sexuality, but they never come to know Jesus, it profits nothing. When they come to know Jesus, the Holy Spirit will begin to deal with their beliefs. Until then, keep the main issue the main issue: where are they with Jesus?

(Note: My emphasis in this chapter is the unsaved individual. I'm not talking about those who call themselves Christians but hold to a revisionist interpretation of the Bible that justifies homoerotic behavior. In that case, the main issue is the truth of God's Word, and it would be entirely appropriate to engage the revisionist arguments addressed in chapter 4.)

People often ask me how to witness to an LGBTQ-identified person. I tell them, "The same way you witness to anyone else." I don't try to get the alcoholic to stop drinking so he can receive Jesus. I get him connected to Jesus, and when the Holy Spirit comes to live inside him, He will deal with his drinking problem. I don't try to get the promiscuous girl to stop sleeping with any guy who says he loves her. I get her connected to Jesus, and when the Holy Spirit comes to live inside of her, He will deal with her sexual promiscuity. The same holds true for a selfish person, an arrogant person, or one who adopts an LGBTQ identity and sins sexually. Jesus doesn't require anyone to clean up their act before they get saved. Once they get saved, He will deal with their sexuality in the context of relationship with Him.

That said, a common obstacle for LGBTQ-identified people is a skewed view of God based on past hurts. Some were rejected by church leaders when they confessed their struggles openly. Some were rejected by Christian family members. Others have become disillusioned with God because they prayed for years for God to remove their feelings, but nothing changed. That's how some came to identify as "gay Christians" and now believe that God condones gay partnerships. One of the greatest things you can pray for your LGBTQ-identified friend or loved one is for them to encounter the heart of God and see Him as He really is. Pray that they will have a prodigal son "aha" moment where they realize they are eating the slop of pigs (i.e., acting on their disordered desires doesn't satisfy the deep hunger in their soul) and that they are persuaded to come home to their loving heavenly Father.

Be patient and remember that the LGBTQ-identified person often has much to lose when it comes to following Christ, especially if their only support network is the LGBTQ community. If they don't have solid relationships in the body of Christ, it can be difficult to sever ties with the only community that has affirmed them. Following Jesus might involve losing their LGBTQ friends and their social life—not to mention giving up the core identity that has shaped their life in recent years. Laying all those things down to entrust themselves to the body of Christ can be scary, especially if their only concept of Christians is the Westboro Baptist Church caricature that labels them as perverts, reprobates, and an abomination. Put yourself in your friend's or loved one's shoes and imagine what it would be like to potentially lose everything that's familiar to you and risk entering a new community.

If your friend or loved one is in a romantic relationship, the thought of breaking off ties can be especially daunting. If they "married" their partner, they will eventually have to face the consequence of getting a legal divorce when they follow through in surrendering all to Jesus. (By the way, I wouldn't make severing relationships a prerequisite to receiving Jesus as Savior. Lead them to the Lord, and the Holy Spirit will begin dealing with everything connected to their old life.)

Give your friend or loved one space to count the cost. Don't compromise the truth of the gospel and what it means to submit to Jesus as Lord. Be sure you communicate the truth in such a way that your friend or loved one knows you love them whether or not they choose to receive the truth. They are not the enemy. Christ died for them and loves them infinitely more than you or I ever could.

Most of all, love well and don't be in a rush. Ask God to use your relationship with them to reveal His heart. Remember, we get hurt in relationship, and we get healed in relationship. It can take a long time for someone with past hurts to open up and trust people, let alone trust God. Sometimes people need to experience the gospel in the context of community before they are willing to surrender their lives—much less their sexuality—to Christ.

**2. Build relationship and ask lots of questions.**

Invest in LGBTQ-identified friends and loved ones just as you would anyone else who doesn't know Jesus. Ask them questions about their life to get to know them better: "What was your family like growing up? Did you go to church?" I love asking questions like that and seeing where the conversation goes. If they grew up going to church, I'll ask if they still go now and why or why not. That can lead to some interesting conversations about past church hurt and where they are now with God.

Another great conversation starter is, "Tell me your story." Take a genuine interest in hearing how they arrived at embracing an LGBTQ identity. Ask them what they were feeling along the way. Listen to their heart, empathize with their struggles, and love them the same way Jesus has loved you and me in our brokenness. If they are in a same-sex relationship, ask them how they met their partner. Consider inviting them both over for dinner. You're not condoning someone's sin by taking a genuine interest in them. Even Jesus ate with sinners and tax collectors (Matthew 9:10–12).

Some Christians are concerned as to whether their interactions with LGBTQ-identified friends and loved ones are compromising the gospel. As a litmus test, it helps to remove the stigmatizing label of LGBTQ and insert a different scenario. For example, if you live next door to a male/female couple who live together without being married, would you be condoning their immorality by inviting them over for dinner? Does inviting your Muslim neighbor into your home condone Islam? What about hosting an atheist in your home? Loving others doesn't mean we agree with everything they believe. We simply love them where they are the same way God loves us.

### 3. Avoid gay-bashing jokes and trite phrases.

A college student who struggled with same-sex attractions told me about the time he was going to share his struggles with his Bible study and ask for prayer. Before the study began, his friends started making gay-bashing jokes. Shocked by their jesting, the student decided to keep to himself and continued to struggle in silence, unbeknownst to his friends.

There's no context where gay/trans-bashing jokes are ever appropriate. Jesus died for us all, and our conversations ought to reflect His heart to see everyone reconciled to Him. Some may think it's funny to say, "it was Adam and Eve, not Adam and Steve," but it's not. You never know who's in the room and how your insensitivity may affect them.

We must be mindful about our language and consider what it communicates to others. Christians sometimes say, "love the sinner, hate the sin." The phrase may be well-intended, but we need to realize the person who identifies as LGBTQ may interpret that phrase as, "you hate me," because they see no distinction between their sexual desires and their identity; they consider them one and the same.

Likewise, the term "gay lifestyle" can come across as pejorative and misinformed. What is the gay lifestyle? There are gay-identified people who march in parades and live wildly promiscuous lives, but there are also gay-identified people who live quiet lives as lonely singles. There is no uniform experience for those who identify as LGBTQ.

When I was growing up, I used to hear Christians say, "If you're gay, it's your choice." But I didn't choose to have those feelings. I could choose whether or not I acted on them, but the very experience of those feelings was not something I could control. Hopefully, after reading this book, you have a better understanding as to why that phrase is misinformed and hurtful to those who experience disordered sexual desires.

### 4. When appropriate, apologize for the way Jesus has been misrepresented.

Unfortunately, some people have been deeply wounded by fringe groups like Westboro Baptist Church and Christians who condemn those who embrace an LGBTQ identity. Most Christians I know are doing their best to love LGBTQ-identified people well, so don't concede to the erroneous stereotype that all Christians are haters. There are Christians out there who respond with compassion and represent Jesus well.

But some Christians have failed in that regard, and we need to recognize the hurt they have caused. If, in the course of conversation, I discover that my friend or loved one has been hurt by those who misrepresented Jesus, I listen intently and empathize with them as they express the pain they've experienced. I apologize for how Jesus has been grossly misrepresented to them, and I let them know I am not coming in that spirit. I respond to their pain with the compassion of Christ. At the same time, I don't apologize for the gospel or for God's design for sexuality. I can't apologize for the truth—only for the way my friend or loved one may have been treated in a hurtful manner by those who misrepresented the heart of Christ.

### 5. When disagreement arises, talk about ideas, and avoid personal attack.

Over the course of time, LGBTQ matters may arise in conversation. You may feel pressure to agree with your friend or loved one since they likely operate in today's mindset of, "if you disagree with me, you hate me." It takes skill not to fall into that trap and to keep the conversation in the realm of ideas to avoid personal attack.

One option to avoid personal attack is to move the conversation away from the heated topic of LGBTQ and use a less-triggering comparison. For example, I was once asked to speak to an auditorium full of people who were likely to oppose my perspective, so I asked the Holy Spirit what I should do to first disarm the opposition in the room and gain a hearing. I sensed the Lord directing me to start with cupcakes. (Random, I know.)

To ease the tension, I introduced myself as a lover of chocolate and asked if there were any fellow chocolate lovers present. Then I asked, if we were to have chocolate or vanilla cupcakes for lunch, who would choose vanilla over chocolate every time. Several hands went up, but not as many as for chocolate (because we all know chocolate is superior to vanilla). I then asked one of the vanilla lovers whether we could be friends, even though they always choose vanilla, and I always choose chocolate. Is it possible to agree to disagree agreeably about our flavor choices?

Of course, it is. Disagreement is not denigration.

In fact, if I force you to agree with me, I am no longer operating in love (where you retain your free will) but rather coercion (forcing your will to conform to mine). By definition, I cannot truly "tolerate" someone or appreciate "diversity" and "inclusion" *unless* I disagree with them in some way yet still choose to love and respect them as a fellow human being made in the image of God.

What makes the cupcake illustration effective is keeping the argument in the realm of ideas. I may disagree with *your idea* that vanilla is superior to chocolate, but I still love you *as a person*. Likewise, I may disagree with your *ideas* on sexual morality, but I can still love you *as a person*.

Another way to keep the conversation in the realm of ideas and avoid personal attack is to use the "affirmation sandwich" approach:

- Bottom piece of bread: "I love you; you're my friend."
- Meat: "I disagree with *the idea* of (fill in the blank—same-sex marriage, transgender surgeries for children, biological men competing against females, etc.)." Keep the conversation focused on *ideas*, and avoid using the word *you* (i.e., "I disagree with you"), which comes across as a personal attack when discussing ideas.
- Top piece of bread: "I still love you, and you're my friend, even if we disagree about an *idea*."

If you keep the conversation grounded in the realm of *ideas*, while still affirming your love for the *person*, it diminishes the potential to interpret your disagreement as a personal attack.

### 6. Don't force change on those who don't want it.

There will always be people who choose to embrace an LGBTQ identity and don't want to hear the message of transformation. Respond to them in the same way Jesus responded to us before we knew Him. He didn't force himself on us or coerce us to change our mind. He worked gently, softening our heart, and winning us to the truth. We must learn to do the same. Pray for your LGBTQ-identified friends and loved ones, asking the Holy Spirit to open their eyes to God's truth and bring healing to their wounded hearts. Ask the Lord to grant you His compassion to see them through His eyes so they know you love them for who they are, whether or not they ever change. Just as you cannot force someone to want to surrender to Jesus, you cannot force your LGBTQ-identified loved one to want transformation for themselves.

This can be especially difficult for parents, as they want what is best for their child. But if parents try to force their will on a child, it can backfire and make their child more resistant to the truth. The battle must be won in prayer, for only the Holy Spirit can change a child's heart.

## Closing Thoughts

Keep in mind that no matter how loving and compassionate you are, your LGBTQ-identified friends and loved ones may still reject you. It helps to remember that we are not battling flesh and blood and that those who have come under the deceitful influence of a demonic stronghold will naturally oppose those who represent God. Don't take it personally.

Not everyone whom Jesus invited chose to follow Him. Even His own brothers didn't believe in Him during His time on earth (John 7:5). If Jesus lost followers and family members, you will, too. Don't believe the lie that success in the kingdom means everyone will like you. The cost of following Jesus means that even members of our own household may be among our enemies (Matthew 10:36). Follow Jesus's example. Pray earnestly, love well, speak the truth with compassion, and trust God with the results. Sometimes our LGBTQ-identified friends and loved ones need to go through a period of total rebellion before they realize nothing compares to the Father's love.

### Tips for Engaging with LGBTQ-Identified Friends and Loved Ones

1. Focus on connecting them to Christ, not on changing their views about sexuality.
2. Build relationship and ask lots of questions.
3. Avoid gay-bashing jokes and trite phrases.
4. When appropriate, apologize for the way Jesus has been misrepresented.
5. When disagreement arises, talk about ideas, and avoid personal attack.
6. Don't force change on those who don't want it.

## DISCUSSION QUESTIONS

1. When engaging with unsaved LGBTQ-identified friends and loved ones, why is it important to focus on Jesus and the gospel instead of sexuality?
2. What are some questions you can ask to get to know your LGBTQ-identified friend or loved one better?
3. In what ways have you seen Jesus misrepresented to the LGBTQ community?
4. Why is it important to not force change on those who don't want it?
5. Take some time and pray together for your LGBTQ-identified friends/loved ones.

15

# CULTURAL CONUNDRUMS: CHURCH INVOLVEMENT, WEDDINGS, AND PRONOUNS

We're facing cultural conundrums today that we could never have imagined even just a decade ago. This book does not afford space to address every possible scenario, so I will narrow the focus of this chapter to three common concerns: church involvement, whether to attend a gay wedding, and what pronoun to use with those who identify as transgender.

## Church Involvement

Hopefully your church is engaging with the lost on a regular basis, which means you may have unsaved visitors who identify as LGBTQ. Rather than creating a separate category for LGBTQ, apply the same principles for involvement and leadership that you would to any other area of sexuality. Can fornicators or adulterers serve in church leadership? No. Scripture is very clear that those in church leadership are to live above reproach and yield their sexuality to God's design (1 Timothy 3:1–13). That principle applies across the board to any form of sexual sin outside of a one-man-one-woman covenant marriage. Gay "marriage," though recognized as a legal marriage in the U.S. and other countries, is not a marriage according to Scripture. You are not treating homosexuality as a different category of sin; you are being consistent with the Word regarding any sexual activity outside of marriage.

Apply a similar litmus test for volunteer positions. If a boyfriend and girlfriend are sleeping together before marriage, can they serve in a volunteer role? Use the same standard for same-sex couples who ask to serve as volunteers. Similarly, if someone is struggling to overcome a pornography addiction and is genuinely repentant and open to accountability, can they serve as a volunteer? Apply the same principle to a believer who struggles with same-sex attractions or transgender desires and is genuinely repentant and open to accountability. (Note: I'm not talking here about those who call themselves Christians yet adopt a gay or transgender identity or who use revisionist arguments to justify LGBTQ ideology. That's an entirely different matter, as noted in the previous chapter.)

Two things to consider regarding volunteer roles are the individual's level of surrender and the type of volunteer role in consideration. Is the individual fully surrendered to Christ, genuinely repentant, and open to accountability, or are they insisting they can continue in sin and follow Christ at the same time? The type of volunteer role matters as well. There's a difference between cleaning the church, working a food pantry, or directing traffic in the parking lot and serving on the worship team, teaching Sunday school, or mentoring teens in the youth group. Each overcomer is at a different place in their healing journey. Seek the Lord for guidance as to whether the overcomer is ready for a role that makes them a visible representation of the church or places them in a position of a spiritual overseer.

During my own journey of transformation, I volunteered in the church and eventually served in leadership. I was not acting on my temptations, nor was I looking for a loophole to justify sin. I was yielded to the Lord, honest with my pastors about my struggles, and I welcomed high accountability. Experiencing temptation doesn't exclude someone from serving. At the same time, my pastors operated in wisdom and didn't put me in a compromising position, such as discipling another gal who struggled with her sexuality. It's important that the overcomer be open and honest with church leadership. That enables the leaders to discern how the overcomer can best serve the body of Christ during their journey of transformation.

## Should a Christian Attend a Gay Wedding?

When I first considered this question years ago, I was in favor of attending a gay wedding as a means of building a bridge for the gospel with my unsaved friend or loved one. I figured sinners are going to sin, and I shouldn't expect them to hold to a Christian sexual ethic if they don't follow Jesus. So, if they want to "marry," I ought to support them by celebrating what's important to them and being present on their special day. After all, who are they hurting?

My perspective radically changed after I read an article by theologian Robert Gagnon entitled "Should You Attend a 'Gay Wedding' if Invited?"[244] Gagnon cites 1 Corinthians 8 and 10 where Paul referred to "strong" believers who wanted to visit temples and eat food sacrificed to idols. They knew the idols had no power, so what harm could it do? Paul forbade them from doing so on two counts: first, their actions could influence a "weaker" believer to incorporate idol worship into their life, as the "stronger" believers sent the message that idol worship wasn't a big deal; second, the "stronger" believers unwittingly aligned themselves with demonic powers by attending a temple where sacrifices were made to idols.

The same principles apply to a gay wedding. If I attend the ceremony, even though I don't condone homosexuality, my presence communicates to onlookers that God's design for sexuality is not important, that homoerotic behavior isn't that big of a deal. Even if I told the couple privately that I don't agree with same-sex marriage and that I'm there simply because I love them, my presence at the ceremony communicates support for same-sex marriage whether that is my intention or not.

Second, the purpose of a public wedding is for a man and woman to establish a lifelong covenant in the presence of other witnesses. As an attendee, I serve as a witness that this is indeed a valid covenant in the eyes of God. That's why ministers used to say, "If anyone knows any reason why this couple should not be joined together in holy matrimony, speak now or forever hold your peace." It's also why some ministers conclude the ceremony by affirming the validity of the covenant: "Therefore what God has joined together, let no one separate" (Mark 10:9).

A gay "marriage" is not a covenant in God's eyes; it's an abomination. (Note: it is the *act* that is an abomination. God still loves the people who act out homosexually, but unless they repent and submit to Jesus's lordship, they cannot inherit the kingdom of heaven [1 Corinthians 6:9–11].) Attending a gay wedding is wholly different from attending a graduation ceremony or birthday celebration, which have nothing to do with validating a covenant in the eyes of God. If I attend a gay wedding, I serve as a witness to affirm what the Bible calls an abomination. In doing so, I unwittingly align myself with demonic powers and strengthen the very demonic stronghold I say I oppose. My actions have implications in both the natural and spiritual realms.

Gagnon points out that Jesus interacted with sexual sinners, but He found morally neutral settings to do so. He never attended a pagan temple or partook in a ritual that celebrated immorality. There are alternative ways to reach out to our LGBTQ-identified friends and loved ones other than attending their wedding ceremony: have them over for dinner, throw them a birthday party, or attend a sporting event or concert together.

I recognize there are well-meaning Christians who have come to a different conclusion. Some consider attending a gay wedding a matter of conscience and cite Romans 14 to support their perspective.[245] I have friends with gay-identified children who grapple with whether they would attend their child's wedding because it's their *child*.

Admittedly, I'm not a parent, so I've never been put in that difficult position. It may sound harsh and unloving not to attend someone's wedding—*especially* when it's your own son or daughter. The fear is that refusing to attend a loved one's wedding may indefinitely sever the relationship. While that's within the realm of possibility, it's also part of the cost of following Jesus:

> Anyone who loves their father or mother more than me is not worthy of me; anyone who loves their son or daughter more than me is not worthy of me. Whoever does not take up their cross and follow me is not worthy of me. Whoever finds their life will

> lose it, and whoever loses their life for my sake will find it. (Matthew 10:37–39)

While I've never had to face that dilemma as a parent, there are times I've had to count the cost of losing a relationship to follow Jesus. It's not easy. I urge you not to believe the lie that your loved one's salvation is dependent on you and your relationship with them; only God can save them. Yes, we want to do all we can to love others and stay in relationship, if at all possible, but loving God is the first and greatest commandment. Everything else must flow from our love relationship with Him.

Unbelievers are not impressed by Christians who compromise the truth to be liked by others. They expect us to hold fast to our convictions and, though they may be understandably hurt when we tell them we cannot attend their wedding, they're usually not surprised. Our allegiance to the Lord at great personal cost sends a powerful message: our Savior who laid down His life for us is worth laying our lives down for Him.

Of course, if you choose not to attend a loved one's wedding, it's important to exercise sensitivity in the way you communicate *why* you won't attend. If possible, talk to your loved one face-to-face so they can see your facial expressions and hear your tone of voice. Communicate with them that this is a difficult decision because you want to stay in relationship with them. You might consider following the affirmation approach mentioned in chapter 14: "I love you and your partner, and I want to stay in relationship with you. I cannot violate my conscience before God and attend the ceremony. But that will never change the fact that I love you and your partner and want to stay in relationship with you." Keep the content of the conversation in the realm of ideas and avoid any language that could be interpreted as a personal attack. If they choose to sever the relationship because you are following your conscience before God, that's beyond your ability to control. Your responsibility is to love well, honor God, and trust Him with the results.

Most of all, remember that we are not battling flesh and blood. The evil one hates God's sacred design for our sexuality, and he is doing all he can to destroy the concept of male and female altogether. Imagine the irreparable damage that would be done to the demonic stronghold sweeping across our nation if Christians took a united stand and refused to acknowledge same-sex marriage as a legitimate covenant.

What struck me most about Gagnon's article was his closing statement: "What good would I be at a 'gay wedding' anyway since I would be visibly weeping my heart out at a ceremony that solemnizes a behavior that puts a loved one at risk of not inheriting God's Kingdom?" Sad but true. We must consider what our presence at a gay wedding communicates both in the natural and spiritual realms.

## What About Transgender Pronouns?

I used to approach transgender pronouns like I did gay weddings. I figured unbelievers have no reason to conform to their God-given gender, so I may as well call them by their preferred name or pronoun to build trust. How will they ever be open to the gospel if I force them to adopt a Christian sexual ethic first? I resolved to make the gospel the focus, not their external behavior or preferred name/pronoun.

There may be believers who, as a matter of conscience, agree with my former perspective. Accommodation proponents (see chapter 12) refer to the above as "pronoun hospitality."[246] I believe in building bridges with lost people to love them toward Christ. However, my perspective changed when I took into consideration the ramifications in both the natural and spiritual realms. For the same reason that I would not attend a gay wedding, I would not affirm the lie that someone's biological sex is contrary to who God created them to be. Sex is sacred, and I cannot concede otherwise. I will not willfully participate in a known lie. My allegiance is to Jesus, not to the demonic stronghold influencing our culture to destroy God's design for sexuality. At the same time, I want to love the trans-identified person in front of me and not unnecessarily offend or hinder them from coming to know Christ.

I found Andrew Walker's article "He, She, Ze, Zir? Navigating Pronouns While Loving Your Transgender Neighbor" especially helpful.[247] Walker starts with four biblical foundations:

1. Love rejoices in the truth (1 Corinthians 13:6), and we ought to speak truthfully about the matter.
2. We are commanded to love our neighbors as ourselves (Mark 12:31), and that includes speaking the truth in love.
3. We are to obey our conscience and what we know to be true (Romans 2:14–16).
4. We are to live at peace with others and not be needlessly combative (Romans 12:18).

With those principles in mind, think of three concentric circles that represent three levels of relational collateral we may have with others. The innermost circle represents those closest to us, like family members or church members, with whom we have the most trust and relational collateral. The middle circle represents those who are not as close but with whom we interact on a semi-regular basis, such as neighbors and coworkers. The outermost circle represents strangers or acquaintances we meet for the first time, with whom we have no relational collateral. The level of trust I have with someone determines how I approach their name or pronouns.

### Strangers

Once a year, I get my golf clubs regripped at a local sports store, and the same man helps me each time. When I dropped off my clubs last year, the clerk looked drastically different. He had long hair, had grown breast tissue, and his name tag said, "Teresa." I don't remember what his name was before, but I know it wasn't Teresa!

My heart went out to him in that moment. I felt the cultural pressure fueled by demonic strongholds to call him Teresa and refer to him as "ma'am." But it would not be loving for me to participate in a known lie and reject his God-given identity. At the same time, I recognize there's deep pain behind his decision to identify as a woman, especially when he doesn't even pass well as one. I have zero relational collateral with him, so it would be entirely inappropriate for me to exclaim, "Your name isn't really Teresa, and you're not a woman!" There's no need to unnecessarily offend. At the same time, I don't want to strengthen the very demonic stronghold I say I oppose.

With all that in mind, I looked into his eyes with compassion and said, "Thank you so much for your prompt service. You always get my clubs done early, and I so appreciate that. You do such excellent work. I hope you have a great day." I didn't have to use a name or a gendered pronoun when speaking directly to him. I simply loved him where he was in the middle of his brokenness, the same way Jesus loves me. As I turned and walked away, I prayed for him to come to know Jesus and find healing for the deep pain in his heart.

### Family Member or Fellow Believer

My response would be completely different if the person were in the innermost circle of trust, such as an immediate family member or a fellow believer. Let's say I'm a parent, and my son Tommy wants to "transition" and change his name to "Teresa." Under no circumstances would I affirm my child in a false identity contrary to God's design. However, I need wisdom from the Holy Spirit as to how to navigate that conversation. Tommy has likely put a lot of thought into his decision, and it may have taken a lot of courage for him to say something to me. A dogmatic reply of, "No, I'm not calling you Teresa, so just stop it!" may make Tommy feel ostracized and reinforce his decision to pursue that path.

Remember, we're not battling flesh and blood. The evil one is the enemy, not Tommy. What Tommy needs most is for me to join with him against the enemy who is attempting to destroy his identity. Wounds of rejection are often at the root. Rather than condemning Tommy and contributing to further rejection, I respond with compassion and curiosity: "Tell me more about that. Why would you want to be a girl? What do you dislike about being a boy?"

My job as a parent is to come alongside Tommy in his formative years, helping him discover the man God created him to be and affirming him in his unique personality temperament and talents. Many times, boys who adopt a female persona feel like a failure as a male and are made fun of at school, further reinforcing their sense of failure. So, I ask the Holy Spirit for some open-ended questions to encourage dialogue and expose the lies that are compelling Tommy to reject who God created him to be. I would do the same for a daughter adopting a male persona, though the roots may be different. She may be experiencing ROGD, or there may be other factors contributing to traditional gender dysphoria. (See chapter 7 for more detail.)

We respond similarly to a fellow believer who confesses transgender feelings, knowing their struggle is likely rooted in wounds of rejection. Rather than encouraging them to transition socially (taking on a false name or false pronouns) or surgically alter their body, we ask the Lord to expose the deep-seated wounds that feed their disidentification with their own sex and their idolatry of the opposite sex.

The situation is much like an anorexic girl who thinks she's fat, even though she isn't. She's deceived in her thinking. It would be unloving to reinforce her anorexic mindset by agreeing that she's fat and offering to pay for liposuction. At the same time, we don't chastise and condemn her. Rather, we start by gently engaging her in conversation and exploring what's going on in her mind. It will take some time to resolve the wounds in her soul that have led her to that extreme, but we bear with her in love through the process of healing and transformation, without affirming her in a false identity.

### Neighbor or Coworker

Navigating names/pronouns with a neighbor or coworker can be the most challenging. Let's say the man who wants to be called "Teresa" moves in next door to me. I can avoid using a name/pronoun if I only see him in the store once a year, but if I get to know him as my neighbor, I'm going to have to call him something besides "you."

When my neighbor first introduces himself to me as "Teresa," I may suspect that's not his real name, but I don't have an option but to call a new acquaintance by the name they give me. As I get to know "Teresa," I may joke around with him and ask if I can call him "T" as a fun nickname. But if he prefers that I call him Teresa, then I honor his request the same as I would honor your request to call you whatever name you give me.

Names can change with culture. When I was a kid, Jordan was predominantly a boy's name. Today, girls are named Jordan. Similarly, Chris and Kelly can be used for men or women. I may call my neighbor Teresa because it's the name he gives me, but I won't refer to him as "she/her" (or "they/them"). Again, if I'm talking directly to my neighbor, there's no need for a pronoun except for "you." However, if I'm talking to another neighbor about Teresa, I'll simply repeat the name Teresa instead of using "she/her" pronouns. "That's *Teresa's* car," instead of "That's *her* car," so as not to reinforce a false identity. At the same time, I don't want to unnecessarily offend, so I don't say "That's *his* car."

Repeating the name can become cumbersome since pronouns are a way of condensing conversation. There may come a point when Teresa or another neighbor asks why I never use a feminine pronoun in reference to him. I would respond truthfully yet tactfully, saying,

> I'm glad we can have an honest conversation about this as friends. I hope you know by now that I love you, though we may not share the same beliefs. I

> believe God is our Creator and that He knit me together in my mother's womb with a divine purpose as a female. I believe the same is true for you as a male. That's why I don't refer to you with feminine pronouns. However, I recognize that you may not share my beliefs, so I'm doing my best to honor your choices without imposing my conscience on you. As your friend, I hope you will extend the same courtesy to me.

That's a tough conversation to have, but when asked, I will speak the truth in love. Hopefully, I will have already built enough trust and relational collateral with my neighbor that he will receive my answer in the spirit it is given so that we can continue our relationship. But there's a risk that he will take offense and cut off our relationship.

Jesus took the same risk when He spoke the truth in love. Some weren't willing to receive the truth, as in the case of the rich young ruler and those who deserted Jesus after He spoke of eating His flesh and drinking His blood (Mark 10:17–23; John 6:60–69). But some not only received the truth but were so completely transformed by the truth that they couldn't help but share it with others, as in the case of the woman at the well and the disciples in the book of Acts (John 4:1–42; Acts 4:19–20).

Some of us are afraid to have conversations like that because we fear man more than we fear God. We forget that Romans 2:15 says the law of God is written on everyone's heart, even that of LGBTQ-identified people. When we affirm a trans-identified person in their God-given sex, the Holy Spirit who came to convict the world of sin, righteousness, and judgment (John 16:8) is right there with us to quietly reinforce the truth in their heart.

However, if we refuse to speak the truth in love when the opportunity arises, we cave to the spirit of intimidation and hinder that person from experiencing the Holy Spirit's conviction through our conversation. Fearing people more than we fear God is ultimately an act of selfishness: we care more for our own reputation than for the state of someone else's eternal soul. Our compliance with darkness energizes the very stronghold we say we oppose. We must consider the ramifications in both the natural and spiritual realms.

## Closing Thoughts

Obviously, there are dozens of cultural conundrums like this that we face on a regular basis. I wish there were a formula as to how to respond in each situation. But the good news is that the Holy Spirit is with us in every moment. As we seek Him for guidance, He will grant us grace to be as wise as serpents and as innocent as doves (Matthew 10:16–20) and to love others as He loves us (1 John 4:19).

## DISCUSSION QUESTIONS

1. When considering cultural conundrums, does it help you to replace the sin of homoerotic behavior with another sin like a boyfriend and girlfriend having sex before marriage? Why or why not?
2. Have you ever been invited to a gay wedding? If so, how did you respond? What are your thoughts after reading this chapter?
3. Have you ever been in a situation where you've had to navigate pronouns with a person who identifies as transgender? If so, how did you respond? What are your thoughts after reading this chapter?

CONCLUSION

# RECLAIMING THE RAINBOW

A traditional rainbow has seven colors: red, orange, yellow, green, blue, indigo, and violet. Seven is the number of perfection, representing God and His covenant promise never again to flood the earth because of our wickedness. It's no coincidence that the LGBTQ community uses the rainbow as its icon, akin to an "in your face" to God.

Years ago, I was driving behind a car with a bumper sticker of an LGBTQ flag, and for some reason I decided to count how many colors were in that rainbow. To my surprise, there were only six—representing the number of man. Then it struck me. Satan left a subtle imprint, proudly reminding us that he is behind the scheme to destroy our sacred sexuality.

Interestingly, the Hebrew word for "rainbow" (*qesheth*) is the same word for a battle "bow" used to shoot arrows.[248] A rainbow hangs across the clouds, as if God were hanging up His battle bow and declaring His covenant of peace.[249] In a figurative sense, Satan seeks to steal the battle bow by distorting the symbol of God's covenant promise and exploiting it to brand his evil agenda. For arrows, Satan uses human pawns whom he has deceived into proudly embracing perverted sexuality at odds with their Creator's design.

And yet, God remains true to His promise: never again will He flood the earth because of our wickedness—even when we become enemies of God and use His covenant symbol against Him. What a picture of God's mercy in light of the wrath our sin deserves. All of us who have come to faith in Jesus were once enemies of God (Colossians 1:21). All of us like sheep have turned to our own way; yet while we were still sinners, Christ died for us (Isaiah 53:6; Romans 5:8). God's covenant promise shines brightly against the dark backdrop of our stormy rebellion.

As ones who have been shown mercy, may we demonstrate God's compassion toward those who embrace all things LGBTQ. At the same time, may we hold fast to God's Word, refusing to compromise on His sacred design for sexuality that images the gospel. Such compassion without compromise reflects God's heart and leads to transformation.

APPENDIX A

# QUICK GUIDES FOR MINISTRY LEADERS

The following reference guides, known as ReStory Quick Guides, were designed with ministry leaders in mind. To view an interactive PDF or print a copy of each quick guide, visit restoryministries.org. The ReStory website has additional quick guides along with training videos, tough topic papers, book recommendations, and other resources.

APPENDIX B

# WHEN SOMEONE SAYS, "I EXPERIENCE SAME-SEX ATTRACTIONS"[250]

**REASSURE:** Thank them for their honesty and let them know that their struggles do not change how you see them. Reassure them that experiencing same-sex attractions is not a sin, though acting on such desires is (James 1:14–15).

**REMIND** them that all believers experience temptation that must be resisted (1 Corinthians 10:13) and that rather than focusing on our fallen desires, our goal in life is to know Jesus and live a life yielded to Him (John 17:3; Galatians 5:17). Teach them how to connect with the Lord through daily Bible reading and prayer. Encourage them to pursue the baptism in the Holy Spirit and pray in tongues on a regular basis to strengthen their connection with the Lord and release their burdens to Him (1 Corinthians 14:4; Jude 20).

**REFRAME** their perspective. They are not gay (as in the world's definition of an inborn, immutable orientation); they are experiencing deceitful desires and are on a journey of sanctification, dying to the old self with its deceitful desires, being made new in the attitude of their minds, and putting on the new self, created to be like God in true righteousness and holiness (Ephesians 4:22–24). Transformation is a lifelong journey of being conformed to the image of Christ (Romans 8:29; 12:2). Know that, as a leader, your job is not to set the overcomer free but to connect them with Jesus, His body, and resources that put them on a lifelong trajectory toward transformation.

**RELATIONSHIPS:** Help them form relationships with believers of the same sex who can affirm them as a man among men or a woman among women. At their root, same-sex attractions are not a sexual issue but often result from an emotional-relational disconnect with the same-sex parent or parental figure. In short, we get hurt in relationships, and we can receive healing through healthy relationships. In addition to peer relationships, it's helpful to connect younger believers with older believers in the local church who can love them like spiritual parents. Toward that end, it also helps to cultivate healthy relationships with the opposite sex, especially for those who have been wounded earlier in life by the opposite sex.

**RESOURCE:** Connect them with resources highlighting testimonies of other believers who have experienced transformation in the area of same-sex attractions so that they know they are not alone on their journey. *The Such Were Some* *of You* documentary is a great resource. We also recommend *The Broken Image* for everyone, *Desires in Conflict* for men, and *Restoring Sexual Identity* for women.

**REFER** them to professionals who can help. Many overcomers benefit from meeting with a Christian counselor or therapist (especially one skilled in inner healing and deliverance) to help them process issues that may contribute to the development of same-sex attractions, such as dysfunctional family patterns, codependency, or abuse. If you don't already have a trusted Christian counselor locally, the Restored Hope Network can offer suggestions of people with expertise in counseling those with same-sex attractions.

**REAFFIRM** that you love the fact that they're saying "no" to what so much of the world is saying "yes" to, that you're there for them as they continue, that you're honored to walk alongside them, and that your only expectation of them is that they'll continue growing in faith and becoming the person God intends them to be (Philippians 1:6).

## APPENDIX C

# WHEN SOMEONE SAYS, "I STRUGGLE WITH MY GENDER IDENTITY"[251]

**REASSURE:** Thank them for their honesty and let them know that their struggles do not change how you see them. Reassure them that experiencing gender dysphoria is not a sin, though acting on such desires or rejecting our God-given biological sex is (Deuteronomy 22:5; Isaiah 45:9).

**REMIND** them that all believers experience temptation that must be resisted (1 Corinthians 10:13) and that rather than focusing on our fallen desires, our goal in life is to know Jesus and live a life yielded to Him (Galatians 5:17; John 17:3). Teach them how to connect with the Lord in the secret place through daily Bible reading and prayer. Encourage them to pursue the baptism in the Holy Spirit and pray in tongues on a regular basis to strengthen their connection with the Lord and release their burdens to Him (1 Corinthians 14:4; Jude 20).

**REFRAME** their perspective by helping them understand that God created us male and female for a purpose (Genesis 1:26–27). Our biological sex is not a mistake; God knit us together in our mother's womb, and we are fearfully and wonderfully made (Psalm 139:13–16). When someone experiences gender dysphoria from a young age, it's often due to emotional factors that affect their gender identity development. The answer is not to change the body to match the fallen mind but rather to renew the mind to match the body God gave them (Ephesians 4:22–24). Know that, as a leader, your job is not to resolve their gender dysphoria but to connect the overcomer with Jesus, His Body, and resources that put them on a lifelong trajectory toward transformation.

**RELATIONSHIPS:** Help them form relationships with believers of the same sex who can affirm them as a man among men or a woman among women. At its root, gender dysphoria is not a sexual issue but a matter of healing wounds in the soul that affect our gender identity. In short, we get hurt in relationships, and we can receive healing through healthy relationships. Toward that end, it also helps to cultivate healthy relationships with the opposite sex, especially for those who have been wounded earlier in life by the opposite sex.

**RESOURCE:** Connect them with resources sharing testimonies of other believers who once struggled with their gender identity and have made peace with their God-given gender so that they know they are not alone on their journey. The *TranZformed* documentary is a great resource in addition to other resources from Linda Seiler, Walt Heyer, and Help4Families.

**REFER** them to professionals who can help. Many overcomers benefit from meeting with a Christian counselor or therapist (especially one skilled in inner healing and deliverance) to help them process issues that may contribute to the development of gender dysphoria such as being teased for their personality temperament, dysfunctional family patterns, or abuse. If you don't already have a trusted Christian counselor locally, the Restored Hope Network can offer suggestions of people with expertise in counseling those with gender identity issues.

**REAFFIRM** that you love the fact that they're saying "no" to what so much of the world is saying "yes" to, that you're honored to walk alongside them, and that your only expectation of them is that they'll continue growing in faith and becoming the person God intends them to be (Philippians 1:6).

## APPENDIX D

# RAPID-ONSET GENDER DYSPHORIA (ROGD): WHY TEEN GIRLS TRANSITION[252]

...............

### THE PHENOMENON

Over the past decade, the US has witnessed a 1,000 percent increase in teen girls who announce they are nonbinary (don't identify as male or female) or transgender (identify as the opposite sex). Most of these girls have no previous history of gender dysphoria (being unhappy as a female) or gender nonconformity (acting more like a male). Thus, their announcement often comes as a shock to parents.

### ORIGIN

Researcher Lisa Littman coined the term "Rapid-Onset Gender Dysphoria" (ROGD) in a 2018 study analyzing the phenomenon. In the study, parents describe a sudden gender identity change in their teenage daughters along with friends who adopt alternative identities. ROGD appears to be a social contagion that spreads among peers and via social media apps like Tumblr, TikTok, Reddit, and Instagram.

## CONTRIBUTING FACTORS

In her book *Irreversible Damage: The Transgender Craze Seducing Our Daughters*, Abigail Shrier describes several factors that may account for the rise in ROGD among teen girls: 1) the invention of the smartphone spreads social media contagion among peers; 2) discomfort with their developing bodies can make girls feel like they don't measure up to cultural standards of feminine beauty, which makes them vulnerable to the suggestion they may not be "real" women; 3) exposure to violent pornography makes womanhood seem undesirable; and 4) comorbid mental health issues such as depression and suicidal thoughts compel teens to seek alternative ways to alleviate painful emotions. These are the same girls who in past decades may have sought relief through maladaptive coping mechanisms like eating disorders and cutting.

## WHY TEEN GIRLS "TRANSITION"

Adopting a nonbinary or transgender identity is a trendy way for teen girls to dissociate from emotional pain. A girl battling feelings of rejection receives immediate affirmation when she announces her alternative identity on social media. This gives her a rush of euphoria and the impression that being "born again" in her new identity will resolve all her troubles. It also shields her from further peer rejection because teens celebrate LGBTQ identities. In some states, she can access testosterone injections without parental consent, and the injections can take the edge off her emotional pain, further confirming her assumption that transitioning will resolve her problems. Some girls may begin to bind their breasts and even go so far as to have a double mastectomy and hysterectomy.

## THE HARSH REALITY

Search "detransition" on YouTube, and sadly, you'll see dozens of girls who realized "transitioning" didn't resolve their problems. And yet, they must live with the permanent effects of testosterone injections such as a lowered voice, receding hairline, and increased facial and body hair—not to mention the irreversible consequences of mastectomies and hysterectomies.

## HOW TO HELP

Today's generation of teen girls desperately needs guidance from parents and pastoral influences to help them process the pains of life in healthy ways so that girls can push through the awkward years of puberty and peer rejection to discover who God created them to be when He knit them together in their mother's womb (Psalm 139:13–16). We recommend the books *Desist, Detrans, Detox: Getting Your Child Out of the Gender Cult* and *Irreversible Damage: The Transgender Craze Seducing Our Daughters*, which offer practical tips, such as expressing support for your child without affirming a false identity, limiting your child's social media use (especially unsupervised, private chat rooms), increasing family connection and communication, encouraging your child to prioritize in-person relationships over virtual ones, and addressing any underlying mental health concerns.

# GLOSSARY

**Androgynous:** having both masculine/feminine traits; blurring the lines between male/female.

**Asexual:** someone who experiences little or no sexual attraction to either sex; also known as "ace."

**Autogynephilia:** *auto* (self) + *gyne* (woman) + *philia* (love) = to love oneself as a woman; the condition in which a man is aroused by the thought of himself as a woman; often associated with transvestism/cross-dressing; most autogynephilic men are sexually attracted to women.

**Biological sex:** also known as natal sex or sex at birth; male or female as determined by chromosomes, external anatomy, and internal sex organs. (Pro-gay activists use the term "sex assigned at birth" to suggest that sex can change.)

**Bisexual:** someone who experiences attraction to both sexes.

**Bottom surgery:** surgery that involves genital mutilation and cosmetic construction to mimic the genitalia of the opposite sex; referred to as vaginoplasty for men (which includes castration and penile inversion) or phalloplasty for women (which includes stripping skin from the forearm or thigh to construct a nonfunctional penis).[253]

**Cisgender:** someone whose gender identity (feeling male or female) aligns with their biological sex; also known as "cis."

**Conversion therapy:** a pejorative term coined by pro-gay activists to describe change-allowing therapy or ministry efforts to resolve unwanted same-sex attractions; the term is typically used to villainize those who believe that disordered sexual desires or gender insecurity can change.

**Cross-sex hormones:** hormones of the opposite sex used in hormonal transition (i.e., biological women taking testosterone and biological men taking estrogen).

**Deadname:** to call a transgender person by their original name (i.e., using the name Bruce Jenner instead of Caitlyn Jenner).

**Desister:** a term describing someone who once identified as transgender but has returned to identifying by their birth sex.

**Detransition:** the act of embracing one's God-given sex after having transitioned hormonally or surgically to appear as the opposite sex.

**Drag king:** a female entertainer who dresses as a male and exaggerates masculine stereotypes.

**Drag queen:** a male entertainer who dresses as a female and exaggerates feminine stereotypes.

**Gender affirmation surgery (or gender confirmation surgery):** formerly known as "sex reassignment surgery," which involves genital mutilation and cosmetic surgery to appear as the opposite sex. Surgery alters the body but does not affect the chromosomes. No one can "become" the opposite sex.

**Gender binary:** the existence of only two genders, male and female.

**Gender dysphoria:** the experience of distress when one's mental concept (or subjective feelings) of being male or female conflicts with one's biological sex.

**Gender expression:** how one communicates his or her sense of masculinity or femininity through clothing, mannerisms, speech, behavior, etc.

**Gender identity:** one's mental concept (or subjective feeling) of being male or female.

**Gender nonconformity:** not aligning with cultural stereotypes for masculinity (males) or femininity (females).

**Gender-fluid:** someone whose gender identity or gender expression fluctuates.

**Genderqueer:** someone whose gender identity or gender expression falls outside of traditional stereotypes for masculinity/femininity.

**Gnosticism:** a heretical belief system that grew concurrently with early expressions of Christianity and often in the same locations; espousing a dualism between physical matter and the spiritual realm, based upon the presumption that all matter, including the human body, is inherently evil, while the spirit is inherently good. Accordingly, evil actions done with the body have no bearing on salvation since, according to gnostic dualism, God only cares about the spirit.

**Hermaphrodite:** an outdated term referring to a person born with both testicular and ovarian tissue. Also known as ovotesticular syndrome.

**Intersex:** a rare, congenital (present from birth) disorder of sexual development that can affect chromosomes, hormones, reproductive organs, or genitalia.[254] Formerly called hermaphroditism, intersex conditions are physiological, whereas gender dysphoria is psychological.

**LGBTQ:** an all-inclusive acronym for lesbian, gay, bisexual, transgender, queer/questioning, and additional identities that continue to emerge. Some include the "plus" sign (LGBTQ+) to allow for ever-expanding descriptors of alternative sexual identities.

**Mixed-orientation marriage:** a male-female marriage in which one spouse experiences sexual attractions to the same sex.

**Nonbinary:** someone who does not identify as male or female.

**Pansexual:** someone who remains open to sexual attraction to anyone, including those who identify as nonbinary or transgender.

**Puberty blockers:** hormonal intervention designed to suppress puberty so that a child does not develop secondary sex characteristics. Puberty suppression increases the risk of sterility, cancer, coronary disease, cardiovascular disease, and osteoporosis, among other conditions.[255]

**Revisionist:** someone who changes (i.e., revises) Scripture to justify homoerotic behavior.

**ROGD:** acronym for rapid-onset gender dysphoria, a social contagion prevalent among teen girls whereby they suddenly adopt a nonbinary or transgender identity.

**Sexual orientation:** a psychological term describing the direction of one's sexual attractions toward the same sex (homosexual), the opposite sex (heterosexual), both sexes (bisexual), or neither sex (asexual).

**TERF:** Trans-Exclusive Radical Feminist; the term originally referred to feminists who reject men who identify as transgender women. TERF has become a slur applied to anyone who rejects transgender ideology.

**Top surgery:** surgery to make the upper torso appear as that of the opposite sex—mastectomy (women) or breast enhancement (men).

**Traditional (homophilic) gender dysphoria:** *homo* (same) + *philia* (love) = to love the same sex; feeling like the opposite sex in one's mind and sexually attracted to the same sex.

**Transgender:** an umbrella term that describes someone whose mental concept of being male/female does not align with one's biological sex.

**Transition:** the process of rejecting one's biological sex to identify as the opposite sex. Social transition involves changing one's name, pronouns, and external appearance. Hormonal transition involves cross-sex hormone injections. Surgical transition involves top and bottom surgery.

**Transman:** a biological woman who identifies as a man; also known as FTM (female to male).

**Transsexual:** an outdated term used to refer to someone who underwent surgical procedures to appear as the opposite sex.

**Transvestite:** a biological man who finds it sexually arousing to dress as a woman (most often associated with autogynephilia).

**Transwoman:** a biological man who identifies as a woman; also known as MTF (male to female).

# ACKNOWLEDGMENTS

Though my name is on the cover, this book has been a team effort. I'll be forever grateful for my college campus pastor, John Swanson, who is now with the Lord. His response of compassion without compromise nearly three decades ago set me on a trajectory of transformation upon which others could build.

Pastor Dave Short, thank you for introducing me to the baptism in the Holy Spirit and responding with grace and truth when I confessed my sin. Mama Carol, thanks for making the trip to Crossroads Campus Church and teaching us how to flow in the gifts of the Spirit. The night you "read my mail" changed my life forever. Pastors Russ and Nan, I am who I am today because you loved me well and prayed me through some of the darkest moments of my life. I love you both so much. Emily, Sherilyn, Tata, Bob, and Sean—thank you for loving me intentionally and affirming my womanhood. Pastor Dale Crall, the years I spent in Carbondale changed my life forever. Thank you for never giving up on me and being among my most faithful intercessors. Calvary Campus Church family, your intercession was key to my transformation. I'm grateful for your continued prayer covering.

Jim Klein, thank you for investing in me and showing me the compassionate heart of the Lord. I think of you often when I see a lighthouse. Mark Sandford, I cannot praise God enough for your expertise in inner healing and deliverance and how He used you to transform my life. Thank you for your investing in me and this book. Bonnie Blake, though you are with the Lord, I carry your spiritual DNA and cherish your final words to me about God's call on my life. You knew. Marleen Troyer, you are a blessing beyond words. Your prayers, spiritual wisdom, and concern for my well-being mean the world to me. Kimberley Knochel, you are an amazing support to me as I continue in my journey of sanctification.

Madison Cantey, you did an amazing job proofing the final manuscript. I'm grateful for your expertise, attention to detail, and generous gift of your time. Carla Harshman, only the Lord knows how many hours you've invested in this book. Thank you for serving selflessly to build the kingdom. Tim Beals and Credo House, I so appreciate your patience with me since 2016. It has been a joy working with you.

To all my professors at AGTS, thank you for enriching my life, modeling what it looks like to be a scholar practitioner, and showing me that "seminary" is not synonymous with "cemetery." To the dozens of people who served on my book review team, thank you for your significant time investment and thoughtful feedback. This book is better than it could have been because of you. To my local intercessors who meet in my living room every month, it's been a joy to share this journey with you. You are among my greatest treasures. Mom and Dad, thank you for loving me and being my biggest cheerleaders. I love you with all my heart.

My highest praise goes to You, Jesus. I cannot thank You enough for saving me, transforming me, and allowing me the privilege to partner with You. What a joy to see the fruit of what You spoke to my heart twenty-one years ago in the back corner of that auditorium. To You alone be all the glory.

# ABOUT THE AUTHOR

Linda Seiler is an ordained Assemblies of God minister and nationally appointed US missionary with Chi Alpha (XA). A former high school English teacher turned missionary, Linda served as a XA staff associate at the University of Illinois and Southern Illinois University before leading a team to pioneer XA at Purdue University in 2007. She served as the XA director there until 2020, when she stepped into a new role as a national XA field specialist, training campus missionaries and student leaders in matters of applied theology and culture. Linda also serves as the executive director of ReStory Ministries, which was established to equip churches to address LGBTQ.

Linda graduated with her BA from the University of Illinois and earned a PhD in intercultural studies from the Assemblies of God Theological Seminary. She is an avid golfer, dark chocolate lover, and cat mom to feline Facebook sensations Bo and Tabby.

For more info about Dr. Seiler as well as helpful resources on LGBTQ, visit *lindaseiler.com* and *restoryministries.org*.

# ENDNOTES

...............

Please note that the provision of sources cited does not constitute the author's endorsement of the individuals or organizations associated with each source. Some may hold perspectives that conflict with the author's.

### Introduction

1 Today's term is "gender affirmation surgery." See glossary.

2 Linda Ann Seiler, "An Investigation of Factors That Contribute to Sexual Orientation Change through Religious Mediation," *ProQuest* Dissertation, Assemblies of God Theological Seminary (2020), https://www.proquest.com/openview/b3c8f4935022264126380 51fc34b8742/1?pq-origsite=gscholar&cbl=51922&diss=y.

### Chapter 1: Trans-Formed

3 Gender dysphoria is a state of dis-ease or dissatisfaction with one's biological sex. See glossary.

4 I'm using terminology from the 1980s since that's all I knew at the time. No one used the terms "sex reassignment surgery" or "gender affirmation surgery" back then.

5 As an instance of role reversal, in a turnabout dance the girls invite the boys to the dance.

6 "Drag" is slang for dressing in clothes of the opposite sex. See glossary.

7 It's common for those who struggle with their sexuality to have a distorted view of God based on feelings of guilt, shame, and condemnation.

8 To hear the full story, click on the "Baptism in the Holy Spirit" message at lindaseiler.com.

9 Thankfully, that prophetic message was caught on cassette tape, and I play the digitized recording in my seminar series.

10 This is what Leanne Payne, author of *The Broken Image,* calls the "cannibalism complex," which helped me understand my attractions were not a sexual issue, but an emotional-relational issue rooted in gender insecurity.

## Chapter 2: How Our Sexuality Images the Gospel

11 Some argue that the plural pronouns in Genesis 1:26 refer to God and His angels or to a heavenly court. However, Genesis 1 makes no prior reference to angels or a heavenly court, and v. 27 specifies that God made mankind in *His* image, not in the image of angels or of a heavenly court. See Gregory A. Boyd and Paul R. Eddy, *Across the Spectrum: Understanding Issues in Evangelical Theology*, 2nd ed. (Grand Rapids: Baker Academic, 2009), 106–07. Further, the verb tenses in the creation narrative referring to God are singular, not plural, even though *Elohim* is plural. Genesis 5:1–3 uses terminology similar to Genesis 1, describing Adam and Eve made in the image of God and Seth made in the image of Adam. Just as plants and animals reproduce after their own kind, God made humans in His image (after His kind, so to speak), and, accordingly, humans have the capacity to reproduce after their own kind.

12 Larry Crabb describes God as a "divine community" in his book *Fully Alive: A Biblical Vision of Gender That Frees Men and Women to Live Beyond Stereotypes,* noting that he drew insights from theologian Stanley Grenz.

13 I do not intend to communicate that the only purpose for sex is procreation or that couples who choose not to have children do not image God's character and nature. Whether or not it results in children, the marital act images unity in diversity and an exclusive covenant relationship that reserves sexual intimacy for one's spouse.

14 Tim Bulkeley, "Jesus and the Father," *Asian Journal of Pentecostal Studies* 17, no. 2 (2014): 145–47, accessed April 16, 2023, https://www.aptspress.org/wp-content/uploads/2018/06/14-2_Tim_Bulkeley-_3.pdf.

15 I am not referring to the Incarnation here.

16 Tim Bulkeley, "God as Mother? Ideas to Clarify before We Start," *Asian Journal of Pentecostal Studies* 17, no. 2 (2014): 111, accessed April 16, 2023, https://www.aptspress.org/wp-content/uploads/2018/06/14-2_Tim_Bulkeley_-1.pdf.

17 Aside from the moral argument against gay "marriage," another detriment is that gay "marriage" robs a child from understanding the full expression of God's love, since God reveals Himself to us through both fatherly and motherly love.

18 Bulkeley, "Jesus and the Father," 139.

19 See "hermaphrodite" in glossary.

20 Mary Stewart Van Leeuwen, *Gender & Grace: Love, Work & Parenting in a Changing World* (Downers Grove, IL: InterVarsity Press, 1990), 213–14. Includes quotation from Lewis B. Smedes, *Sex for Christians: The Limits and Liberties of Sexual Living*, Rev. ed. (Grand Rapids: W.B. Eerdmans, 1994), 31.

21 Dennis P. Hollinger, *The Meaning of Sex: Christian Ethics and the Moral Life* (Grand Rapids: Baker Academic, 2009), 97.

## Chapter 3: What About Sexual Orientation and Gender Identity?

22 Sam Killermann, "The Genderbread Person," accessed May 19, 2023, https://www.itspronouncedmetrosexual.com/2011/11/breaking-through-the-binary-gender-explained-using-continuums/. I'm using an earlier rendition for ease of explanation. See also the Gender Unicorn found at https://transstudent.org/gender/ (accessed April 12, 2023).

23 Francis Mark Mondimore, *A Natural History of Homosexuality* (Baltimore: Johns Hopkins University Press, 1996), 27–28.

24 See glossary.

25 David Haig, "The Inexorable Rise of Gender and the Decline of Sex: Social Change in Academic Titles, 1945–2001," *The Official Publication of the International Academy of Sex Research* 33, no. 2 (2004): 89, 93, https://dx.doi.org/https://doi.org/10.1023/B:ASEB.0000014323.56281.0d.

26 Christopher West, "21. Gender, Generation, and Genitals . . . Duh!," January 20, 2015, accessed May 8, 2021, http://corproject.com/21-gender-generation-and-genitals-duh/.

27 Albert Mohler, "Biblical Theology and the Sexual Crisis," September 16, 2014, accessed April 12, 2023, http://www.albertmohler.com/2014/09/16/biblical-theology-and-the-sexuality-crisis/.

28 Stanley J. Grenz, *Sexual Ethics: An Evangelical Perspective* (Louisville, KY: Westminster John Knox Press, 1997), 26.

29 Mohler, "Biblical Theology."

30 I use quotes when referring to gay "marriage" because the Bible defines marriage exclusively as between a man and a woman.

31 For more information, see Larry Crabb's book *Fully Alive: A Biblical Vision of Gender That Frees Men and Women to Live Beyond Stereotypes*.

32 See "bottom surgery" in glossary, describing vaginoplasty and phalloplasty.

33 Leonard Sax, "How Common Is Intersex? A Response to Anne Fausto-Sterling," *Journal of Sex Research* 39, no. 3 (2002), https://dx.doi.org/10.1080/00224490209552139.

34 LGBTQ stands for Lesbian, Gay, Bisexual, Transgender, Queer/Questioning and is a common acronym for the gay community. Some include the "plus" sign (LGBTQ+) to allow for ever-expanding descriptors of alternative sexual identities.

## Chapter 4: The Bible and Homosexuality

35 Michael L. Brown, "What the Bible Really Says About Homosexuality," *Charisma News*, October 31, 2014, accessed March 24, 2023, www.charismanews.com/opinion/in-the-line-of-fire/45975-what-the-bible-really-says-about-homosexuality.

36 Named for Nicolaus Copernicus.

37 Matthew Vines, *God and the Gay Christian: The Biblical Case in Support of Same-Sex Relationships* (New York: Convergent Books, 2014), 22–25, Kindle edition.

38 Vines, *God and the Gay Christian*, 14, 17, 19, 58.

39 John Boswell, *Christianity, Social Tolerance, and Homosexuality: Gay People in Western Europe from the Beginning of the Christian*

*Era to the Fourteenth Century* (Chicago: University of Chicago Press, 1980), 93–95.

40 Justin Lee, *Torn: Rescuing the Gospel from the Gays-vs.-Christians Debate* (New York: Jericho Books, 2012), 171–74.

41 Robert A. J. Gagnon, *The Bible and Homosexual Practice: Texts and Hermeneutics* (Nashville: Abingdon Press, 2001), 73.

42 *NIV Cultural Backgrounds Study Bible: Bringing to Life the Ancient World of Scripture* (Grand Rapids: Zondervan, 2016), 75.

43 "Strange flesh" could refer to angels, but the Sodomites did not know the visitors were angels, and Jewish tradition did not refer to angels as having flesh. See Craig S. Keener, *The IVP Bible Background Commentary: New Testament* (Downers Grove, IL: InterVarsity Press, 1993), 754.

44 Robert Jamieson, A.R. Fausset, and David Brown, *Jamieson, Fausset, and Brown's Commentary on the Whole Bible* (N.p.: Delmarva Publications, Kindle, 2013), loc. 87509.

45 Gagnon, *The Bible and Homosexual Practice: Texts and Hermeneutics*, 75.

46 Boswell, *Christianity, Social Tolerance, and Homosexuality*, 100–02.

47 Gagnon, *The Bible and Homosexual Practice*, 111.

48 Gagnon, *The Bible and Homosexual Practice*, 121.

49 Boswell, *Christianity, Social Tolerance, and Homosexuality*, 109.

50 Lee, *Torn*, 183, 205.

51 Gagnon, *The Bible and Homosexual Practice*, 290–91.

52 Gagnon, *The Bible and Homosexual Practice*, 350.

53 *1946: The Mistranslation that Shifted a Culture*, 2023, accessed May 23, 2023, https://www.1946themovie.com.

54 Vines, *God and the Gay Christian*, 123.

55 James B. DeYoung, *Homosexuality: Contemporary Claims Examined in Light of the Bible and Other Ancient Literature and Law* (Grand Rapids: Kregel Publications, 2000), 195.

56 Gagnon, *The Bible and Homosexual Practice*, 316.

57 Robert A.J. Gagnon, "Don't Be Silly," First Stone Ministries, last modified November 2, 2021, accessed April 12, 2023, https://www.firststone.org/articles/post/dont-be-silly.

58 For more on eunuchs, see A. Philip Brown II, "Does Jesus' Reference to Eunuchs Affirm Transgender People?," Answers in Genesis, last

modified December 1, 2017, accessed August 19, 2022, https://answersingenesis.org/answers/in-depth/v12/does-jesus-reference-to-eunuchs-affirm-transgender-people/.

## Chapter 5: What Science Says

59 Lady Gaga, *Born This Way*, Interscope Records (2011).

60 Life's Little Mysteries Staff, "The Lady Is a Champ: Lady Gaga Sets Twitter Record," Live Science, May 18, 2011, accessed April 12, 2023, https://web.archive.org/web/20130702233957/http://www.livescience.com/33288-lady-gagas-world-records.html.

61 See my dissertation for a detailed chapter on scientific research.

62 D. H. Hamer et al., "A Linkage between DNA Markers on the X Chromosome and Male Sexual Orientation," *Science* 261, no. 5119 (1993), https://dx.doi.org/10.1126/science.8332896.

63 George Rice et al., "Male Homosexuality: Absence of Linkage to Microsatellite Markers at Xq28," *Science* 284, no. 5414 (1999), https://dx.doi.org/10.1126/science.284.5414.665.

64 Niklas Långström et al., "Genetic and Environmental Effects on Same-Sex Sexual Behavior: A Population Study of Twins in Sweden," *The Official Publication of the International Academy of Sex Research* 39, no. 1 (2010), https://dx.doi.org/10.1007/s10508-008-9386-1. See also Stanton L. Jones, "Same-Sex Science: The Social Sciences Cannot Settle the Moral Status of Homosexuality," *First Things* (February 2012), accessed April 12, 2023, https://www.firstthings.com/article/2012/02/same-sex-science.

65 Långström et al., "Genetic and Environmental Effects on Same-Sex Sexual Behavior: A Population Study of Twins in Sweden," 79.

66 E.M. Drabant et al., "Genome-Wide Association Study of Sexual Orientation in a Large, Web-Based Cohort," 23andMe, Inc., 2012, accessed April 12, 2023, https://blog.23andme.com/wp-content/uploads/2012/11/Drabant-Poster-v7.pdf.

67 Andrea Ganna et al., "Large-Scale GWAS Reveals Insights into the Genetic Architecture of Same-Sex Sexual Behavior," *Science* 365, no. 6456 (2019): 6, https://dx.doi.org/10.1126/science.aat7693.

68 Andrea Ganna et al., "Research Article Summary: Large-Scale GWAS Reveals Insights into the Genetic Architecture of Same-Sex

Sexual Behavior," *Science* 365, no. 6456 (2019): 1, https://dx.doi.org/https://doi.org/10.1126/science.aat7693.

69 William R. Rice, Urban Friberg, and Sergey Gavrilets, "Sexually Antagonistic Epigenetic Marks That Canalize Sexually Dimorphic Development," *Molecular Ecology* 25, no. 8 (2016), http://dx.doi.org/10.1111/mec.13490.

70 Lisa M. Diamond, and Clifford J. Rosky, "Scrutinizing Immutability: Research on Sexual Orientation and U.S. Legal Advocacy for Sexual Minorities," *The Journal of Sex Research* 53, no. 4–5 (2016): 366, https://dx.doi.org/10.1080/00224499.2016.1139665.

71 Simon LeVay, "A Difference in Hypothalamic Structure between Heterosexual and Homosexual Men," *Science* 253, no. 5023 (1991), https://dx.doi.org/10.1126/science.1887219.

72 David Gelman, "Homosexuality: Born or Bred?," *Newsweek* (February 23, 1992), accessed April 14, 2023, http://www.newsweek.com/homosexuality-born-or-bred-200636.

73 David Nimmons, "Sex and the Brain: Neurobiologist Simon Levay Found a Link between Brain Structure and Homosexuality," *Discover* (March 1, 1994), accessed April 14, 2023, https://www.discovermagazine.com/mind/sex-and-the-brain.

74 Gelman, "Homosexuality: Born or Bred?"

75 Lutz Jancke, "Music Drives Brain Plasticity," *International Journal of Psychophysiology* 108 (2016), https://dx.doi.org/10.1016/j.ijpsycho.2016.07.155.

76 Bogdan Draganski et al., "Neuroplasticity: Changes in Grey Matter Induced by Training," *Nature* 427, no. 6972 (2004): 311, https://dx.doi.org/10.1038/427311a.

77 Fight the New Drug Inc., "How Porn Changes the Brain," Fight the New Drug website, accessed April 14, 2023, https://fightthenewdrug.org/how-porn-changes-the-brain/.

78 Susan L. Andersen et al., "Preliminary Evidence for Sensitive Periods in the Effect of Childhood Sexual Abuse on Regional Brain Development," *Journal of Neuropsychiatry and Clinical Neurosciences* 20, no. 3 (2008): 298, https://dx.doi.org/10.1176/appi.neuropsych.20.3.292.

79 Fight the New Drug, "How Porn Changes the Brain."

80 Biological men who have had surgery to appear like a woman.

81 Biological women who have had surgery to appear like a man.

82 Lawrence S. Mayer and Paul R. McHugh, "Sexuality and Gender: Findings from the Biological, Psychological, and Social Sciences," *The New Atlantis*, no. 50 (Fall 2016): 102, accessed January 17, 2019, https://www.thenewatlantis.com/publications/number-50-fall-2016.

83 Phoenix, C. H. Phoenix et al., "Organizing Action of Prenatally Administered Testosterone Propionate on the Tissues Mediating Mating Behavior in the Female Guinea Pig." *Endocrinology* 65 (1959): 369-82.

84 To read more about intersex conditions, see N.E. Whitehead and B.K. Whitehead, *My Genes Made Me Do It! Homosexuality and the Scientific Evidence* (Whitehead Associates: 2018), 102–13, accessed January 22, 2019, http://www.mygenes.co.nz/download.html; Sax, "How Common Is Intersex? A Response to Anne Fausto-Sterling."; Mayer and McHugh, "Sexuality and Gender: Findings from the Biological, Psychological, and Social Sciences," 91–115.

85 Linda Titus-Ernstoff et al., "Psychosexual Characteristics of Men and Women Exposed Prenatally to Diethylstilbestrol," *Endocrinology* 14, no. 2 (2003): 155, https://dx.doi.org/10.1097/01.EDE.0000039059.38824.B2; Melissa Hines, "Prenatal Endocrine Influences on Sexual Orientation and on Sexually Differentiated Childhood Behavior," *Frontiers in Neuroendocrinology* 32, no. 2 (April 2011), https://dx.doi.org/10.1016/j.yfrne.2011.02.006; Rebecca Troisi et al., "Gender Identity and Sexual Orientation Identity in Women and Men Prenatally Exposed to Diethylstilbestrol," *Archives of Sexual Behavior* 49, no. 2 (2020): 453.

86 Mayer and McHugh, "Sexuality and Gender," 37.

87 Mayer and McHugh, "Sexuality and Gender," 7.

88 L. Diamond, "Just How Different Are Female and Male Sexual Orientation?" (paper presented at the Human Development Outreach and Extension Program, Cornell University, October 17, 2013), accessed February 20, 2017, http://www.cornell.edu/video/lisa-diamond-on-sexual-fluidity-of-men-and-women; Lisa Diamond, "Sexual Fluidity in Male and Females," *Current Sexual Health Reports* 8, no. 4 (2016), accessed April 14, 2023, https://

dx.doi.org/10.1007/s11930-016-0092-z; Diamond and Rosky, "Scrutinizing Immutability: Research on Sexual Orientation and U.S. Legal Advocacy for Sexual Minorities"; Sabra L. Katz-Wise, "Sexual Fluidity in Young Adult Women and Men: Associations with Sexual Orientation and Sexual Identity Development," *Psychology and Sexuality* 6, no. 2 (August 2015), accessed April 14, 2023, https://dx.doi.org/10.1080/19419899.2013.876445; Miles Ott et al., "Stability and Change in Self-Reported Sexual Orientation Identity in Young People: Application of Mobility Metrics," *The Official Publication of the International Academy of Sex Research* 40, no. 3 (2011), accessed April 14, 2023, https://dx.doi.org/10.1007/s10508-010-9691-3; R.C. Savin-Williams and G.L. Ream, "Prevalence and Stability of Sexual Orientation Components During Adolescence and Young Adulthood," *The Official Publication of the International Academy of Sex Research* 36, no. 3 (2007), accessed April 14, 2023, https://dx.doi.org/10.1007/s10508-006-9088-5; R.C. Savin-Williams, K. Joyner, and G. Rieger, "Prevalence and Stability of Self-Reported Sexual Orientation Identity During Young Adulthood," *The Official Publication of the International Academy of Sex Research* 41, no. 1 (2012), accessed April 14, 2023, https://dx.doi.org/10.1007/s10508-012-9913-y.

89 Jones, "Same-Sex Science."

## Chapter 6: How Same-Sex Attractions Develop

90 Susan Miller, "Gen Z is Driving Force among Adults Identifying as LGBTQ, Poll Shows. Here's a Breakdown," *USA Today* (February 22, 2023), https://www.usatoday.com/story/news/nation/2023/02/22/gallup-poll-lgbtq-identification/11309075002/.

91 George Barna, "New Insights into the Generation of Growing Influence: Millennials in America," Foundations of Freedom. (October 2021), accessed August 26, 2022, https://www.arizonachristian.edu/wp-content/uploads/2021/10/George-Barna-Millennial-Report-2021-FINAL-Web.pdf.

92 Paul Bond, "Nearly 40 Percent of U.S. Gen Zs, 30 Percent of Young Christians Identify as LGBTQ, Poll Shows," *Newsweek* (Oct. 20,

2021), accessed Mar 28, 2022, https://www.newsweek.com/nearly-40-percent-us-gen-zs-30-percent-christians-identify-lgbtq-poll-shows-1641085.

93 Gerard J. M. van den Aardweg, "On the Psychogenesis of Homosexuality," *The Linacre quarterly* 78, no. 3 (August 2011): 330, https://dx.doi.org/10.1179/002436311803888267.

94 Sometimes hormonal disorders such as polycystic ovary syndrome (PCOS) can affect bodily appearance in biological women. Those with PCOS may have higher androgen levels than the average woman, resulting in a deeper voice, severe acne, or more body hair than the average woman. This is different than an intersex condition, which affects both genotype (chromosomes) and phenotype (external appearance). Women with PCOS have normal XX chromosomes.

95 Daryl J. Bem, "Exotic Becomes Erotic: A Developmental Theory of Sexual Orientation," *Psychological Review* 103, no. 2 (April 1996), https://dx.doi.org/10.1037/0033-295X.103.2.320.

96 I am summarizing multiple study outcomes here, including Laura Baams, "Disparities for LGBTQ and Gender Nonconforming Adolescents," *Pediatrics* 141, no. 5 (May 2018), https://dx.doi.org/10.1542/peds.2017-3004. See my dissertation for full documentation of the original studies over the past four decades.

97 Elizabeth Moberly, "Homosexuality: Structure and Evaluation," *Theology* 83, no. 693 (1980), https://dx.doi.org/10.1177/0040571X8008300304.

98 Jay Stringer's book *Unwanted: How Sexual Brokenness Reveals Our Way to Healing* (Colorado Springs: NavPress, 2018) explains this phenomenon as it pertains to heterosexual promiscuity and pornography addiction.

99 Moberly, "Homosexuality," 179.

100 Mayer and McHugh, "Sexuality and Gender," 7.

101 Even if molestation does not result in the development of same-sex attractions, the fact remains that childhood sexual abuse always creates damage that will need healing.

102 Joe S. McIlhaney and Freda McKissic Bush, *Hooked: New Science on How Casual Sex Is Affecting Our Children* (Chicago: Northfield Publishing, 2008), Kindle location 407–49.

103 Valerie Voon et al., "Neural Correlates of Sexual Cue Reactivity in Individuals with and without Compulsive Sexual Behaviours," *PLoS ONE* (2014), https://dx.doi.org/10.1371/journal.pone.0102419; Carolyn Ross, "Overexposed and under-Prepared: The Effects of Early Exposure to Sexual Content," *Psychology Today* (Aug 13, 2012), accessed April 14, 2023, https://www.psychologytoday.com/us/blog/real-healing/201208/overexposed-and-under-prepared-the-effects-early-exposure-sexual-content.

104 Whitehead and Whitehead, *My Genes Made Me Do It!*, 87.

105 Whitehead and Whitehead, *My Genes Made Me Do It!*, 179.

## Chapter 7: How Transgender Desires Develop

106 The World Health Organization now uses the term "gender incongruence," which moves away from a mental health classification (dysphoric feelings that can be resolved) toward a sexual health classification (a physiological condition that must be affirmed); see https://www.who.int/standards/classifications/frequently-asked-questions/gender-incongruence-and-transgender-health-in-the-icd.

107 The terminology keeps changing to the point that some use *trans** (the asterisk indicating that trans manifests in a variety of ways) as an umbrella term to encompass a wide range of descriptions, such as non-binary, gender-fluid, bigender, genderqueer, and so forth. By the time this book is published, there will likely be even more terms invented, illustrating the chaos and confusion in a culture that has rejected God's design for sexuality. Ironically, the definition for each alternative sexuality or gender identity necessarily uses terms describing how it deviates from the gender binary, reinforcing the reality of God's original design of male and female.

108 J. Michael Bailey and Ray Blanchard, "Gender Dysphoria Is Not One Thing," 4th Wave Now (December 7, 2017), accessed March 21, 2020, https://4thwavenow.com/2017/12/07/gender-dysphoria-is-not-one-thing/.

109 Louise Perry, "What Is Autogynephilia? An Interview with Dr Ray Blanchard," *Quillette* (Nov 6, 2019), accessed March 9, 2021, https://quillette.com/2019/11/06/what-is-autogynephilia-an-interview-with-

dr-ray-blanchard/. Rather than "androphilic gender dysphoria," I'm using the term "homophilic," which applies to both sexes.

110 D. N. Ruble et al., "The Role of Gender Constancy in Early Gender Development," *Child Development* 78, no. 4 (Jul-Aug 2007), https://dx.doi.org/10.1111/j.1467-8624.2007.01056.x. Kohlberg's theory is based on Piaget's theory of cognitive development in contrast to Freudian psychology; See Kolberg's chapter in Eleanor E. Maccoby et al., *The Development of Sex Differences, Stanford Studies in Psychology*, vol. 5 (Stanford, CA: Stanford University Press, 1966).

111 P. T. Cohen-Kettenis, H. A. Delemarre-van de Waal, and L. J. Gooren, "The Treatment of Adolescent Transsexuals: Changing Insights," *Journal of Sex Medicine* 5, no. 8 (Aug 2008), https://dx.doi.org/10.1111/j.1743-6109.2008.00870.x; American College of Pediatricians, "Gender Dysphoria in Children," last modified November 2018, accessed June 7, 2023, https://acpeds.org/position-statements/gender-dysphoria-in-children.

112 Perry, "What Is Autogynephilia? An Interview with Dr. Ray Blanchard."

113 Sexologist Ray Blanchard asserts that the converse in women (autoandrophilia) refers to women who are sexually aroused at the idea of being a gay man: https://twitter.com/blanchardphd/status/986235912127467520?lang=en (accessed April 15, 2023). Additionally, there is controversy as to whether women can have sexual fetishes, which may be why there is little research on autoandrophilia. Fetishes may be more prevalent in men because they are primarily visually stimulated, whereas women are often focused more on an emotional connection that precipitates sexual desire.

114 One of the people I interviewed for this book is a woman who transitioned to appear as a man yet remained attracted to men. Her background includes a distant relationship with her mother yet an unusually deep relationship with her father, who was able to connect with her heart. Her desire to transition was partly rooted in her jealousy of her brother.

115 Anne A. Lawrence, "Erotic Target Location Errors: An Underappreciated Paraphilic Dimension," *Journal of Sex Research* 46, no. 2–3 (2009), https://dx.doi.org/10.1080/00224490902747727.

116 Jerry Leach, *Flight toward Woman* (Lexington, KY: Reality Resources Publications, 2001), 41, 54, 62.

117 Booth Moore, "For Caitlyn Jenner, an Old-School Vision of Beauty," *Los Angeles Times* (June 1, 2015), accessed March 21, 2020, https://www.latimes.com/fashion/alltherage/la-ar-caitlyn-jenner-old-school-beauty-20150601-story.html; Ravi Somaiya, "Caitlyn Jenner, Formerly Bruce, Introduces Herself in Vanity Fair," *New York Times* (June 1, 2015), accessed March 21, 2020, https://www.nytimes.com/2015/06/02/business/media/jenner-reveals-new-name-in-vanity-fair-article.html.

118 Pure Passion Media, "Walter Heyer Pt 1—from Walt to Laura to Walt—a Transgender's Story," (2016), accessed March 21, 2020, https://www.youtube.com/watch?v=pMcROI-IUAk.

119 Leach, *Flight toward Woman*, 74–77.

120 Lisa Littman, "Rapid-Onset Gender Dysphoria in Adolescents and Young Adults: A Study of Parental Reports," *PLoS ONE* 13, no. 8 (2018), https://dx.doi.org/10.1371/journal.pone.0202330.

121 Kenneth J. Zucker, Anne A. Lawrence, and Baudewijntje P.C. Kreukels, "Gender Dysphoria in Adults," *Annual Review of Clinical Psychology* 12 (2016): 217, https://dx.doi.org/10.1146/annurev-clinpsy-021815-093034.

122 Nastasja M. de Graaf et al., "Sex Ratio in Children and Adolescents Referred to the Gender Identity Development Service in the UK (2009-2016)," *Archives of Sexual Behavior* 47, no. 5 (2018), https://dx.doi.org/DOI:10.1007/s10508-018-1204-9.

123 Tony Grew, "Inquiry into Surge in Gender Treatment Ordered by Penny Mordaunt," *The Sunday Times*, September 16, 2018, accessed Mar 30, 2022, https://www.thetimes.co.uk/article/inquiry-into-surge-in-gender-treatment-ordered-by-penny-mordaunt-b2ftz9hfn.

124 Jonathan Kay, "An Interview with Lisa Littman, Who Coined the Term 'Rapid Onset Gender Dysphoria,'" *Quillette* (March 19, 2019), https://quillette.com/2019/03/19/an-interview-with-lisa-littman-who-coined-the-term-rapid-onset-gender-dysphoria/; Riittakerttu Kaltiala-Heino et al., "Two Years of Gender Identity Service for Minors: Overrepresentation of Natal Girls with Severe Problems

in Adolescent Development," *Child and Adolescent Psychiatry and Mental Health* (2015), https://dx.doi.org/doi.org/10.1186/s13034-015-0042-y.

125 Bailey and Blanchard, "Gender Dysphoria Is Not One Thing." An autistic girl may have difficulty with abstract concepts and be more likely to believe her discomfort as a girl means there's only one solution: she must be a boy. She may fixate on that solution to the neglect of alternative explanations.

126 The Rubin Report, "Exposing the Reality of the Transgender Craze in Teen Girls with Abigail Shrier," (December 20, 2020), accessed March 21, 2023, https://www.youtube.com/watch?v=YIFdWhRwfFg&list=WL&index=33&t=14s.

127 Kerry Smith, "Testosterone & Young Females: What is Known About Lifelong Effects?," 4th Wave Now (June 18, 2018), accessed April 16, 2023, https://4thwavenow.com/2018/06/18/testosterone-young-females-what-is-known-about-lifelong-effects/.

128 https://www.restoredhopenetwork.org

129 Joe Dallas, *When Homosexuality Hits Home: What to Do When a Loved One Says, "I'm Gay"* (Eugene, OR: Harvest House Publishers, 2004).

130 www.help4families.org

131 www.sexchangeregret.com

132 Pure Passion Media, *Such Were Some of You*, YouTube (2018), accessed April 15, 2023, https://www.youtube.com/watch?v=VKSFPdyH8x4.

133 Pure Passion Media, *How Do You Like Me Now?* , YouTube (2019), accessed April 15, 2023, https://www.youtube.com/watch?v=hgg65Ocnjhc&t=6s.

134 Pure Passion Media, *TranZformed: Finding Peace with Your God Given Gender*, YouTube (2019), accessed April 15, 2023, https://www.youtube.com/watch?v=Ebodf8rWpv4&t=5415s.

## Chapter 8: How Transformation Happens: Theologically Speaking

135 Movement Advancement Project, "Equality Maps: Conversion Therapy Laws," accessed March 22, 2023, http://www.lgbtmap.org/equality-maps/conversion_therapy.

136 Brian Bird, "Canada's Ban on Conversion Therapy Could Impact Far More Than That," *Policy Options* (January 28, 2022), accessed February 17, 2023, https://policyoptions.irpp.org/magazines/january-2022/canadas-ban-on-conversion-therapy-could-impact-far-more-than-that/.

137 In their 2017 formal complaint to the Federal Trade Commission, the National Task Force for Therapy Equality exposes the intentional fabrication of "conversion therapy" stories to influence legislation. See National Task Force for Therapy Equality, "In Their Own Words: Lies, Deception, and Fraud—Southern Poverty Law Center, Human Rights Campaign, and the National Center for Lesbian Rights' Hate Campaign to Ban Psychotherapy for Individuals with Sexual and Gender Identity Conflicts," 2017, accessed April 15, 2023, http://www.therapyequality.org/national-task-force-therapy-equality-complaint-ftc-report.

138 For more about the "conversion therapy" controversy, see the ReStory Ministries "Tough Topics" paper at https://restoryministries.org/tough-topics/.

139 Carl R. Trueman, "Into the Anthropological Chaos: The Moral Turn of Revoice," *World News Group* (October 24, 2022), accessed October 29, 2022, https://wng.org/opinions/into-the-anthropological-chaos-1666613075.

140 I use the word "overcomer" instead of "struggler" because the former implies the believer is on a journey of progressive sanctification leading toward resolution/victory; the latter implies a perpetual battle with no hope for resolution/victory.

141 David Kyle Foster, a former gay prostitute, wrote a fantastic article describing the process of change: David Kyle Foster, "Transformation of a Homosexual: What Change Looks Like," Charisma News, 2014, accessed November 11, 2022, https://www.charismanews.com/opinion/46000-transformation-of-a-homosexual-what-change-looks-like.

## Chapter 9: How Transformation Happens: Practical Application

142 Foster, "Transformation of a Homosexual: What Change Looks Like.", "Transformation of a Homosexual."

143 Visit lindaseiler.com resource page for a message on the baptism in the Spirit.

144 I highly recommend the article "Is Masturbation a Sin?," by Mark Sandford and John Sandford, Elijah Rain Ministries (2019), accessed April 15, 2023, https://elijahrainministries.org/blogs/miscellaneous-articles/is-masturbation-a-sin. Additionally, the booklet "Emotional Dependency" helps the overcomer understand the characteristics of an emotionally dependent relationship and how to find freedom (www.restoryministries.org/resources).

145 Similarly addressed by Jay Stringer, *Unwanted: How Sexual Brokenness Reveals Our Way to Healing* (Colorado Springs: NavPress, 2018).

## Chapter 10: Redemptive Relationships

146 www.restoredhopenetwork.org

## Chapter 11: Inner Healing

147 From a neuroscience perspective, inner healing occurs when pain that has been trapped in the limbic brain integrates with the cognitive brain (prefrontal cortex). This aligns with the scriptural concept of renewing the mind. My dissertation expands more on that phenomenon.

148 Elijah Rain Ministries www.elijahrainministries.org; Elijah House Ministries www.elijahhouse.org;

149 Inner-healing ministries often use a client intake form that has specific questions designed to uncover potential roots. This article explains why examining our past can be helpful in revealing roots to bad fruit: Mark Sandford, "Why Should We Look at the Past?," (March 5, 2021), accessed April 15, 2023, https://elijahrainministries.org/blogs/inner-healing-and-deliverance/healing-past-roots.

150 The Gender Dysphoria Support Network, https://genderdysphoriasupportnetwork.com/resources.

151 Again, see Stringer, *Unwanted.*

152 David Kyle Foster, "Essentials Series," MasteringLife.org (2020), accessed May 29, 2023, https://www.masteringlife.org/resources/the-divine-marriage.

153 David Kyle Foster, "The Truth About the Transgender Movement," Virtue Online (July 5, 2017), accessed May 29, 2023, https://virtueonline.org/truth-about-transgender-movement.

## Chapter 12: The Five Streams

154 For example, see https://web.archive.org/web/19981205192027/http://www.bridges-across.org/ba/divide.htm and https://strengthofhismight.wordpress.com/2018/01/06/side-b-vs-side-y/#_ftn3.

155 Jason Thompson, "Differing Views on Christians Doctrine, Identity, and Homosexuality," Portland Fellowship, 2023, accessed April 15, 2023, https://www.portlandfellowship.com/clarity.php; Andrew Rodriguez, "4 Different Views on Homosexuality & Gender Identity in the Church," YouTube, 2021, accessed April 15, 2023, https://www.youtube.com/watch?v=SDGkLPWBKbo&t=81s.

156 From an academic perspective, this chapter addresses the missiological concept of contextualization. Think of a Venn diagram in which theology, human culture, and missiology intersect. Our mission to the lost and resulting pastoral care must be based on the truth of God's Word and the truths revealed in God's world. My thesis in this chapter is that the transformation approach demonstrates sound contextualization based on the truth of God's Word and truths revealed in biology, psychology, and anthropology. The other approaches either under-contextualize (often leading to legalism) or over-contextualize (known as syncretism).

157 Joshua Kors, "'God Hates Fags': Q&A with Pastor Fred Phelps," *Huffington Post* (August 20, 2010), accessed April 15, 2023, https://www.huffpost.com/entry/god-hates-fags-qa-with-pa_b_689430.

158 https://web.archive.org/web/20190301060707/http://godhatesfags.com/

159 Brian Tashman, "Swanson Defends Uganda's Anti-Homosexuality Bill, Lauds Country as Model," Right Wing Watch, last modified November 30, 2012, accessed April 12, 2019, http://www.rightwingwatch.org/post/swanson-defends-ugandas-anti-homosexuality-bill-lauds-country-as-model/; Miranda Blue, "Kevin Swanson Aghast That Christians Support 'Death Penalty Crime' of Gay Marriage," Right

Wing Watch, last modified December 6, 2017, accessed April 12, 2019, http://www.rightwingwatch.org/post/kevin-swanson-aghast-that-christians-support-death-penalty-crime-of-gay-marriage/; Curtis M. Wong, "Pastor Blames California Wildfires on State's Embrace of LGBTQ Rights," *Huffington Post* (August 6, 2018), accessed April 12, 2019, https://www.huffpost.com/entry/kevin-swanson-california-wildfires_n_5b68552ae4b0de86f4a391ae; Lindsey Bever, "Pastor Refuses to Mourn Orlando Victims: 'The Tragedy Is That More of Them Didn't Die,'" *The Washington Post* (June 15, 2016), accessed April 12, 2019, https://www.washingtonpost.com/news/acts-of-faith/wp/2016/06/14/pastor-refuses-to-mourn-orlando-victims-the-tragedy-is-that-more-of-them-didnt-die/; Martin E. Comas, "Lake County Church Hosting 3-Day 'Make America Straight Again' Event," *Orlando Sentinel* (June 13, 2019), accessed January 29, 2020, https://www.orlandosentinel.com/news/os-ne-lake-county-pastor-make-america-straight-again-20190613-q55c22mqxjf3djdmg6orqdwjru-story.html?fbclid=IwAR344UhzX2gV_vorzw7MAn0SHha5qFYScYFy8EFiHr9Xi2Hh0vfpPeOS2HE.

160 Syncretize = attempt to "sync," or reconcile, two opposing concepts or ideas. This is a missiological concept referring to improper contextualization of the gospel.

161 https://reformationproject.org

162 Greg Johnson, *Still Time to Care: What We Can Learn from the Church's Failed Attempt to Cure Homosexuality* (Grand Rapids: Zondervan, 2021), chapters 1–4; Wesley Hill, *Spiritual Friendship: Finding Love in the Church as a Celibate Gay Christian* (Grand Rapids: Brazos Press, 2015), chapter 2.

163 Misty Irons, "New Testament Gentiles and Gay Christians," The Center for Faith, Sexuality, and Gender (April 22, 2022), accessed June 1, 2023, https://www.centerforfaith.com/blog/new-testament-gentiles-and-gay-christians.

164 Mark Galli, "Revoice's Founder Answers the LGBT Conference's Critics: Orientation Is Not Necessarily Sexual, Nate Collins Says," *Christianity Today* (July 25, 2018), accessed January 15, 2020, https://www.christianitytoday.com/ct/2018/july-web-only/revoices-founder-answers-lgbt-conferences-critics.html.

165 Hill, *Spiritual Friendship*, 75.

166 Gregory Coles, *Single, Gay, Christian: A Personal Journey of Faith and Sexual Identity* (Downers Grove, IL: InterVarsity Press, 2017), 47, italics mine.

167 Hill, *Spiritual Friendship*; "Discern Your Call," Family of Brothers Monastery website, Nashville. http://familyofbrothers.org/discern-your-call/; Wesley Hill, "Spiritual Friendship," Biola University Chapel, 2014, accessed April 1, 2023, https://www.youtube.com/watch?v=glkykQYEy0w&t=808.

168 I use the word "struggler" versus "overcomer" in this context because they are not on a path toward overcoming.

169 Hill, *Spiritual Friendship: Finding Love in the Church as a Celibate Gay Christian*, 87–88.

170 Nate Collins, *All but Invisible: Exploring Identity Questions at the Intersection of Faith, Gender & Sexuality* (Grand Rapids: Zondervan, 2017), 86.

171 Anne Kennedy, "Identity and Obedience in Revoice 2021," *Christian Research Journal*, Last modified March 9, 2023 (February 1, 2022), accessed Feb 12, 2022, https://www.equip.org/article/identity-and-obedience-in-revoice-2021/?fbclid=IwAR3DUM0sANG3bu-EYgWv_I_7BuUKtVXVuzU6xFBBKOl42EmsJrRneupXaTI.

172 This video demonstrates the disturbing dynamics of a "spiritual friendship": Evangelical Dark Web, "Revoice Conference Exposed 1," recorded April 8, 2021, YouTube, accessed May 26, 2022, https://www.youtube.com/watch?v=Phus7d4ewDM&t=272s. See also Eve Tushnet, "Hope Is the Thing with Feather Boas: Two Small Gay Catholic Thoughts," @evetushnet, last modified January 30, 2023, accessed April 1, 2023, https://www.patheos.com/blogs/evetushnet/2023/01/hope-is-the-thing-with-feather-boas-two-small-gay-catholic-thoughts.html.

173 Preston Sprinkle, "Faith, Sexuality, and Gender," (March 6, 2020), accessed Oct 13, 2021. YouTube time code 3:00-4:43, https://www.youtube.com/watch?v=B5_xtBwF0oU; Preston Sprinkle, "Same-Sex Attraction, Deconstruction, and the Problem of Evil: Tony Scarcello," (July 26, 2020), accessed Oct 13, 2021. YouTube time code 37:38–38:26, https://www.youtube.com/watch?v=ILqXI6Rx0dw.

174 Justin Brierly, "Transgender People and the Church: Preston Sprinkle & Christina Beardsley," (Feb 5, 2021), accessed Oct 13, 2021. YouTube time code 46:39–46:54, https://www.youtube.com/watch?v=5aNz4-y7lwE.

175 Sprinkle, "Faith, Sexuality, and Gender,"time code 3:18–4:43.

176 Brierly, "Transgender People and the Church: Preston Sprinkle & Christina Beardsley," time code 42:50–44:52.

177 "Differing Views: "Preston Sprinkle and Jason Thompson," https://vimeo.com/521622676/05b848ba84.

178 Revoice Conference, 2018, https://web.archive.org/web/20180828014500/http://revoice.us/.

179 Tim Challies, "The Controversy Behind the Revoice Conference," www.challis.com, last modified June 15, 2018, accessed November 26, 2018, https://www.challies.com/articles/the-controversy-behind-the-revoice-conference/.

180 Mark Yarhouse, "Reflections on Revoice 2019," June 9, 2019, accessed April 24, 2023, https://psychologyandchristianity.wordpress.com/2019/06/09/reflections-on-revoice-2019/.

181 Leslie serves as the gender identity expert for the Posture Shift ministry team: https://postureshift.com/team/.

182 Mary Jackson and Todd Vician, "Identity Crisis: Ascendant Gender Ideology Undermines Group Trying to Balance Homosexuality and Biblical Orthodoxy," *World News Group* (October 21, 2021), accessed March 6, 2023, https://wng.org/articles/identity-crisis-1666367393.

183 Preston Sprinkle, *Embodied: Transgender Identities, the Church, and What the Bible Has to Say* (Colorado Springs: David C Cook, 2021), 9, 16, 26–27. Kindle edition.

184 Jackson, and Vician, "Identity Crisis: Ascendant Gender Ideology Undermines Group Trying to Balance Homosexuality and Biblical Orthodoxy."

185 For a thorough critique of Revoice, see M.D. Perkins, "A Little Leaven: Confronting the Ideology of the Revoice Movement," American Family Association (2021), accessed April 15, 2023, https://afa.net/media/595378/afa_alittleleaven_perkins_2021.pdf.

186 Rosaria Butterfield, "You Are What—and How—You Read," The Gospel Coalition (Feb. 13, 2014), accessed Feb 16, 2022, https://www.thegospelcoalition.org/article/you-are-whatand-howyou-read/.

187 See Association of Certified Biblical Counselors (ACBC), known prior to 2013 as the National Association of Nouthetic Counselors (NANC). Nouthetic counseling began in the 1970s with Jay Adams' book *Competent to Counsel* (https://biblicalcounseling.com/about/history/).

188 Christopher Yuan, *Holy Sexuality and the Gospel: Sex, Desire, and Relationships Shaped by God's Grand Story* (Colorado Springs: Multnomah, 2018), 46.

189 Sam Allberry, *Is God Anti-Gay?* (N.p.: The Good Book Company, 2013), Kindle location 874.

190 Butterfield, "You Are What—and How—You Read."

191 Personal communication, January 14, 2002.

192 https://watch.revoice.org/revoice19-talks-1/season:5/videos/friday-workshop-mission-and-sexuality-rachel-gilson;https://watch.revoice.org/videos/greg-coles-rachel-gilson-terminology.

193 Jesse T. Jackson, "'Are All Sexual Orientations Created by God?' Jackie Hill Perry Answers Preston Sprinkle at Exiles in Babylon Conference," Church Leaders, last modified April 5, 2022, accessed April 22, 2023, https://churchleaders.com/news/421288-are-all-sexual-orientations-created-by-god-jackie-hill-perry-answers-preston-sprinkle-at-exiles-in-babylon-conference.html; Preston Sprinkle, "#706—a Conversation with Jackie Hill Perry," November 12, 2018, in *Theology in the Raw*, https://theologyintheraw.com/podcast/706-a-conversation-with-jackie-hill-perry/; https://christian-sexuality.com.

194 Yuan, *Holy Sexuality and the Gospel*, 38.

195 Greg Koukl, "Sexuality and Gender: Rosaria Butterfield Interview with Greg Koukl," Stand to Reason (December 14, 2016), accessed April 29, 2019, https://www.str.org/article/rosaria-butterfield-interview-greg-koukl#.XMeFSi-ZNAY.

196 Butterfield, "You Are What—and How—You Read."

197 Rosaria Butterfield, "Retraction of My Position on Reparative Therapy and Ex-Gay Organizations," (2022), accessed March 6, 2022, https://static1.squarespace.com/static/5a81dca7d55b41d51ee756c3/t/62cdd566fd9ed703c736fdb7/1657656678694/Retraction+FINAL+EDIT+PDF.pdf.

198 Rachel Gilson, *Born Again This Way: Coming out, Coming to Faith, and What Comes Next* (The Good Book Company, 2020), 137.

199 Gilson, *Born Again This Way*, 82.

200 Jackie Hill Perry, "Jackie Hill Perry," Cru at University of Wisconsin-Stevens Point, Live Stream Recording (March 7, 2019), accessed June 7, 2021. YouTube timestamp 1:01:00–1:01:26, https://www.youtube.com/watch?v=7R430L_oqH0.

201 Sean Doherty, "Does Living out Support Gay Cure or 'Conversion Therapy'?," Living Out, 2019, accessed April 23, 2019, https://web.archive.org/web/20190401071351/http://www.livingout.org/does-living-out-support-gay-cure-or-conversion-therapy; This is another example of how streams can merge, as accommodation proponents embrace the idea of an immutable sexual orientation.

202 Denny Burk, and Heath Lambert, *Transforming Homosexuality: What the Bible Says About Sexual Orientation and Change* (Phillipsburg, NJ: P&R Publishing, 2015), 39–59, Kindle edition.

203 In early 2023, much controversy erupted over the concept of concupiscence. See Douglas Wilson, "Concupiscence Is as Concupiscence Does," Blog & Mablog: Theology that Bites Back, last modified January 11, 2023, accessed April 22, 2023, https://dougwils.com/books-and-culture/books/concupiscence-is-as-concupiscence-does.html.

204 Yuan, *Holy Sexuality and the Gospel*, 46.

205 Trinity Broadcasting Network, "Jackie Hill Perry Testimony: Delivered from Sexual Sin," *Praise* (Sep 28, 2021), accessed Oct 13, 2021, https://www.facebook.com/watch/?v=1420480101686895&ref=sharing.

206 I'm not a fan of the term "ex-gay" because it presupposes that gay is an identity. Furthermore, the term is too simplistic, as if one flips a switch to go from gay to straight. I prefer to use terms like "disciple" or "overcomer" in the context of progressive sanctification.

207 Exodus International, a forerunner of the transformation stream, was birthed during the charismatic renewal.

208 The General Council of Assemblies of God, "Homosexuality, Marriage, and Sexual Identity," (2014), accessed Feb 18, 2022, https://ag.org/Beliefs/Position-Papers/Homosexuality-Marriage-and-Sexual-Identity.

209 Warren Throckmorton, "Alan Chambers: 99.9% Have Not Experienced a Change in Their Orientation," (January 9, 2012), accessed April 15, 2023, https://wthrockmorton.com/2012/01/09/alan-chambers-99-9-have-not-experienced-a-change-in-their-orientation/.

210 Exodus International provided decades of effective ministry until Chambers became president and began to steer the organization away from biblical truth. In 2012, a group of orthodox leaders within Exodus pulled out to form the Restored Hope Network. Former Exodus president Joe Dallas shares his insights about Exodus in Joe Dallas, "What I've Always Wanted to Say About Ex-Gay Ministry," YouTube (Feb 21, 2022), accessed Feb 22, 2022, https://www.youtube.com/watch?v=uTOg5hbe8fo.

211 In holding therapy, the therapist holds the client by hugging the client or having the client lie in the therapist's lap. Exodus publicly renounced the method—see David Roberts, "Confirmed: Exodus Met with Richard Cohen, Original Statement Pulled," July 3, 2008, accessed Feb 25, 2022, https://exgaywatch.com/2008/07/confirmed-exodus-met-with-richard-cohen-original-statement-pulled/.

212 Anna Silman, "8 People on Surviving Gay Conversion Therapy," The Cut (Aug 10, 2018), accessed Feb 25, 2022, https://www.thecut.com/2018/08/8-gay-conversion-therapy-survivors-on-cameron-post.html.

213 Nico Lang, "Conversion Therapy Provider Must Dissolve, Pay Millions, Judge Rules," *NBC News* (June 12, 2019), accessed Feb 25, 2022, https://www.nbcnews.com/feature/nbc-out/conversion-therapy-provider-must-dissolve-pay-millions-judge-rules-n1016856.

214 National Task Force for Therapy Equality, "In Their Own Words," https://www.therapyequality.org.

215 Peter Sprigg, "Truth Matters in Ex-Gay Debate," *LifeSite News* (Sep 2, 2014), accessed Feb 25, 2022, https://www.lifesitenews.com/opinion/truth-matters-in-ex-gay-debate/; David Pickup, "Sam Brinton Exposed!! Visit Www.Sambrintonhoax.Com for More!," (October 20, 2017), accessed March 20, 2019, https://www.youtube.com/watch?v=gx9A7L-bpZE.

216 Geneva Sands, Maegan Vazquez, and Jeremy Diamond, "Top Energy Department Official No Longer Employed after Luggage Theft Accusations," *CNN* (Dec 13, 2022), accessed March 6, 2023, https://www.cnn.com/2022/12/13/politics/sam-brinton-department-of-energy/index.html.

217 Brandon Showalter, "Christian Authors Blast Amazon for Banning Their Books, Selling Pedophilia Titles," *The Christian Post*, August 30, 2019, accessed Apr 1, 2022, https://www.christianpost.com/news/christian-authors-blast-amazon-banning-their-books-selling-pedophilia-titles.html; Doug Mainwaring, "Ex-Gays Petition Amazon to Stop Banning Books That Help with Unwanted Same-Sex Attraction," *LifeSite News*, July 8, 2019, accessed April 22, 2023, https://www.lifesitenews.com/blogs/ex-gays-petition-amazon-to-stop-banning-books-that-help-with-unwanted-same-sex-attraction.

218 Brandon Showalter, "Facebook Shuts Down Christian Ministry's Page with No Explanation," *Christian Post*, October 8, 2020, accessed Apr 1, 2022, https://www.christianpost.com/news/facebook-shuts-down-christian-ministrys-page-with-no-explanation.html.

219 Janko Roettgers, "Under Pressure, Google Removes Gay Conversion Therapy App," *Reuters*, March 29, 2019, accessed April 22, 2023, https://www.reuters.com/article/variety-idUSL3N21G5E5.

220 Banned by Amazon.

221 Banned by Amazon.

222 https://www.restoredhopenetwork.org/purepassion; https://www.youtube.com/c/DavidKyleFoster/playlists.

223 https://restoryministries.org.

224 Restored Hope Network, "Frequently Asked Questions (FAQs): How Did Restored Hope Network Form?," (2022), accessed Feb 18, 2022, https://www.restoredhopenetwork.org/frequently-asked-questions; Restored Hope Network, "Frequently Asked Questions (FAQs): How Did Restored Hope Network Form?"

225 https://www.portlandfellowship.com.

226 https://changedmovement.com.

227 Rosaria Butterfield's recent recantation regarding her criticisms of change-allowing therapy demonstrates the potential for solidarity between the mortification and transformation streams. It's less likely

that the accommodation stream would unite with the mortification or transformation streams due to its progressive ideology.

## Chapter 13: Spiritual Warfare

228 Pew Research Center, "Same-Sex Marriage, State by State," (2023), accessed April 15, 2023, http://www.pewforum.org/2015/06/26/same-sex-marriage-state-by-state/.

229 Bill Chappell, "Trans Athlete Laurel Hubbard Has Made Olympic History Competing in Individual Event," *NPR* (August 2, 2021), accessed Aug 07, 2021, https://www.npr.org/sections/tokyo-olympics-live-updates/2021/08/02/1023724506/trans-weightlifter-laurel-hubbard-tokyo-olympics.

230 Drag Story Hour, "What is Drag Story Hour?," (2023), accessed June 5, 2023, https://www.dragstoryhour.org/about; Dave Nethers, "Planned 'Drag Queen Story Hour' Raises Controversy in Local Community," Fox 8 News (March 7, 2023), accessed April 15, 2023, https://fox8.com/news/planned-drag-queen-story-hour-raises-controversy-in-local-community/.

231 Anagha Srikanth, "AMA Doctors, Experts Recommend Removing Sex Designation from Birth Certificatesl," *The Hill* (August 6, 2021), accessed June 5, 2023, https://thehill.com/changing-america/respect/equality/566767-ama-doctors-experts-recommend-removing-sex-designation-from/#:~:text=Now%2C%20the%20American%20Medical%20Association%20is%20recommending%20no%20longer%20designating,racial%20hierarchies%2C%20and%20prohibit%20miscegenation.

232 Christopher Tremoglie, "Hershey's Puts the 'Man' in 'Woman' with New Promotional Candy Bar," *The Washington Examiner* (March 7, 2023), accessed March 8, 2023, https://www.washingtonexaminer.com/opinion/hersheys-puts-the-man-in-woman-with-new-promotional-candy-bar.

233 Doha Madani, "J.K. Rowling Accused of Transphobia after Mocking 'People Who Menstruate' Headline," *NBC News* (June 7, 2020), accessed June 5, 2023, https://www.nbcnews.com/feature/nbc-out/j-k-rowling-accused-transphobia-after-mocking-people-who-menstruate-n1227071.

234 John Kass, "Why Are We Calling Mothers 'Birthing Persons'?," *The Baltimore Sun* (Jun 21, 2021), accessed April 15, 2023, https://www.baltimoresun.com/opinion/op-ed/bs-ed-op-0621-katz-birthing-mothers-20210621-4lvc7jtpnrd37ci24oikwattc4-story.html. [Only subscribers can see even part of this article.]

235 Azura Goodman, "It's Time to Add 'Chestfeeding' to Your Vocabulary," *Today's Parent* (Jun 09, 2021), accessed Aug 07, 2021, https://www.todaysparent.com/baby/breastfeeding/chestfeeding-faq/.

236 Gwen Aviles, "J.K. Rowling Faces Backlash after Tweeting Support for 'Transphobic' Researcher," *NBC News* (Dec 19, 2019), accessed Aug 07, 2021, https://www.nbcnews.com/feature/nbc-out/j-k-rowling-faces-backlash-after-tweeting-support-transphobic-researcher-n1104971.

237 I'm using quotes here to indicate the irony that today's concept of "tolerance" is anything but tolerance. It tolerates everything except the Christian worldview.

238 D. A. Carson, *The Intolerance of Tolerance* (Grand Rapids: Eerdmans, 2012), 6–7.

239 Carson, 12–13.

240 Carson, 27.

241 Visit https://www.therapyequality.org for a detailed report exposing the lies behind fabricated stories to justify the banning of so-called "conversion therapy."

242 Movement Advancement Project, "Equality Maps: Conversion Therapy Laws."

243 Oswald Chambers, "Greater Works | October 17th," *My Utmost for His Highest* (1992).

## Chapter 15: Cultural Conundrums

244 Available on resource page at lindaseiler.com. See also Robert Gagnon, "Encore: Is It Loving for a Faithful Christian to Go to a 'Gay Wedding'?," *Christ Over All* (March 17, 2023), accessed April 16, 2023, https://christoverall.com/article/concise/is-it-loving-for-a-faithful-christian-to-go-to-a-gay-wedding/.

245 Gagnon, "Encore: Is It Loving for a Faithful Christian to Go to a 'Gay Wedding'?"

246 Sprinkle, *Embodied: Transgender Identities, the Church, and What the Bible Has to Say*, 203–11.

247 Andrew T. Walker, "He, She, Ze, Zir? Navigating Pronouns While Loving Your Transgender Neighbor," The Goodbook.com (August 31, 2018), accessed April 16, 2023, https://www.thegoodbook.com/blog/interestingthoughts/2018/08/31/he-she-ze-zir-navigating-pronouns-while-loving-you/.

## Conclusion

248 James Strong, *Strong's Exhaustive Concordance of the Bible* (Iowa Falls, Iowa: World Bible Publishers, 1992), p.185 (H7198).

249 John F. Walvoord and Roy B. Zuck, *The Bible Knowledge Commentary: An Exposition of the Scriptures by Dallas Seminary Faculty*, 2 vols. (Wheaton, IL: Victor Books, 1983), 40.

## Appendixes

250 © 2023 ReStory Ministries, Inc. All Rights Reserved. Used with permission. Visit restoryministries.org to print the original and see more Quick Guide resources like this one.

251 © 2023 ReStory Ministries, Inc. All Rights Reserved. Used with permission. Visit restoryministries.org to print the original and see more Quick Guide resources like this one.

252 © 2023 ReStory Ministries, Inc. All Rights Reserved. Used with permission. Visit restoryministries.org to print the original and see more quick guide resources like this one.

## Glossary

253 Brandon Showalter, "Reporting on the Transgender Movement: A Report from the Front," Ruth Institute (September 1, 2020), accessed April 11, 2023, https://ruthinstitute.org/tell-ruth-the-truth/reporting-on-the-transgender-movement-a-report-from-the-front/.

254 Sax, "How Common Is Intersex?"

255 Paul W. Hruz, Lawrence S. Mayer, and Paul R. McHugh, "Growing Pains: Problems with Puberty Suppression in Treating Gender Dysphoria," *The New Atlantis* (Spring 2017), accessed April 11, 2023, https://www.thenewatlantis.com/publications/growing-pains; Kiley Crossland, "Doctors: Puberty Blockers Are a Dangerous Experiment," *World News Group* (June 23, 2017), accessed April 11, 2023, https://wng.org/roundups/doctors-puberty-blockers-are-a-dangerous-experiment-1617229035.

Made in the USA
Coppell, TX
04 September 2024